Innovation and Creativity

Innovation and Creativity

Pillars of the Future Global Economy

Edited by

Filip De Beule and Ysabel Nauwelaerts

KU Leuven, Belgium

Edward Elgar
Cheltenham, UK • Northampton, MA, USA

Published by
Edward Elgar Publishing Limited
The Lypiatts
15 Lansdown Road
Cheltenham
Glos GL50 2JA
UK

Edward Elgar Publishing, Inc.
William Pratt House
9 Dewey Court
Northampton
Massachusetts 01060
USA

A catalogue record for this book
is available from the British Library

Library of Congress Control Number: 2012943747

This book is available electronically in the ElgarOnline.com
Business Subject Collection, E-ISBN 978 1 78100 433 3

ISBN 978 1 78100 432 6

Typeset by Servis Filmsetting Ltd, Stockport, Cheshire
Printed by MPG PRINTGROUP, UK

Contents

Contributors

Nathalie Avallone, Université François Rabelais – GERCIE, IUT de Tours, France

Oscar Afonso, University of Porto, Portugal

Ana Paula Africano, University of Porto, Portugal

Nathalie Beckers, KU Leuven, Belgium

René Belderbos, KU Leuven, Belgium; UNU-MERIT, Maastricht University, the Netherlands

Katarina Blomkvist, Uppsala University, Sweden

John Cantwell, Rutgers Business School, USA

Séverine Chédor, ADIS, IUT Sceaux, Université Paris Sud, France

Martine Cools, KU Leuven, Belgium; Rotterdam School of Management, the Netherlands

Filip De Beule, KU Leuven, Belgium

Axèle Giroud, Manchester Business School, UK

Yoo Jung Ha, York Management School, University of York, UK

Stijn Kelchtermans, Hogeschool-Universiteit Brussel, KU Leuven, Belgium

Bart Leten, KU Leuven; Vlerick Leuven Gent Management School, Belgium

Jens O. Meissner, Lucerne University of Applied Sciences and Arts, Switzerland

Jean-Louis Mucchielli, Sorbonne Center of Economics, University of Paris 1 Panthéon-Sorbonne-CNRS, France

Ysabel Nauwelaerts, KU Leuven, Belgium

Armando Silva, University of Porto and Polytechnic of Porto, Portugal

Roger Smeets, Rutgers Business School, USA

Dieter Somers, KU Leuven, Belgium

Martin Sprenger, Lucerne University of Applied Sciences and Arts, Switzerland

Peter Teirlinck, Federaal Wetenschapsbeleid and Hogeschool-Universiteit Brussel, KU Leuven, Belgium

Ilke Van Beveren, KU Leuven, Belgium

Alexandra Van den Abbeele, KU Leuven, Belgium

Elena Vijfeyken, KU Leuven, Belgium

Mo Yamin, Manchester Business School, UK

1. Innovation and creativity: statement of the issues

Filip De Beule and Ysabel Nauwelaerts

1.1 INTRODUCTION

This book was inspired by the European Year of Creativity and Innovation and by the Lisbon Agenda. The purpose of the Lisbon Agenda was to make the EU the most competitive, knowledge-based economy in the world by 2010. The member states were to formulate national reform programs, and use these as their main instrument in order to reach this goal. The Lisbon strategy put forward quite ambitious targets for Europe in terms of innovation and growth of innovative capacity. Firms have to be ambidextrous; they must be able to exploit their capabilities and explore new ones. In a globalizing world where more and more firms from more and more countries are joining this rat race, it is increasingly difficult to make your mark. Firms therefore need to create an advantage over their competitors. A firm's competitive advantage thereby depends more and more on its ability to be creative and innovative. Innovation is thereby the creation of better or more effective products, processes, services, technologies or ideas that are accepted by markets, governments and society. This can take different forms, ranging from administrative versus technical innovation, product versus process innovation, and radical versus incremental innovation. In general, the modern world puts more and more emphasis on better use of knowledge and rapid innovation as the way forward. Innovation is the process which follows on creativity, and it can thus be seen as the implementation of creative ideas. Creativity is therefore a critical step in the innovation process. This need for and emphasis on better use of knowledge and rapid innovation also requires a broadening of creative skills. In particular, there is a need for skills and competences that enable people to embrace change as an opportunity and to be open to new ideas in a culturally diverse, knowledge-based society. Innovation and creativity therefore make up the foundation for the future of the global economy. As a result, both firms and governments should put more emphasis on innovation and creativity.

1

This volume has brought together a set of chapters that tackle some of the most important aspects of innovation and creativity. The first set of chapters takes a country-level perspective and analyzes how well European countries, for example Belgium, and policies have fared. The second set of chapters takes a firm-level approach and analyzes various aspects of the internationalization of innovation and its effects on the firm. The third set of chapters looks into multinational companies in particular, and tries to analyze research and innovation at the headquarters and subsidiary level, and the linkages between them. The last set of chapters delves into management of innovation in firms and subsidiaries which helps us to gain more insight into how firms can innovate more and/or more effectively and efficiently while looking at innovation initiatives within MNEs or at the role of management control and culture in stimulating creativity as an important driver of innovation. In the end, it is hoped that the volume will help researchers, government officials and managers to be more creative and innovative.

1.2 COUNTRY-LEVEL STUDIES

Nathalie Avallone, Séverine Chédor and Jean-Louis Mucchielli found in their study (Chapter 2) that the European Lisbon strategy gave disappointing results in terms of R&D expenditures and patents. In their chapter titled 'International trade in disembodied technology: trends, patterns, and comparisons for European and OECD countries', the authors ask whether the EU displays some characteristics concerning its connection to global markets for knowledge and technology. Indeed during the 1990s, exchanges of technology across organizations, across industries and across countries have emerged and increased. OECD data allowed the authors to depict some interesting characteristics. First they found that R&D expenditures of the European Union lag behind Japan, the United States and other OECD countries, with the exception of Sweden and Finland. However, R&D financed from abroad in the EU is significantly higher. Second, co-inventions are particularly superior. The US has great performers in terms of R&D expenditures and patents, with large openness to foreign collaboration, and weak R&D financed from abroad. Japan seems successful in innovative activities while being quite isolated from global research networks. The European Union, on the other hand, seems to be in the opposite situation but with differentiated positions depending on the European countries. Finally, Technology Balance of Payments (TBP) statistics give some additional results. While the EU15 used to exhibit a TBP deficit, the situation has changed since 2006, and the EU15 now registers a surplus. Nonetheless, this performance relies mainly on Germany, Sweden and Austria, which are the main exporters of technology among European countries. The chapter proves clearly the urgent need for more innovation initiatives and performance in the EU and it also tells us which European countries can be viewed as 'examples' in terms of innovation.

As in most of the other EU member states, Peter Teirlinck specifies that Belgium translated the 3 per cent Lisbon objective into a national objective and – since the start of the Lisbon Agenda – a broad range of initiatives at different government levels have been taken. Seen from a European Commission perspective, most policy making in Belgium is done through a bottom-up process where interest groups lobby for increased support for one or more areas related to scientific research and its commercial exploitation. Unfortunately, over the last decade this has been done without a clear understanding of the knowledge demand needs (why, in what fields, for whom and to what end is one seeking to increase knowledge production) and in a context of weak assessment of the outputs and results of research programs.

For about a decade, impact assessment exercises of public funding for research and innovation in Belgium (as in most other EU member states) has occurred on an ad hoc basis, mainly depending on the government level and on the level of the ministerial department/agency. Also there is no systematic reflection being carried out to make a better causal link between indicators and policy objectives. Therefore, there is clearly room for improvement in this area.

In terms of policies, there are indeed a number of bottlenecks impeding the promotion of innovation and creativity. First, innovation policy has to a large extent focused on science and technology, and has neglected innovation in less knowledge-intensive industries. As there is a widespread belief that the high-tech industries are primarily the growing and thriving industries of tomorrow for high-income economies, the dominant view is that such high-tech industries hold the key to the future, whereas the low- and medium-tech sectors are usually regarded as being based on low levels of knowledge and without any real future in many industrialized economies. Low-tech industries are sometimes even called sunset industries, indicating that these industries are seen as declining and relocating to emerging economies, and eventually perhaps even vanishing from Western countries. In a similar vein, only the high-tech sectors are supposed to offer prospects for development, and therefore it makes sense that research should focus on these sectors and that policy makers should favor them (European Commission, 2008).

In spite of this widespread focus on high-tech industries, high-tech

manufacturing and high-tech services only provide a marginal contribution to Western economies. Quantitatively between 90 and 97 per cent
of GDP is accounted for by low- and medium-tech sectors in Western
European countries (Kaloudis et al., 2005; Hirsch-Kreinsen et al., 2005).
Despite a perception of the opposite, the relative share of high-tech industries has only increased marginally.

In fact, the generation, diffusion and utilization of knowledge has
become a core characteristic of firms and economic activity as a whole.
It is not only high-tech sectors but also traditional sectors that have
undergone change. The result is that many mature, low-tech, allegedly
threatened industries are not only still located in their industrialized home
countries, they continue to contribute the lion's share of employment
and value-added (De Beule and Van Beveren, 2009). One of the primary
explanations put forward for the sustained competitiveness is innovation
and creativity. As such, innovations are not confined to firms in high-tech
industries. Rather, firms in low-tech industries often rely on innovations,
not only in the form of new processes but also by developing new products
(Christensen, 2010).

The second issue is the accelerated internationalization of innovation
and the intertwining of regional and national innovation systems and
the emergence of international systems (like the EU) presenting a new
context for innovation policy making, as indicated in the chapter by Peter
Teirlinck (Chapter 3). Despite the Lisbon Strategy, for instance, Europe
has been unable to reduce its (business) R&D deficit within the triad and
is challenged by newly emerging economies such as China and India. Over
the last decades, policy responses in Europe to reduce the R&D deficit
were mainly characterized by a domestic focus. However, this territorially
based view is not completely in line with the ideas suggested by innovation
system(s) thinking to integrate regional, national and international innovation networks into broader, global ones.

The domestic focus of policies ignores the reality of a changing landscape for R&D in which Europe will take a less dominant position and
in which R&D activities of business enterprises (in particular those of
multinational enterprises) are increasingly footloose and beyond policy
makers' control. European-based companies have indeed good reasons
for moving parts of their R&D capacities abroad, ranging from nearness to foreign local markets to the need to be exposed to new ideas and
intellectual resources. Despite the fact that beneficial returns from inward
foreign direct investment (FDI) in R&D are not automatic and that
outward FDI in R&D should not be considered a priori as being negative,
actual policy measures towards FDI in R&D in the EU member states are
largely biased towards the attraction of inward FDI and do not target the

valorization of outward FDI, and, in more general terms, of knowledge developed outside Europe (Teirlinck, 2009).

The ignorance of opportunities of outward FDI in R&D is also recognized by the 'Expert Group Knowledge for Growth' (European Commission, 2006) highlighting the need for policy makers in Europe to give greater consideration to how Europe can take advantage of foreign knowledge, located both at home and abroad. A similar remark can be made regarding open innovation or knowledge exchange across national borders. Here as well, no arguments exist for policy makers to (try to) restrict policy measures to their own territory as is actually the case (European Commission, 2007).

At present there are serious biases in data collection in favor of 'inward' science, technology and innovation (STI) flows and their effects. The measurement and effects of (cross-border) 'outward' STI flows are somewhat ignored. Also, some aspects of open innovation, for example the outsourcing of R&D and its effects on the internal R&D, are under-investigated (Teirlinck et al., 2010). Therefore, policy makers should stimulate further efforts to measure and collect internationally comparable data on cross-border R&D and (open) innovation, and to investigate the implications for the domestic R&D and innovation base.

This is in fact borne out in the chapter by Filip De Beule, Dieter Somers and Ilke Van Beveren in their analysis of the innovation performance of firms located in Belgium (Chapter 4). A comparison of the ownership and innovative characteristics of firms shows that not only is most research and development carried out by either foreign subsidiaries in Belgium or Belgian multinational groups, but also innovative performance is much higher for companies that are part of multinational groups, either foreign or Belgian. The figures regarding collaboration also show that foreign multinationals and Belgian groups reported that they had collaborated more often than stand-alone firms.

De Beule et al.'s analysis of firms in Belgium, based on the Community Innovation Survey data for three successive waves, also suggests that firms seem to enjoy a significantly positive impact from increased sectoral concentration on innovation. When they compare high-tech manufacturing firms with low-tech manufacturing firms and high-tech service firms with low-tech service firms, they notice that the high-tech firms significantly outperform their low-tech counterparts in terms of innovative activities. However, further results suggest that this difference can potentially be explained by the higher average funding opportunities for high-tech firms. Furthermore, other results (De Beule and Van Beveren, 2012) with regard to sectoral differences have shown that – after controlling for funding, and so on – low-tech manufacturing and service sectors benefit from localization economies in their innovation process, while medium- and high-tech sectors do not. This is in line with recent research that has increasingly shown the sustained competitiveness and innovativeness of low-tech sectors in high-wage European countries (Hansen and Winther, 2011). Highly knowledge-intensive service firms, on the other hand, seem to benefit most from urbanization economies in the form of heterogeneity across sectors within their region.

These findings have implications for both firms and policy makers. For firms, this means that research and development could be put to better use as the return on investment in innovation – that is expenditure on research and development – is potentially more productive in regions with relatively more sectoral agglomeration. These regionally agglomerated sectors accumulate sources of spillovers, which in turn attract innovators and support innovation. This is, however, more so for low-tech manufacturing and service industries than for high-tech industries. Yet, highly knowledge-intensive service firms also seem to be able to benefit from larger, more diverse regions in their innovation process. Given that these industries are still predominant in Belgium, much progress can be made.

For policy makers, this implies that agglomeration can be an important channel in the overall promotion of innovation. Policy focus is, however, often on high-technology industries and not on low-tech sectors. Funding at regional, national and European level, for instance, is currently mostly awarded to firms in less-agglomerated, high-tech manufacturing industries and least to firms in low-tech service and manufacturing industries. Although it is encouraging to see that R&D funding has a significantly positive effect on innovation (except for high-tech manufacturing industries), their results suggest that funding could be used more effectively and efficiently in more agglomerated and low-tech industries, in particular (De Beule and Van Beveren, 2012). This, in turn, suggests that Belgian (regional) innovation policy, which currently invests relatively more efforts into the fast and effective development of high-tech industries, should not overlook the stimulus of innovation in low-tech sectors, especially given its importance in terms of employment and value-added. The results indicate that policies should focus more on the innovation of (medium) low-tech industries, although perhaps not at the expense of high-tech sectors.

Finally, given that subsidiaries of foreign – as well as Belgian – multinationals outperform purely domestic companies, both companies and governments should take steps towards increasing the internationalization of firms in order to improve their innovativeness.

1.3   INNOVATION AND INTERNATIONALIZATION

The existence of a positive relationship between the level and the growth of technological knowledge and foreign exposure has been documented before. There is general agreement that this positive connection results from the highly competitive pressure of international markets, which require firms' constant technological updating and adaptation.

In a study on Portuguese firms (Chapter 5), Armando Silva, Oscar Afonso and Ana Paula Africano show that firms that are more globally engaged have a higher ability to innovate. This study also finds that the access to knowledge information flows has a systematically higher impact on innovation ability than knowledge inputs, which is in line with previous studies. Moreover, their study reveals that the importance of knowledge information sources varies with both the type of innovation output indicator considered and the level of firms' global engagement. In fact, Portuguese firms access the global knowledge stock through three main channels: internal pool of information (especially for multinational firms), and market contacts with clients and suppliers (especially for exporters).

Furthermore, their analyses have allowed them to verify that the existing knowledge stock is not uniformly accessible throughout the world, and that the more engaged firms have both more access to it and a higher capacity for taking advantage of it. This logic is often called the 'paradox of openness' (Laursen and Salter, 2007): on the one hand, the innovation creation requires firms' 'openness', resulting in additional importance for the ability to access and adopt others' ideas – knowledge information flows – and, on the other hand, in order to apply and benefit from those innovations, firms also need to obtain returns from their innovative ideas, which in turn requires their own internal effort and absorptive capacity.

Furthermore, it is becoming increasingly important also to focus on the international performance resulting from innovation and creativity. Especially in the European economy, it appears vital that the SMEs succeed in bringing their creative innovations to the international markets and in being competitive and successful on these foreign markets. Recent studies show that, for many different – well-known and less known – reasons, European firms often do not excel in selling their innovations successfully on the international markets. In particular the small creative SMEs are often confronted with many difficulties in exporting their innovative products or services to the competitive global markets. Since the international performance of our creative firms is of utmost importance for our European economy to flourish, governments have a crucial role to play in stimulating and supporting these SMEs in their international adventures.

In the chapter by Nauwelaerts and Vijfeyken (Chapter 6), the authors investigate the export performance of Flemish creative SMEs from a resource-based view. They focus on the effects of support actions by a governmental organization, 'Flanders Investment and Trade' (FIT), also taking into account the effects of internal firm resources. The resource-based model used for the study mainly follows Wilkinson and Brouthers (2006), who demonstrate the linkage between the difficulties experienced by smaller firms on international markets and their ability to overcome these difficulties through the development of internal and external resources. In the study, the authors test more precisely the effects of export-stimulating programs of FIT organized in the home and in the host country on the export satisfaction of Flemish creative SMEs, also taking into account the effects of internal firm resources on their export performance satisfaction.

The results show that on the side of the export promotion instruments, only the so-called 'product sample booths' seem to have a consistent significant positive effect. These typically sector-oriented export promotion activities, sending a representative of the firm to international trade fairs, seem to be the most effective export-stimulating initiative. The use of 'trade missions, prospection and business trips' and the 'invitation of foreign buyers' seem not immediately useful, since they are negatively and/or insignificantly related to the export performance of SMEs in the creative sector. These programs are often not sector specific and therefore less useful than 'product sample booths' which are, in contrast, mostly sector specific. Furthermore they find that 'marketing reserves' are clearly significant for the 'purely creative firms'. These results suggest that extra marketing efforts are particularly effective to promote and stimulate exports in the creative firms and the design sectors.

Besides, recent studies have shown that the 'creative industry' is a booming industry with high growth rates in terms of employment and value-added (Guiette et al., 2010). As such, creative industries have become increasingly more important, deserving growing attention. Besides, creativity in firms as well as management in the creative sectors is relatively underdeveloped and under-researched. Several chapters in this edited volume will therefore give special attention to the role of organizational creativity and culture to stimulate innovation within companies.

1.4   MULTINATIONAL FIRMS AND INNOVATION

In the chapter by Stijn Kelchtermans, Bart Leten and René Belderbos (Chapter 7), the effects of basic research on the technological performance of firms, in the pharmaceutical sector in particular, are examined. It is demonstrated that firms that perform basic research may benefit from 'first-mover advantages'. First-mover advantages refer to a wide set of advantages that firms can obtain from being the first to possess new knowledge resulting from basic research, such as the acquisition of valuable assets (whose value becomes apparent from the new knowledge) or the creation of new products and production processes which, in the case of effective patent protection, may (at least temporarily) block competing firms. In addition, firms can improve the efficiency of their technology activities by doing basic research. Scientific knowledge, resulting from basic research activities, helps firms to gain a better understanding of the technological landscape in which they search for new inventions, informs them about the most profitable directions for applied research, and helps them to better interpret findings of applied research. Internal basic research capabilities also allow firms to better monitor, interpret and absorb scientific knowledge that is conducted externally to firms.

Their analysis draws on a unique panel dataset (1995–2002) on the R&D, patent and publication activities of 33 large US, European and Japanese pharmaceutical firms. The analyses show that pharmaceutical firms can increase their technological performance by conducting more basic research, and that the magnitude of this effect is substantial. Technological performance is a monotonously increasing function of basic research intensity (measured by the number of basic research publications per million US dollars invested in R&D), with the largest marginal gains present at lower levels of basic research (including cases of no investments in basic research). This finding suggests that the benefits of basic research, such as the creation of absorptive capacity to recognize and utilize the fruits of external basic science and improved search heuristics for applied research, may not require relatively large investments in basic research to materialize. After the large initial gains from getting involved in basic research, technological performance is further enhanced if involvement in basic research becomes more intense, yet the marginal effects of greater involvement are smaller.

In terms of spillovers, the cumulative ambiguity in empirical results regarding the productivity-enhancing effects of inward foreign direct investment has led scholars to start investigating such effects in more detail (Smeets, 2008). Some studies try to disentangle the knowledge diffusion channels through which such effects allegedly take place, while others have considered the moderating role of factors such as the absorptive capacity of local firms or the geography of inter-firm patterns of location. A more recent stream of literature has approached the issue by acknowledging the fact that multinationals and their foreign subsidiaries are not homogeneous, and as such they may generate different (productivity) effects on host-country firms (Feinberg and Keane, 2005).

In the chapter by Cantwell and Smeets (Chapter 8), they propose that, contrary to recent empirical evidence, FDI motivated by a technology-seeking strategy is at least as likely to induce positive productivity effects in the host country as technology exploiting FDI. They support this proposition by three arguments: first, a number of recent empirical microeconomic studies have demonstrated that the R&D and innovation intensity of MNE subsidiaries with a technology-seeking mandate is substantial, and even likely to outperform that of technology-exploiting subsidiaries. Second, there is increasing theoretical and empirical evidence that productivity leaders rather than laggards engage in technology-seeking FDI, implying high knowledge spillover potential. Third, it has been demonstrated that productivity spillovers are most likely to be mutual, flowing not only from the MNE to domestic firms but also the other way around. This implies that to seek technology successfully, subsidiaries also have to be prepared to diffuse some of their own.

Overall, Cantwell and Smeets' empirical results provide quite consistent support for their hypothesis on technology-seeking FDI. They find consistent positive and significant productivity effects of technology-seeking FDI. Regarding technology-exploiting FDI, they find no significantly positive effects on innovation.

In the next chapter (Chapter 9), Katarina Blomkvist looks at the reverse side in analyzing reverse technology diffusion from the subsidiary to the headquarters. According to recent research in the field of international business, developing and diffusing technology throughout the MNE network constitutes one of its most important policies and sources of competitive advantage. The general story often depicts the MNE as an increasingly interconnected and superior creature for leveraging technology domestically as well as internationally, where autonomous innovative activity by foreign subsidiaries serves as an important source for the technological development of the MNE as a whole.

The ability of the MNC to leverage knowledge from geographically dispersed foreign subsidiaries is perceived as a must for firms' success, and global diffusion of capabilities is viewed by several scholars as the main *raison d'être* of MNEs. Consequently, the importance of reverse diffusion has increased as it allows the MNE to draw upon the knowledge and capabilities residing in its network and to take advantage of the scope economies of learning within the entire multinational group.

The main results suggest an increased speed of reverse diffusion, that is, the diffusion from foreign advanced subsidiaries to headquarters has become faster over time. The findings support those who have argued that the reason why MNEs exist and succeed is their ability to develop and leverage knowledge efficiently across borders, and foreign subsidiaries' function as important sources of technological capabilities for headquarters and the entire multinational group. Moreover, the results of an increased speed in reverse diffusion agree with previous research arguing that enhanced international competition and shortened product life cycles have contributed to increasingly rapid transfer of technology within the MNE. The observed hazard rate suggests a substantial increase over time in the speed of diffusion of technological capabilities from competence-creating subsidiaries to headquarters.

The results also demonstrate a clear difference between greenfield and acquired competence-creating subsidiaries regarding the diffusion speed to headquarters of technological capabilities emerging in these subsidiaries. This supports previous research arguing that acquisitions are often used in order to gain access to new technologies and that headquarters therefore take a great interest in their technological assets and capabilities. Several of the control variables showed results that were in line with those expectations; however, they were not significant. The diffusion speed from foreign subsidiaries to headquarters is higher from large and substantial markets, such as the automotive or pharmaceutical industry.

1.5   INNOVATION AND CREATIVITY

Axèle Giroud, Yoo Jung Ha and Mo Yamin focus their study on the determinants and outcomes of the innovation initiative within foreign subsidiaries in South Korea. Very often, the innovative capacity is related to the presence of and interaction between internal and external forces and their organizational strength within the MNE. The authors consider innovation as the process through which new products or processes are introduced within the firm. It represents the end of a process of knowledge sourcing and transformation, as well as the beginning of a process of exploitation which may result in an improvement in the performance of the innovating firm. In this chapter (Chapter 10), the authors investigate the drivers of innovation initiative in foreign subsidiaries located in South Korea, balancing internal and external drivers to innovation, before investigating its outcome on innovation output and performance of the subsidiary, as well as the level of intra-MNC knowledge sharing with the HQ or other units of the MNC. Their findings demonstrate that the external technological environment in South Korea and MNC internal embeddedness are conducive to subsidiary initiative, and that innovation arising in South Korea is shared with other units of the MNC. Given the rising investments from

Asian countries in European firms, the results of this study also offer interesting insights and lessons to be learned in terms of innovation for European firms.

Organizational creativity is recognized as another important driver for innovation. It is defined as the ability to manage individual creativity to improve performance. Organizational creativity could induce a regular flow of new ideas to nurture new product development processes. Creativity results from the coordination between the individual level and organizational level through the group level (Woodman et al., 1993).

In their chapter (Chapter 11), Nathalie Beckers, Martine Cools and Alexandra Van den Abbeele investigate the role of management control instruments to stimulate creativity in an organizational context. The first aim of this chapter is to review the management accounting and control literature related to fostering creativity as well as innovation, since both concepts are highly intertwined. The second aim is to identify research gaps related to management control and creativity that merit future research. The authors formulate potential avenues for future research at four levels of analysis: the individual level, the group level, the firm level and the inter-firm level.

Finally, in the last chapter of this book (Chapter 12), Jens Meissner and Martin Sprenger present a more applied case study where they show the linkages between Innovation Process and Culture in a large service company. Two trends in innovation management influenced the basic idea of this chapter: first, the increasing number of managerial attempts to design linear innovation management processes that can be derived from literature and practice, and secondly, the increasing acceptance of innovation culture dynamics as a key driver for innovations. The two approaches partly contrast each other. Studies explaining the link between innovation culture and innovation project management seem to be quite rare. Indeed the study of Brown and Eisenhardt (1995) gives an excellent overview of the innovation management research, but the issue regarding innovation culture is lacking. This missing link between innovation process design and innovation culture on the firm level represents the theoretical field of this chapter. The research question focuses on how basic assumptions of team members occur in managed organizational innovation activities and how they influence the effectiveness of the innovation process. The authors conducted a single case study in a Swiss telecommunications company and used two series of interviews for data gathering. The main contribution of this chapter is the suggestion that innovation managers in large service firms might apply a dynamic role model for innovation management to be successful.

We can conclude this introduction by saying that innovative capacity and creativity really seem to be important drivers of competitiveness. Since most European firms and regions are not performing well in terms of innovation, it is hoped that this book can help managers, politicians and academics to gain better or new insights in how we can enhance countries' and firms' innovative capacity. The book shows that not only technical knowledge but also creative capacity, intercultural performance and the interaction between internal and external sources of creativity within firms can be important drivers of innovation.

REFERENCES

Brown, S. and K. Eisenhardt (1995), 'Product development: past research, present findings, and future directions', *Academy of Management Review*, **20**(2), 343–78.
Christensen, J.L. (2010), 'Low-tech, high-performing clusters in knowledge-based economies', paper presented at 'Opening up innovation: strategy, organization and technology', DRUID Summer Conference, London Business School, 16–18 June.
De Beule, F. and I. Van Beveren (2009), 'Belgium's diamond of competitiveness: a comparison between foreign and domestic companies', in D. Van Den Bulcke, A. Verbeke and W. Yuan (eds), *Handbook on Small Nations in the Global Economy: the Contribution of Multinational Enterprises to National Economic Success*, Cheltenham, UK and Northampton, MA, USA: Edward Elgar Publishing, pp. 30–49.
De Beule, F. and I. Van Beveren (2012), 'Does firm agglomeration drive product innovation and renewal? An application for Belgium', *Tijdschrift voor Economische en Sociale Geografie – Journal of Economic and Social Geography*, forthcoming.
European Commission (2006), 'Globalization of R&D: linking better the European economy to "foregin" sources of knowledge and making EU a more attractive place for R&D investment', Experts Group 'Knowledge for growth', Brussels: European Commission.
European Commission (2007), 'Europe in the global research landscape', Brussels: European Commission.
European Commission (2008), 'ERA indicators and monitoring', Brussels: European Commission.
Feinberg, S. and M. Keane (2005), 'The intra-firm trade of US MNCs: findings and implications for models and policies towards trade and investment', in T.H. Moran, E.M. Graham and M. Blomström (eds), *Does Foreign Direct Investment Promote Development?*, Washington, DC: Institute for International Economics, pp. 245–71.
Guiette, A., A. Schramme and K. Vandenbempt (2010), 'Creatieve industrieën in Vlaanderen anno 2010: een voorstudie', Flanders District of Creativity.
Hansen, T. and L. Winther (2011), 'Innovation, regional development and relations between high- and low-tech industries', *European Urban and Regional Studies*, **18**(3), 321–39.
Kaloudis, A., T. Sandven and K. Smith (2005), 'Structural change, growth

and innovation: the roles of medium and low-tech industries 1980–2000',
in G. Bender, D. Jacobson and P. Robertson (eds), *Non-Research-Intensive
Industries in the Knowledge Economy*, Lublin (Poland): Catholic University.

Hirsch-Kreinsen, H., D. Jacobson, S. Laestadius and K. Smith (2005), 'Low-tech
industries and the knowledge economy: the analytical issues', in H. Hirsch-
Kreinsen, D. Jacobson and S. Laestadius (eds), *Low-tech Innovation in the
Knowledge Economy*, Frankfurt: Peter Lang, pp. 11–30.

Laursen, K. and A.J. Salter (2007), 'The paradox of openness appropriability
and the use of external sources of knowledge for innovation', paper presented
at 'Appropriability, proximity, routines and innovation', DRUID Conference,
2007, Copenhagen, 18–20 June.

Smeets, R. (2008), 'Collecting the pieces of the FDI knowledge spillovers puzzle',
World Bank Research Observer, **23**, 107–38.

Teirlinck, P. (2009), 'Foreign direct investment in business R&D in Belgium
in comparison with other EU member states: statistical overview and policy
making', Brussels: Belgian Science Policy Research Series 10.

Teirlinck, P., M. Dumont and A. Spithoven (2010), 'Corporate decision-making
in R&D outsourcing and the impact on internal R&D employment intensity',
Industrial and Corporate Change, March.

Wilkinson, T. and L.E. Brouthers (2006), 'Trade promotion and SME export performance', *International Business Review*, **15**, 233–52.

Woodman, R.W., J.E. Sawyer and R.W. Griffin (1993), 'Toward a theory of
organizational creativity', *The Academy of Management Review*, **18**(2), 293–321.

2. International trade in disembodied technology: trends, patterns and comparisons for European and OECD countries

Nathalie Avallone, Séverine Chédor and Jean-Louis Mucchielli

2.1 INTRODUCTION

The 1990s have witnessed the emergence of global markets for knowledge and the increasing exchange of technology across organizations, across industries and across countries (Gambardella et al., 2007). International trade in technology increases with internationalization of patent activity via multinational enterprises strategies since 1990. Moreover new actors have emerged on the international market of technology. For instance, in 2006 China's Gross Domestic Expenditure on Research and Development (GERD) reached 1.43 per cent and China aims at a goal of 2 per cent in 2010. International trade in technology is a major tool for globalization of innovation and knowledge. In 2000 European countries launched ambitious objectives to become the most competitive knowledge-based economy in the world. Unfortunately its results for R&D expenditures and patents were disappointing. In prospect of the assessment of the Lisbon Agenda in 2010, it seemed important to assessing the situation of the European countries about international trade in technology and knowledge. In other words, what about European countries' connection to global research?

Disembodied technologies or knowledge refer to 'technologies that are protected by intellectual property rights, but can be purchased by a firm and included in its production process' (Chang and Robin, 2006). These include patented technologies, licensed technologies and royalty-inducing technologies. Trade in disembodied technologies, particularly international trade on technology services, has been rather neglected by economists. The aim of this chapter is to characterize technology transfers at the European level. This subject is particularly important for two reasons. While there is an extensive body of literature dealing with technology and knowledge spillovers and their impact on productivity, the issue of disembodied trade in technology (measured by the balance of technological payments) seems to remain marginal in the literature. Nonetheless, international trade in technology is more and more important, and few papers dealing with this issue conclude that it has positive effects on productivity (Deardoff and Djankov, 2000; Veugelers and Cassiman, 2004; Lee, 2006; Mendi, 2007; Criscuolo et al., 2010). The chapter will be organized as follows. First we will present as carefully as possible the important concepts depicting international technology and knowledge diffusion. Secondly, we will indicate trends and patterns of international trade in technology for European countries compared with OECD countries in order to highlight their specificities.

2.2   GLOBAL TRADE IN KNOWLEDGE AND TECHNOLOGY: DEFINITIONS AND IMPACT

It is important to distinguish two important channels of technology and knowledge diffusion: transfers and spillovers. While transfers are easier to appraise because they rely on market transactions, the issue of technology spillovers receives greater attention in the empirical literature.[1] Nonetheless the study of disembodied knowledge trade, and particularly the analysis of international trade on technology services (international patent licensing, technical assistance, engineering and external R&D services, know-how contracts), is increasingly important. Indeed, as Onodera (2008, pp. 48–9) emphasizes: 'stronger innovation and diffusion of innovation is important for addressing global challenges such as meeting increased demands for energy and food, and in particular for meeting the challenges presented by climate change'. To the extent that disembodied knowledge trade constitutes a more direct transfer means of innovation and knowledge, it therefore constitutes a fundamental matter of analysis.

In this section, we will first present important definitions concerning international diffusion of technology and knowledge. Then we will introduce some empirical studies that assess knowledge and technology diffusion effects on productivity and innovative performances.

2.2.1   Defining International Technology Diffusion

The aim of this section is to explain what we mean by international trade in technology. Following Maskus (2003, p. 14), it is possible to define a technology as the information needed 'to achieve a certain production outcome from a particular means of combining or processing selected inputs'. Technology diffusion may rely on transfers or spillovers (Shih and Chang, 2008; Keller, 2004). *Technology transfers* refer to any process by which one party gains access to a second party's information, and successfully learns and absorbs it into his or her production function. Taschler and Chappelow (1999, p. 30) define technology transfer as 'the managed, interpersonal, and systematic process of passing control of a technology from one party to its adoption by another party as evidenced by a strong emotional and financial commitment to sustained, routine use'. Consequently, 'technology transfer occurs between willing partners in voluntary transactions' (Maskus, 2003, pp. 14–15). Conversely, *technology spillovers* are defined as 'technological knowledge being learned and absorbed into competition in such a way that the benefits do not fully accrue to the original owner of the technology' (Shih and Chang, 2008, p. 2). Technology or knowledge spillovers come from the fact that 'technological investments frequently create benefits to individuals other than the inventor', that is to say they generate positive externalities. (Shih and Chang, 2008, p. 2)[2]

More and more technology transfers occur at international level mainly because multinational enterprises (MNEs) are performing a growing share of their R&D abroad (UNCTAD, 2005, p. 121). It is then important to distinguish two types of international transfer of technology: first, the market-mediated international transfer of technology (through licensing, R&D contracting and company sell-offs and cooperation in R&D) and secondly the intra-group transfer of technology. On the one hand, a market-mediated mechanism means that some form of formal transaction underlies the technology movement (Maskus, 2003).[3] On the other hand, intra-group transfer of technology consists in exchange of technology between parent company and affiliates.

A common classification of technology relies on the distinction between embodied and disembodied technology. *Embodied technology* refers to 'new technology [. . .] embodied in an asset [. . .] such as new personnel or (parts of) other firms or equipment' (Cassiman and Veugelers, 2000, pp. 1–3). In other words, 'Technology can be embodied in intermediate inputs, capital goods, or people' (Mendi, 2007, p. 121). Conversely, *disembodied technology* refers to codified technology (in the form of formulas, blueprints, drawings, patent applications, and so on) or in an uncodified form (in the sense of requiring implicit know-how from personnel) (Maskus, 2003, p. 14; Shih and Chang, 2008, pp. 2–3).

On the basis of these previous definitions, three ways of transferring technology and knowledge internationally can be identified: licensing, collaboration and movement of technical and managerial personnel.

Licensing 'involves the purchase of production or distribution rights (protected by some intellectual property right) and the technical information and know-how required to make effective the exercise of those rights'. License contracts can

> cover a variety of transactions, including technical assistance, codified knowledge, know-how, establishment of turnkey operations, and intellectual property rights. Licenses may be offered for a fixed fee, a franchise fee, a royalty schedule (for example, sliding share of sales), or a share of profits. They may offer rights to produce for, or distribute to, a limited geographical territory for a given period of time. The terms of a license contract may involve performance requirements of the licensee, such as non-disclosure mandates, 'no-compete' clauses for personnel, and grant-back provisions on adaptive innovations (Maskus, 2003, p. 15 and p. 26).

International *collaboration* is also a means of disembodied technology transfer. It consists in partnership among researchers that can 'take place either within a multinational corporation (providing research facilities in several countries) or through a research joint venture (JV) among several firms or institutions (collaboration between universities or public research organizations)' (OECD, 2008, p. 30).

Another significant channel of international technology and knowledge transfer is *cross-border movement of technical and managerial personnel*. Indeed, many technologies cannot be effectively or affordably transferred without the complementary services and know-how of engineers and technicians that must be on-site for some period of time.

Thus a firm can obtain new disembodied technology through a licensing agreement or by outsourcing the technology development from an R&D contractor or consulting agency (Cassiman and Veugelers, 2000, p. 3). In other words technical services and assistance provided by skilled employees who have know-how necessary for a successful transfer of technology can be considered as disembodied flows of technology and knowledge.[4]

To sum up, our purpose is to study disembodied knowledge and technology trade, and consequently we are interested in international technological transfers occurring through market channels, namely those implying a formal transaction underlying the technology movement. Before considering trends and patterns of trade in disembodied technology for European and OECD countries, a brief review of empirical studies (Mucchielli et al., 2009) is required to understand the importance of trade in knowledge as it can result in improved productivity and innovative performance.

2.2.2 Empirical Studies: Impacts of International Diffusion of Knowledge and Technology

In this brief review we focus on empirical papers dealing with international diffusion of knowledge and technology in European and OECD countries.[5] While obtaining data on transfers of technology is quite easy, the bulk of empirical literature deals with technology spillovers. Indeed firms make royalty payments for their use of patents, licenses and copyrights, and these data are available for major countries in the international services balance (Keller, 2004, p. 758).

Consequently we will first briefly present papers that assess the impact of international technology and knowledge spillovers, and then empirical studies that assess the effect of international trade in disembodied technology.

2.2.2.1 Effects of technology spillovers

Three channels of technology spillovers receive particular attention: trade in goods and in intermediate goods and foreign direct investment.[6] Eaton and Kortum (1996) estimate the importance of international technology diffusion for productivity growth. International technology diffusion is assessed on the basis of patents registration abroad. Several explanatory variables are retained to explain patents: (1) each country's productivity as a source of innovation, (2) diffusion of technology between each country pair, and (3) the returns to patenting an invention, conditional on diffusion. They show that 'the impediments to diffusion [of ideas] account for observed differences in productivity across OECD countries'. In spite of these impediments, their results imply that

> international trade in ideas [through patenting] is a major factor in world growth: every OECD country other than the United States obtains more than 50% of its productivity growth from ideas that originated from abroad, and for all but the five leading research economies (the United States, Japan, Germany, France, and the United Kingdom) the figure is more than 90%.

As for the source of these innovations, the United States, Japan and Germany together drive more than half of the growth of every country in their sample.

At a macro level, Keller (2002, pp. 120–42) investigates for G5 countries whether knowledge spillovers are global or local by examining whether the distance between countries affects the magnitude of productivity gains from each other's R&D spending. Using data on manufacturing industries in 14 OECD countries for the years 1970–95, he shows that R&D spillovers decline with geographic distance.

From a sample of 14 OECD countries over the period 1978–93 for total manufacturing industries, Kim and Lee (2004) examine the differentiated impact of domestic R&D and international R&D spillovers on productivity changes. They underline that spillovers may rely on various channels such as 'technological similarity, patents, foreign direct investment, and the presence of foreign firms'. Their results show that domestic R&D and international R&D spillovers measured by the technological distance have positive and large effects on TFP growth and technical change. When high-R&D-intensive countries are considered, only domestic R&D has a large significant influence on TFP and technical changes. On the other hand, for the low-R&D-intensive countries, spillover variables are the main contributing factors to productivity growth (Kim and Lee, 2004, p. 367).

There are also micro empirical studies, which try to appraise the influence of international technological transfers on a firm's efficiency proxied by its innovative performance. For example, from a sample of 432 American firms, Jaffe (1986) studies the impact of R&D spillovers on the productivity of firm R&D. R&D productivity of the firm is usually explained by its own R&D spending, and also the potential spillovers effect of other firms' R&D. The magnitude of spillovers from other firms' R&D expenditures depends on the similitude of the research areas, while R&D productivity of the firm is proxied by patent applications. Jaffe shows that 'firms whose research is in areas where there is much research by other firms have more patents per dollar of R&D'. In other words, the potential spillover pool has a significant positive effect, both directly and through its influence on the R&D elasticity.

After having observed that spillovers can imply positive effects, what can we say concerning the impact of international transfer of technology?

2.2.2.2 Impact of international transfer of technology

Few empirical studies assess the impact of international trade of disembodied technology. Veugelers and Cassiman (2004) explain technology transfers to the local economy by foreign-based multinationals; access to the international technology market; firm size; effectiveness of protecting know-how; technological origin and innovative profile. From a sample of 445 Belgian firms and for the period 1990–92, they obtain several interesting results. First, *foreign affiliates have a higher probability of being innovation active and having an own R&D base*. Second, and quite intuitively, *they are more likely to source technology internationally, typically from their parent company*. Third, *firms sourcing technology internationally are more active in transferring technological know-how to local firms*. Fourth, *MNEs prefer FDI over licensing to a local firm, because this allows a better control of know-how flows.* In particular, they minimize spillovers by having a low personnel exit rate. In addition, foreign subsidiaries may have lower incentives to transfer technology locally, especially when the host market is not an attractive candidate for providing reciprocal access to know-how as compared to other location sites. And, finally, cooperation between foreign subsidiaries and local firms is an important channel for the host country to benefit from technology transfers.

The paper of Mendi (2007) is the only one to estimate the influence of disembodied trade in technology. Among OECD countries he distinguishes those that belong to the G7 and others. Then, he presents 'evidence on the role of markets for technology in the diffusion process, estimating the effect of imports of disembodied technology – as measured by the Technological Balance of Payment Statistics – on the host-country's total factor productivity (TFP).' TFP will depend on the stock of domestic R&D, the import-weighted stock of foreign R&D,[7] a G7 dummy, the ratio of total imports of country i in time $t-1$ to GDP, the stock of disembodied technology imports[8] and finally the country's GDP per capita relative to that of the US.

The author highlights a differentiated impact of imported disembodied technologies across countries and across time. Indeed the 'stock of imports of disembodied technology is found to have a positive, statistically significant effect on productivity in non-G7 countries. On the contrary, concerning G7 countries, there is no evidence that the stock of imported technology has any significant effect on productivity.' Furthermore,

> this positive effect of technology trade on productivity within non-G7 countries was stronger in the initial years of the sample. This suggests that non-G7 countries were initially relying on imported technology, and were gradually reducing their dependence on foreign technology. This result is consistent with the stock of R&D having a non-linear effect on productivity, in the sense that a minimum level in this stock must be reached before any effect on TFP can be observed.

Several previous studies dealing with disembodied trade in technology try to disentangle the respective influence of several means of international technology diffusion.

Lee (2006) examined the international knowledge diffusion through four different channels: inward FDI, outward FDI, intermediate goods imports, and a disembodied direct channel. Applying non-stationary panel data analysis, he estimates for a sample of 16 OECD countries for the period 1981–2000 the relationship between manufacturing TFP and the four following variables: the domestic R&D capital stock in the manufacturing sector, the foreign R&D capital stock accumulated and embodied in the import flows of intermediate goods, the foreign R&D

capital stocks embodied in the inward and outward FDI, and finally the disembodied knowledge spillovers approximated by a measure of technological proximity and patent citations between countries. The estimation results show that 'the effects of international knowledge spillovers through inward FDI and the disembodied direct channel are significant.' By contrast, 'both outward FDI and import flows are ineffective as international transmission channels for knowledge'. In particular, the significance of the import flows, as found in previous studies, was refuted by considering additional channels for international knowledge spillovers, such as cross-border investments and the disembodied direct channel.

The impact of international trade in technology on the host country's productivity seen previously is due to the consequence of firms' activity. What are those consequences at micro and meso-level? Managerial topics focus on studies at the micro-level such as enhancing capabilities of knowledge acquisition and transfer. Several effects are observed: the impact on the efficiency or on innovative performance of the firm or the industry.

Concerning the direct impact of technological transfer on firms' productivity, Deardorff and Djankov (2000) investigate subcontracting arrangements as a source of knowledge transfer and increased efficiency for Czech firms during 1993–96. They consider that subcontracting enhances knowledge transfers via employee training and improves firm efficiency (increases in productivity and market valuation of firms). Thanks to surveys and interviews conducted with the managers of 373 manufacturing firms, they present some evidence of a positive correlation between subcontracting and knowledge transfer, where the latter results in increased firm efficiency. Subcontracting also increases the cost efficiency of recipient firms (reduction in variable costs), while it does not affect the unit costs for competitor firms. Subcontracting is associated with a price premium on the stock market and a high share of subcontracting activity in a particular industry is associated with increased valuation of firms with foreign partners as investors anticipate more subcontracting arrangements. However, the effect of subcontracting on other firms in the industry is weak.

Furthermore, recently the new empirical trade theory of multinational firms tries to better understand the knowledge and productivity advantage of globally engaged firms, mainly multinationals. For instance, Van Beveren (2008) examines whether firms' innovative output (proxied by innovative sales) differs according to their global engagement status (i.e. globally engaged firms, only exporters, foreign affiliates of multinational firms and home-based multinationals). His approach is particularly interesting as his goal is to highlight if innovative output of firms is mainly driven by the direct effect of firms' global integration or by an indirect effect through higher research spending. From a sample of 2988 firms located in Belgium and during the period 2002–04, he shows that 'exporters and multinational firms in Belgium are found to be significantly more likely to generate innovative output than their domestic counterparts'; nonetheless

in terms of innovative sales intensity, no significant differences emerge between the different types of firms. However, taking into account that internationally engaged firms typically spend more on R&D than national firms [. . .], only exporters are found to be more likely to generate innovative sales, while home-based multinationals are significantly less likely to innovate.

Criscuolo et al. (2010) showed from a sample of 7385 UK enterprises in 2000, first, that globally engaged firms do generate more innovation outputs: more patents, more self-reported innovations and a higher fraction of sales due to innovations. Secondly, globally engaged firms do use more researchers and more knowledge inputs to produce knowledge. Not only do they use more knowledge flows from outside the firm (for instance via market transaction), but they also use more flows within the firm, particularly from enterprises within the enterprise group (twice as much as multi-enterprise domestic firms, for example). To sum up, globally engaged firms generate more innovations that generate higher productivity, largely because they learn more from more sources.

As Castellani and Zanfei (2007) emphasize, those results are consistent with some recent modeling in trade theory and with more consolidated views in the economics of international production, suggesting that more productive firms will self-select into international markets, but also that commitment to foreign markets may boost firms' productivity and propensity to innovate.

Finally, macroeconomic results seem to conclude that international trade in disembodied technology has a positive impact on productivity and efficiency. Nevertheless, microeconomic and meso-economic studies deepen the analysis, as it is indeed possible to observe technology strategies more carefully and to obtain more detailed results as seen in the recent theoretical models.

2.3 TRENDS AND PATTERNS OF TRADE IN DISEMBODIED TECHNOLOGY FOR SOME EUROPEAN AND OECD COUNTRIES

We use several sets of data that allow us to evaluate the situation of European countries regarding disembodied technology and knowledge exchanges. In order to assess the way a country is connected to global research, the OECD examines internationally co-invented patents, cross-border patents, R&D funds from abroad, technology balance of payments and finally foreign doctoral students. Unfortunately most of the time it is not possible to present figures for the European Union as a whole because many countries do not communicate detailed data on these subjects. Even so we will try to give, thanks to available data, an accurate picture of the situation. To do so, we will first start by introducing an innovative input–output analysis that will be completed by data on foreign financing and international cooperation in patenting. In a second step we will examine Technological Balance of Payments statistics.

2.3.1 Innovative Input–Output Analysis

In this section, we will first present the traditional innovative input–output analysis. It roughly consists in examining the innovative efforts made by countries in terms of R&D expenditures, and the results obtained, in terms of patents. Then we will study the international openness of innovative activities, as it is an important characteristic of the European Union.

2.3.1.1 R&D expenditures

During the first half of the 1980s, the intensity of R&D expenditures[9] displays a rise in many OECD countries. Afterwards, countries have experienced a falling R&D intensity, with the exception of Japan, which registered R&D expenditures over 3 per cent of GDP.

On the more recent period (see Table 2.1), the EU27 reached 1.8 per cent when the United States registered 2.77 per cent and Japan spent almost 3.5 per cent. For European countries, Table 2.1 distinguishes three groups of countries. The first group of economies consists of countries that spend more GERD (as a percentage of GDP) than OECD countries, that is Sweden, Finland, Denmark, Austria and Germany. The second group encompasses the countries (France, Belgium and United Kingdom) that exhibit greater R&D expenditures as compared to the EU27. Finally the third group is made up of countries[10] that are below the EU27 average.

Sweden and Finland from the first group exhibit an R&D budget over 3 per cent of GDP. Those two countries are just before Japan, the United States, Denmark, Austria and Germany. Since the beginning of 2000, most countries have increased their expenditures on R&D except France, Belgium, Luxembourg, Poland, Greece, Slovak Republic and the Netherlands, for which it is quite stable.

Beyond this general trend, R&D intensity in the business enterprise sector has decreased in some of the industrialized countries since the 1990s

Table 2.1   *Gross domestic expenditure on R&D in decreasing order (as a percentage of GDP)*

Group of European countries	Countries	2000	2005	2008
1st group	Sweden[a]	–	3.60	3.75
1st group	Finland	3.35	3.48	3.49
	Japan	3.04	3.32	3.42
	USA[b]	2.71	2.57	2.77
1st group	Denmark	–	2.46	2.72
1st group	Austria	1.94	2.45	2.67
1st group	Germany	2.45	2.49	2.64
	OECD total	2.19	2.20	2.33
2nd group	France	2.15	2.10	2.02
2nd group	Belgium	1.97	1.83	1.92
2nd group	UK	1.81	1.73	1.88
	EU27 total	1.74	1.74	1.81
3rd group	Netherlands	1.82	1.79	1.75
3rd group	Slovenia	1.39	1.44	1.66
3rd group	Luxembourg	1.65	1.56	1.62
3rd group	Portugal	0.76	0.81	1.51
3rd group	Czech Republic	1.21	1.41	1.47
3rd group	Ireland	1.12	1.25	1.43
3rd group	Spain	0.91	1.12	1.35
3rd group	Estonia	0.60	0.93	1.27
3rd group	Italy	1.05	1.09	1.18
3rd group	Hungary	0.79	0.94	1.00
3rd group	Poland	0.64	0.57	0.61
3rd group	Greece	–	0.59	0.58*
3rd group	Slovak Republic	0.65	0.51	0.47

Notes:
a. Until 2005, R&D data for Sweden excluded R&D activities of state and local governments; Small and Medium Enterprises were not fully covered, and prior to 1993 the surveys in the Business Enterprise, Government and Private Non-Profit sectors excluded R&D in the social sciences and humanities.
b. For the United States, capital expenditure is not covered and R&D conducted by state and local governments is excluded.
*   Data for the year 2007.

Source: OECD (2010).

(as indicated in Table 2.2). In contrast, Austria, Finland, Japan, Denmark, and to a lesser extent the US have registered an increase.

It is noteworthy that, with the exception of Luxembourg and the United Kingdom, European countries belong to the three same groups as before.

Table 2.2   Business expenditure in R&D (BERD as % of GDP) in main European and OECD countries

Group of European Countries		1990	2000	2005	2008
1st group	Sweden	1.83[a]	3.23[b]	2.62	2.78
1st group	Finland	1.15	2.37	2.46	2.77
	Japan	2.12	2.16	2.54	2.69
	USA	1.87	2.02	1.80	2.01
1st group	Denmark	0.88	–	1.68	1.91
1st group	Austria	–	–	1.71	1.89
1st group	Germany	1.88	1.73	1.72	1.85
	Total OECD	1.54	1.52	1.50	1.63
2nd group	Belgium	–	1.42	1.25	1.32
3rd group	Luxembourg	–	1.53	1.35	1.32
2nd group	France	1.40	1.34	1.30	1.27
	EU27	–	1.11	1.08	1.13
2nd group	UK	1.46	1.18	1.06	1.10
3rd group	Ireland	0.49	0.80	0.82	0.93
3rd group	Netherlands	1.09	1.07	1.01	0.89
3rd group	Portugal	0.13	0.21	0.31	0.76
3rd group	Spain	0.46	0.49	0.60	0.74
3rd group	Italy	0.73	0.52	0.55	0.60
3rd group	Hungary	0.56	0.35	0.41	0.53
3rd group	Slovak Republic	1.05	0.43	0.25	0.20
3rd group	Poland	–	0.23	0.18	0.19
3rd group	Greece	–	0.15	0.18	–
3rd group	Czech Republic	–	–	0.89	0.91
3rd group	Slovenia	–	–	–	–

Notes:
a.   Data for the year 1991.
b.   Data for the year 2001.

Source: OECD (2010).

To conclude, the EU as a whole lags behind the US and Japan with the exception of Sweden and Finland for GERD and BERD, while Denmark, Austria and Germany display greater GERD and BERD compared to OECD countries.

2.3.1.2   OECD statistics on patents
We have highlighted that European countries as a whole spend less on R&D compared to the United States or Japan. In this section we examine

Table 2.3   Number and percentage of triadic patent families[11]

	1990	2000	2007
World	32466	46484	51990
OECD total	32216	45664	50014
USA	11229 (35%)	14348 (31%)	15883 (31%)
EU27 total	9986 (31%)	13921 (30%)	15062 (29%)
Japan	9605 (30%)	14779 (32%)	14665 (28%)
Germany	4119 (13%)	6079 (13%)	6283 (12%)
France	1908	2278	2462
UK	1455	1675	1666
Netherlands	585	989	1043
Sweden	441	685	846
Italy	644	680	769
Canada	289	535	719
Australia	186	362	352
Denmark	125	239	328
Finland	152	372	321
Spain	71	151	236

Source: OECD (2010).

the innovative performances measured by the number of triadic patent families of the OECD.

In 2001, the OECD developed a methodology to produce the OECD triadic patent families, defined as a set of patents taken at the three major patent offices to protect a same invention (the European Patent Office, the Japan Patent Office and the US Patent and Trademark Office).

Compared to the previous results, some differences can be noted (see Table 2.3). The US and Japan are the leaders in terms of patents. The European countries taken separately lag far behind the leaders. Germany, for instance, represents less than half the number of triadic patent families for Japan, while Germany is among the European leaders.

Nonetheless, the EU27 as a whole achieves interesting results. Indeed in 2007 the European Union represented 28.97 per cent of the total number of triadic patent families, Japan 28.21 per cent and the US 30.55 per cent. Therefore, the EU27 registers quite good results compared to its R&D expenditure.

2.3.1.3   International openness of innovative activity

One interesting feature of European innovative activity is that it exhibits a strong openness. Indeed the shares of foreign financing and international cooperation in patenting are particularly high. Multinational enterprises (MNEs) have been major actors of R&D internationalization. Indeed 'the bulk of industrial R&D is conducted by the leading big multinational enterprises' (UNCTAD, 2005). Until recently, R&D activity used to exhibit a strong home bias for several reasons.

> Besides the conventional forces working in favor of R&D centralization (economies of scale, avoidance of high communication and co-ordination costs, close control of the R&D portfolio, proprietary information), the exploitation of firm-specific technological advantages offered by public research institutions in the home market is an important reason why R&D lags behind in the internationalization process (Koopmann and Munnich, 1999, p.276).

'Now, firms are increasingly off-shoring R&D activities to other countries' and the internationalization of R&D activity is illustrated by the rise in international patent activity, out licensing and overseas alliances (OECD, 2009).

Concerning the R&D expenditure, we noticed that Japan is one of the greatest contributors, with more than 3 per cent of GDP, and is a country where business expenditure of R&D is especially high compared with OECD countries (2.69 per cent in 2008). Japan is also the country that exhibits the smallest share of R&D expenditure under foreign control (4.3 per cent see Table 2.4). GERD and BERD of the European Union lag far behind Japan, the US and OECD countries with the exception of Sweden and Finland. Nonetheless R&D financed from abroad is higher in the EU.

Concerning the internationalization of patent activity, it goes back to the 1980s when 'a rapid growth of international patent activity has occurred, while domestic patenting has been stagnant' (Archibugi and Pianta, 1992, p.89). It comes with increased international technological collaboration in the 1990s. It involves both: (1) an intensified technological division of labor via insourcing and outsourcing of R&D activities, and (2) a growing significance of technologically oriented inter-company alliances' (Koopman and Munnich, 1999, p.276).

The OECD has developed two indicators dedicated to assessing international cooperation. The first measure – the *international cooperation in patenting* – relates to the share of patents involving inventors with different countries of residence. As inventors in different countries also differ in their specialization and knowledge assets, they look for knowledge beyond national boundaries to overcome a lack of technological resources. The second index is the *share of patent co-inventors*. It measures the 'share of PCT[12] filings with at least one foreign co-inventor in total patents invented domestically'. 'Patent counts are based on the priority date, the inventor's

Table 2.4   R&D expenditure under foreign control (%) 2004

Rank of European countries GERD as % of GDP	Countries*	Decreasing order (%)
3rd group	Ireland	77.3
3rd group	Hungary	62.5
3rd group	Portugal	51.4
3rd group	Czech Republic	48.7
1st group	Sweden	44.7
2nd group	UK	40.3
3rd group	Spain	35.6
1st group	Germany	27.9
3rd group	Netherlands	27.5
3rd group	Italy	25.9
2nd group	France	25.3
3rd group	Poland	16.8
1st group	Finland	16.4
	EU27	38.2
	USA	14.6
	Japan	4.3

Note: * For Slovenia, Slovak Republic, Denmark, Belgium, Luxembourg and Greece data are not available.

Source: OECD (2008).

country of residence and use simple counts on Patent Cooperation Treaty filings at international phase (European Patent Office designations)' (OECD, 2008, p. 30).

The Compendium of Patent Statistics (OECD, 2008) stipulates that 'the world share of patents involving international co-inventions increased from 5.8% in the mid-1990s to more than 7% in 2003-05' and it reached 7.28 per cent in 2004–06. Figure 2.1 provides information dealing with the share of patents with foreign co-inventors[13] for two periods, 1996–98 and 2004–06. Among the OECD countries, we can notice that both the US and the EU experienced a rise in their share of patents with co-inventors. Japan, which exhibits the smallest share of patent with foreign co-inventors, also faced a serious reduction in the second period.

Figures 2.2 and 2.3 depict ownership of inventions. It is noteworthy that Japan is quite different from the other countries. Indeed domestic ownership of inventions made abroad and Japanese inventions realized abroad are the weakest compared to OECD countries.

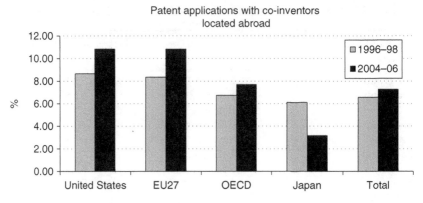

Source: OECD (2009).

Figure 2.1   Patent applications with co-inventors located abroad

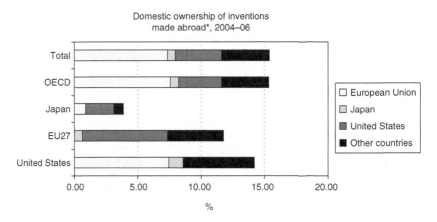

Notes:
Domestic ownership of inventions made abroad: share of patent applications filed under the Patent Cooperation Treaty invented abroad in total patents owned by country residents, by priority date.
Interpretation: For instance, 14 per cent of the inventions made by Americans are performed outside the USA. Around 7 per cent of American inventions are carried out in Europe, 2 per cent in Japan and around 6 per cent in other countries.

Source: OECD (2009).

Figure 2.2   Inventions made abroad

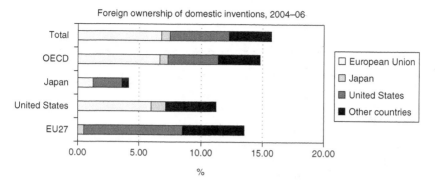

Notes: Foreign ownership of domestic inventions: share of patent applications filed under the PCT owned by foreign residents in total patents invented domestically, by priority date. The EU is treated as one country and excludes intra-EU cooperation; average cooperation is provided for OECD total and total patents. Figures only cover countries with more than 250 patent cooperation treaty filings over 2004–06.

Source: OECD (2009).

Figure 2.3 Domestic inventions owned by foreigners

Foreign and domestic ownership of inventions (Figures 2.2 and 2.3) differs across countries. For the period 1999–2006, the OECD estimated the average foreign ownership of domestic inventions to be around 15 per cent of the total, with 15.72 per cent for the period 2004–06 (Onodera, 2008, p. 6). As already mentioned, Japan appears to be different from the other countries. The US seems, on the other hand, to be particularly active in domestic inventions made abroad (almost 15 per cent compared to 12 per cent for Europe).

The breakdown of patent applications with co-invention for European countries is presented in Table 2.5.

From Table 2.5, it is clear that there is a link between the GERD as percentage of GDP and share of patent applications with co-inventors. Indeed most of the countries that exhibit the greatest share of patent applications with co-inventors belong to the third group and display small gross domestic expenditure on R&D as a percentage of their GDP. Conversely, countries at the bottom of Table 2.5 are characterized by important GERD spending.

Table 2.6 sums up the science and innovation profile of the main OECD countries. It depicts clearly the particularities of the European countries, the United States and Japan. Indeed it is noteworthy that Japan is successful in innovative activities while being quite isolated from the global research network. The European Union seems to be in the

Table 2.5   *Patent applications with co-inventors located abroad, % of GDP, 2004–06*[a]

Group	Country	1996–98	2004–06
2nd group	Belgium	40.79	44.40
3rd group	Poland		34.55
3rd group	Portugal		33.77
3rd group	Ireland	35.66	33.47
3rd group	Czech Republic		31.58
3rd group	Hungary	16.99	30.09
3rd group	Greece		26.40
1st group	Austria	23.98	26.03
2nd group	UK	18.66	24.35
2nd group	France	17.05	21.29
1st group	Denmark	15.40	19.78
3rd group	Spain	18.24	19.37
3rd group	Slovenia		19.27
3rd group	Netherlands	15.33	18.62
1st group	Sweden	12.33	18.55
1st group	Germany	11.83	16.05
1st group	Finland	11.02	15.50
3rd group	Italy	16.37	13.73
	USA	8.66	10.84
	Japan	6.10	3.18
	EU27	8.35	10.82
	OECD	6.75	7.70

Note: a.   Patent counts are based on the priority date and the inventor's country of residence. The EU is treated as one country; intra-EU cooperation is excluded. Average cooperation is provided for OECD total and total patents.

opposite situation. European expenditure in R&D is still weak; nevertheless the percentage of R&D under foreign control is quite important. Furthermore, it is important to notice that global performance of the EU is quite encouraging when we observe expenses in R&D and individual performance of each country.

2.3.2   The Technology Balance of Payments

We have seen previously that innovative activities of European countries are characterized by their great openness to foreign collaboration and financing. In this section, we will examine technology balance of payments data to show the features of European countries as compared to main OECD countries relating to trade in technology.

Table 2.6 Science and innovation profile of the main OECD countries, 2008

Groups of European Countries*	Countries	R&D expenditure (% of GDP)	Business expenditure of R&D (% of GDP)	Patents with foreign co-inventors
	Japan	3.42	2.69	
	USA	2.77	2.01	
1st	Sweden	3.75	2.78	
1st	Finland	3.49	2.77	
1st	Denmark	2.72	1.91	
1st	Austria	2.67	1.89	
1st	Germany	2.64	1.85	
2nd	France	2	1.27	
2nd	Belgium	1.92	1.32	
2nd	UK	1.88	1.10	
3rd	Netherlands	1.75	0.89	
3rd	Slovenia	1.66	1.63	
3rd	Luxembourg	1.62	1.32	
3rd	Portugal	1.51	0.76	
3rd	Czech Republic	1.47	0.91	
3rd	Ireland	1.43	0.93	
3rd	Spain	1.35	0.74	
3rd	Italy	1.18	0.60	
3rd	Hungary	1	0.53	
3rd	Poland	0.61	0.19	
3rd	Greece	0.58	0.1	
3rd	Slovak Republic	0.47	0.2	
	EU 27	1.81	1.13	10.82
	OECD	2.33	1.63	7.70

Note: * The ranking of countries is based on GERD as of GDP.

2.3.2.1 Presentation of the Technology Balance of Payment data

According to Mendi (2007), Technology Balance of Payments (TBP) 'constitutes the only internationally comparable database on trade in disembodied technology' and their aim is 'to provide an accurate measure of trade in technology, removing items without technological content'. The OECD includes the following items in the TBP statistics: patents (purchases and sales); licenses for patents; know-how (unpatented knowledge); models and designs; trademarks (including franchising); technical services; finance of industrial R&D outside national territory. The OECD explicitly excludes from TBP: commercial, financial, managerial and legal assistance; advertising, insurance, transport; films, recordings, and material covered by copyright; design; software.

Technology receipts minus technology payments give the TBP. '*Technology receipts* depend on a country's R&D effort and also correspond to foreign sales of the marketable results of that effort'. 'Over 60% of such technology transfers in the major countries are between parent companies and affiliates'. '*Technology payments* correspond to knowledge that is immediately useable by country's productive system as a technology input' (OECD, 2005, p. 156; OECD, 2006, p. 130).

As an indicator, 'the technology balance of payments reflects a country's ability to sell its disembodied technology abroad and the extent to which it makes use of foreign technologies'. Nonetheless, 'the deficits/surpluses need to be carefully interpreted since they can reflect a wide range of factors including a country's degree of technological autonomy: its ability/inability to assimilate foreign technologies or its high/low levels of technology imports/exports'. Ultimately, a country's technological development can 'reflect the choice between domestic production of technology/inventions (via a high national R&D effort) or foreign absorption (via the acquisition of foreign technologies and the payment of licensing fees and royalties)' (Denis et al., 2006). Consequently a growing deficit does not necessarily indicate low competitiveness in technology. Finally, since most transactions correspond to operations between parent companies and affiliates, the valuation of the technology transfer may be distorted.[14] 'Therefore, additional qualitative and quantitative information are needed to analyze correctly a country's deficit or surplus position' (OECD, 2006) as usual when considering balance of payments statistics.

The examination of the technological balance of payments of the US, Japan and the OECD area as a whole from 1993 to 2006[15] reveals that they have constantly been net technology exporters to the rest of the world. On the other hand the EU's overall technological balance of payments used to be in persistent deficit from 1993. However, the situation changed, as Figure 2.4 shows, and in 2006 the EU exhibited a surplus.

Table 2.7 presents TBP data for selected countries. Because of data non-availability, we do not have figures for the European Union as a whole. Moreover, for some countries data are quite old (France for instance). In decreasing order the countries that record greatest surpluses are: the US, Japan, UK, Germany, Sweden and Austria. The European countries exhibit contrasted situations but the ranking of European countries is not surprising as it fits in with GERD and BERD levels, with the exception of the United Kingdom.

MNEs account for the greater part of international technology flows. Koopmann and Munnich (1999, p. 273) underline for example that

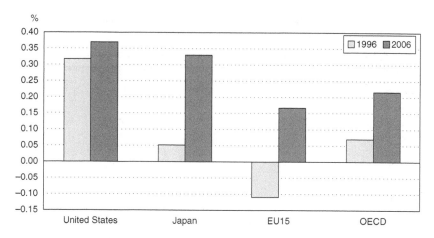

Note: a. For EU and OECD total, including intra-area flows. Excluding: Denmark, Greece, Iceland and Turkey. Data partially estimated.

Source: OECD (2009).

Figure 2.4 *Technology Balance of Payments (1996–2006), % of GDP*[a]

'German companies with foreign subsidiaries in 1997 covered about three quarters of total receipts in manufacturing industry while nearly half of the corresponding payments were met by foreign controlled firms in Germany. In electronics the dominance of multinational corporations was almost complete'. Nonetheless OECD data do not distinguish between arm's-length and intra-group transfers of technology.

2.3.2.2 Geographical patterns of technology payments
The geographical patterns of technology balance of payments are interesting (Table 2.8). Concerning the first group of European countries, we can notice that they always register positive balance of payments, which means they export technology. Among countries that display greatest surpluses, the United States collect more technological receipts from all countries, with the exception of France, in 2008. It is not possible to exploit Japanese and UK data because the geographical breakdown is not available for these countries.

Among European countries, Germany, Sweden and Austria are the main exporters of technology (when data are available). Germany has a deficit with the European Union (EU27) as a whole and the US. Sweden, on the other hand, displays a surplus with the EU27 but a deficit with the US. Austria has surpluses both with the EU27 and the US. Sweden and

Table 2.7 *Technology balance of payments for selected countries, 2008,*
millions of euros

Country/Area	Surplus (+)/Deficit (−)
USA[a]	44 182
Japan[b]	10 988
UK	9993
Germany	6160
Sweden	3797
Austria	2181
France[c]	1732
Finland	852
Italy	374
Czech Republic	102
Portugal	66
Slovak Republic[d]	−214
Greece	−392
Ireland	−470
Hungary	−690
Poland	−1254
Belgium	−1801

Notes:
a. Royalties and license fees.
b. 2007.
c. 2003.
d. 2005.

Source: OECD (2010).

Germany are the best European performers in Asia. While Sweden exports more technology to non-OECD countries, Germany exports to Japan and Korea.

The second group of countries registers more contrasted results. Indeed, for instance France registers a positive balance while it is not the case for Belgium from the second group. Belgium shows a surplus with Ireland. (Ireland exhibits its greatest shortages with the US and OECD countries, whereas it presents surpluses with European Union countries.)

Portugal has an interesting characteristic as it collects a great amount of technology receipts from Africa and the world, while it is in deficit with European and OECD countries.

*Table 2.8 Technology balance of payments by main partner zone/country, 2008, * millions of euros*

Groups of European countries / Partner zone or country	JP	US[b]	1st SE	1st AT	1st DE	2nd FR	2nd BE	3rd IT[a]	3rd CZ	3rd PT	3rd GR	3rd HU	3rd SK	3rd IE
AFRICA			662		511					173				496
Austria (AT)					−794					4			−29	
Belgium (BE)-Luxembourg			225				−140[c]	264	15	5				752
Canada		3557				61						180	5	
China			342	149	647			42						
Czech Republic (CZ)													−108	
Denmark								−23		8				
EUROPEAN UNION (27)[$]	1527	20501	787	835	−399	218	−653	−162	−97	−115	−355	−49	−112	8194
Finland									11					
France (FR)		−345	1018		−369		−143	−320	−103	4	−23	37	−7	2215
Germany (DE)		3413	−292	721			−146	163	−49	−59	−46	−369	−52	
Greece (GR)														
Hungary (HU)					429					−14				
Ireland (IE)					−974	78	130	−26	14	−38			−6	
Israel														159
Italy (IT)						97	−183							−32
Japan (JP)					1017	255	−138		−84	15	−37	85		
Korea		2155			304							−83		
Mexico					487									
Netherlands					363	54	−222	48	39	21	−78			
MIDDLE EAST	198		1022	198						6			−9	1390
NON-OECD ASIA		5730	1838	213	874	68			12	−7		58		
Norway										3				415

Table 2.8 (continued)

Groups of European countries			1st	1st	1st	2nd	2nd	3rd	3rd	3rd	3rd	3rd	3rd	3rd
Partner zone or country	JP	US[b]	SE	AT	DE	FR	BE	IT[a]	CZ	PT	GR	HU	SK	IE
OECD (30)			1021	1165	2617	646	-2389		-123	-115	-348	-340		-1194
Poland				128				40	10				2	465
Portugal (PT)												52		
Russia				147	377				150					
Singapore		2111												
Slovak Republic (SK)									61					
SOUTH AMERICA	334	2336[e]			1052									
Spain					676	130		17		-47		116		
Sweden (SE)						-348				-18		57		
Switzerland		3762	709	304	2118	-54	-97	-106	12	-19				850
Turkey											21			192
UK	3517[d]	3927	-469	-478	-734	127	-218	-303	-50	-5	-106	-277	-16	
USA				104	-1029		-1049	-24	47	15	-51		6	-11208
WORLD	10988	44182	3797	2181	6160	1732	-1801	374	102	66	-392	-690	-214	-470

Notes:
*   Except for Japan, Sweden (2007); Slovak Republic (2005); and France (2003).
$ Europe for Japan, EU25 for Sweden and the US. Data are not available for the UK and Finland. EU15 for France, Poland and Slovak Republic.
a. Figures for OECD (30) unavailable.
b. US royalties and license fees.
c. Luxembourg.
d. North America.
e. South and Central America.

2.4 CONCLUSION

Several facts confirm the growing international trade in technology. Indeed firms are not only developing innovations internationally, they are also exploiting their innovations on world markets by licensing their technologies or by selling their innovations to foreign purchasers (Gassler and Nones, 2008). The balance of payments statistics reflect this tendency as the volume of transactions is increasing.

Concerning empirical analyses, macroeconomic-level studies conclude that there is a positive impact of disembodied technology. Nevertheless, differences are observed between location, development of countries and also level of R&D in countries. For instance, for high-R&D-intensive countries, the growth of total factor productivity is mainly attributable to the increase in domestic R&D. For low-R&D-intensive countries, the international spillovers are the main factors for the TFP growth.

From a statistical point of view, it is not easy to highlight some European specificity because data for the European Union as a whole are missing. Nonetheless, thanks to the OECD data, it is possible to depict some particularities.

Considering the traditional input–output analysis of innovative activities, we notice first that GERD and BERD of the European Union lag behind those of Japan, the United States and OECD countries, with the exception of Sweden and Finland. Second innovative performances as measured by patent triadic families seem to be a little bit smaller for the EU. However, innovative activities in Europe are more internationalized. Indeed R&D financed from abroad in the EU is significantly higher. Moreover, co-inventions are particularly superior.

Technology balance of payments data allow us to expose some additional results. We notice that the European countries for which GERD and BERD as a percentage of GDP are particularly high, always register a positive balance of payments, which means they export technology.

To conclude, it is important to notice that data are missing despite the efforts made by the OECD to collect data on trade in disembodied technology. For instance disaggregated data into affiliated and unaffiliated disembodied transfers of technology are really difficult to obtain. Yet more empirical studies at the firm level are necessary to better understand the specificities, of, respectively, arm's-length and intra-group transfers of technology.

NOTES

1. Keller (2004, p. 758) underlines that many economists believe that most international technology diffusion occurs through externalities (spillovers) and not through market transactions (transfers).
2. According to Shih and Chang (2008), technology spreads internationally through two distinct kinds of spillovers: passive and active technology spillovers. *Passive technology spillovers* consist in the 'implicit usage of the technological knowledge embodied in foreign intermediate goods for final-output production'. *Active technology spillovers* are based on the 'direct international learning or purchasing foreign technological knowledge that involves the explicit usage of disembodied knowledge'. However, in this chapter we will speak of *spillovers* to designate international diffusion of technology, which relies on externalities, and *transfers* of technology and knowledge will refer to the purchase of disembodied technology.
3. According to Maskus (2003, p. 15), international technology transfers can flow through market and non-market mechanisms or otherwise by 'formal' and 'informal' channels. The 'market channels of international technology transfers include: trade in goods and services, foreign direct investment, licensing, joint ventures, cross-border movement of personnel'. The non-market channels or 'informal' channels through which knowledge and technology may flow are: 'a) Imitation b) Departure of employees c) Data in patent applications and test data d) Temporary migration'.
4. On the other hand, hiring a new skilled employee is considered as an embodied flow of knowledge.
5. For greater information concerning empirical studies for other countries, see Mucchielli et al. (2009).
6. See, for example, Blomstrom and Kokko (1998).
7. Weights are imports from country j as a proportion of total imports by country i.
8. According to the author, 'the stock of acquired technology mitigates one disadvantage of the TBP data. These statistics include transactions where ownership of the technology is transferred, as well as other transactions where ownership is retained by the licensor. While the former typically originate lump-sum payments, the latter typically generate variable payments along several periods. Since the proportion of each transaction type is unknown, the stock variable is expected to be a better measure for the imported technology available to a given country in a specific period than the flow variable'.
9. Public and private R&D expenditures (as a share of gross domestic production).
10. In decreasing order: the Netherlands, Slovenia, Luxembourg, Portugal, Czech Republic, Ireland, Spain, Estonia, Italy, Hungary, Poland, Greece, Slovak Republic.
11. The OECD publishes statistics of triadic patent families regularly at www.oecd.org/sti/ipr-statistics.
12. The Patent Cooperation Treaty is an international treaty administered by the World Intellectual Property Organization (WIPO). The PCT makes it possible to seek patent protection for an invention simultaneously in a large number of countries by filing a single 'international application' with a single patent office (i.e. receiving Office). The PCT system simplifies the process of multinational patent filings by reducing the requirement to file multiple patent applications for multinational patent rights. PCT international applications do not result in the issuance of 'international patents' and the International Bureau (IB) does not grant patents. The decision on whether to confer patent rights remains in the hands of the national and/or regional patent offices, and patent rights are limited to the jurisdiction of the patent granting authority. (WIPO, 2008, p. 60).
13. Co-inventions are measured as the share of patent applications filed under the PCT with at least one co-inventor located abroad in total patents invented domestically. Patent counts are based on the priority date and the inventor's country of residence. The EU is treated as one country; intra-EU cooperation is excluded. Average cooperation is provided for OECD total and total patents. Figures only cover countries with more than 250 PCT filings over the periods.

14. For a discussion about TBP limitations see: Mucchielli et al. (2009).
15. Denis et al. (2006) present data from 1993 to 2003.

REFERENCES

Archibugi, P. and M. Pianta (1992), 'Specialization and size of technological activities in industrial countries: the analysis of patent data', *Research Policy*, **21**, 79–93.

Blomstrom, M. and A. Kokko (1998), 'Multinational corporations and spillovers', *Journal of Economic Surveys*, **12**(3), 247–77.

Cassiman, B. and R. Veugelers (2000), 'External technology sources: embodied or disembodied technology acquisition', Working Paper, available at: http://www.econ.upf/edu/docs/papers/downloads/444.pdf.

Castellani, D. and A. Zanfei (2007), 'Internationalisation, innovation and productivity: how do firms differ in Italy?', *The World Economy*, January.

Chang, C. and S. Robin (2006), 'Doing R&D and/or importing technologies: the critical importance of firm size in Taiwan's manufacturing industries', *Review of Industrial Organization*, **29**, 253–78.

Criscuolo, H., J.E. Slaughter and J. Matthew (2010), 'Global engagement and the innovation activities of firms', *International Journal of Industrial Organization*, **28**(2), 191–202.

Deardorff, A. and S. Djankov (2000), 'Knowledge transfer under subcontracting: evidence from Czech firms', *World Development*, **28**(10), 1837–47.

Denis, C., K. McMorrow and W. Röger (2006), 'Globalisation: trends, issues and macro implications for the EU', Directorate-General for Economic and Financial Affairs, no 254, July.

Eaton, J. and S. Kortum (1996), 'Trade in ideas patenting and productivity in the OECD', *Journal of International Economics*, **40**(3–4), Symposium on Growth and International Trade: Empirical Studies, pp. 251–78.

Gambardella, A., P. Giuri and A. Luzzi (2007), 'The market for patents in Europe', *Research Policy*, **36**, 1163–83.

Gassler, H. and B. Nones (2008), 'Internationalisation of R&D and embeddedness: the case of Austria', *Journal of Technology Transfer*, **33**, 407–21, available at: http://www.jstor.org/stable/1816464.

Jaffe, A.B. (1986), 'Technological opportunity and spillovers of R&D: evidence from firms' patents, profits, and market value', *The American Economic Review*, **76**(5), 984–1001.

Keller, W. (2002), 'Geographic localization of international technology diffusion', *The American Economic Review*, **92**(1), 120–42.

Keller, W. (2004), 'International technology diffusion', *Journal of Economic Literature*, **XLII**, September, 752–82.

Kim, J.W. and H.K. Lee (2004), 'Embodied and disembodied international spillovers of R&D in OECD manufacturing industries', *Technovation*, **24** (2004), 359–68.

Koopmann, G. and F. Munnich (1999), 'National and international developments in technology trends, patterns and implications for policy', *Intereconomics*, November/December, 267–78.

Lee, G. (2006), 'The effectiveness of international knowledge spillover channels', *European Economic Review*, **50**(8), 2075–88.

Maskus, E.K. (2003), 'Encouraging international technology transfer', Capacity building project on intellectual property rights and sustainable development, UNCTAD/ICTSD, December.

Mendi, P. (2007), 'Trade in disembodied technology and total factor productivity in OECD countries', *Research Policy*, **36**, 121–33.

Mucchielli, J-L., N. Avallone and S. Chédor (2009), 'Global trade in knowledge: a survey of the literature', OECD Working Paper DSTI/IND/WPGI (2009)6, Working party on globalisation of industry, October.

OECD (2005), *Handbook on Economic Globalization Indicators*, Paris: OECD.

OECD (2006), *Science, Technology and Industry Outlook*, Paris: OECD.

OECD (2008), *Science, Technology and Industry Outlook*, Highlights, Paris: OECD.

OECD (2009), 'The OECD innovation strategy', draft interim report, February, Paris: OECD.

OECD (2010), *Factbook*, Paris: OECD.

Onodera, O. (2008), 'Trade and innovation' a synthesis paper, *OECD Trade Policy Working Paper* no. 72, Paris: OECD.

Shih, H-Y. and T-L.S. Chang (2008), 'International diffusion of embodied and disembodied technology: a network analysis approach', *Technological Forecasting and Social Change*, **76**(6), 821–34.

Taschler, D.R. and C.C. Chappelow (1999), 'Intra-company technology transfer in a multinational industrial firm', *Journal of Technology Transfer*, **22**(1), 29–34.

UNCTAD (2005), *World Investment Report – Transnational Corporations and the Internationalization of R&D*, New York and Geneva: United Nations.

Van Beveren, Ilke (2008), 'Multinational firms, research effort and innovative output: an integrated approach', in *Globalization and Firm Dynamics*, PhD thesis no. 293, Catholic University of Leuven.

Veugelers, R. and B. Cassiman (2004), 'Foreign subsidiaries as a channel of international technology diffusion: some direct firm level evidence from Belgium', *European Economic Review*, **48**, 455–76.

3. A snapshot on STI policies and indicators for Belgium

Peter Teirlinck

3.1 INTRODUCTION

Institutionally speaking, Belgium is a 'mini-Europe': each of the federated authorities (regions and linguistic communities) is singularly competent for the areas of STI (science, technology and innovation) granted to it by the Constitution. The long process of decentralization, which began in the 1970s, has led to a differentiation of institutions and policies adapted to the STI potential, and the social and economic needs of each part of Belgium.

Benchmarked with the total of the European Union, Belgium has a high share of human resources for the knowledge-based economy and is characterized by high labor productivity. Also, involvement in technological innovation is one of the highest in Belgium and the business sector is strongly integrated into the international economy through foreign direct investments. Main weaknesses are the weak entrepreneurial activity and a rather low share of graduates in science and engineering at the first-stage university level. In terms of R&D intensity (R&D expenditures as a percentage of GDP), Belgium is close to the EU average. However, the fact that close to 60 per cent of business research is concentrated within a limited number of large R&D spending multinational firms that have established or took over R&D facilities in Belgium also involves substantial risks of delocalization.

Both STI policy making and statistics are confronted with a number of challenges. First, STI is an increasingly international phenomenon and policy making still is largely based on territorially linked principles. This international context in which multinational enterprises are the key drivers is characterized not only by knowledge development but also by knowledge exchange and valorization (as emphasized by the paradigm of 'open innovation'). Second, especially in policy terms, greater attention is paid to the role of STI to respond to (global) challenges in terms of environment, health, security and energy supply. . . . This forces STI policy making to be considered in a broader policy mix (which actually is not the case) and challenges the evaluation of public funding for research to be based on statistical evidence paying more attention to long-term impacts (that is beyond the currently applied short-term input or output addition-ality views on indicators).

This chapter provides a brief description of the STI institutional and policy system in Belgium (section 3.2) and gives a snapshot on data and trends in indicators on Belgian R&D and innovation (section 3.3). The policy 'mapping' complements the statistical data and will help the reader put into context the choices made by the Belgian authorities in terms of policy objectives and instruments. For each of the authorities, attention is paid to current policy objectives for STI, the main actors and implementa-tion measures of this policy.

A final section (section 3.4) provides some perspectives for STI policy for the small open Belgian economy. This is regarded from a perspective on future orientations of policy, notably in the context of the European Commission's Europe 2020 Strategy, the future European Research & Innovation Plan and the ongoing actions to reinforce the European Research Area (ERA). Topics concerning internationalization, open inno-vation, broader policy mix and evaluation will be addressed.

Dealing with the complex issues of STI policies and indicators is beyond the scope of this chapter. For a broader view on STI statistics and policies for Belgium we refer to *Key Data on Science, Technology and Innovation Belgium 2010* (Belgian Science Policy Office, 2010a) and the *Belgian Report on Science and Technology 2010* (Belgian Science Policy Office, 2010b). These reports are the sources for the STI policy description and the statistical evidence presented here. For more detailed insights into broad STI policy trends in an international context we refer to the 'OECD STI Outlook' (OECD, 2009c).

The insights presented – especially those concerning perspectives for STI policy making – are written to stimulate debate and represent the author's personal opinions.

3.2 INSTITUTIONS AND COMPETENCES IN SCIENCE, TECHNOLOGY AND INNOVATION POLICY IN BELGIUM

In this section attention is paid to the repartition of responsibilities in the Belgian STI policy system (section 3.2.1) and to the general STI policy orientations of the main policy actors (section 3.2.3). To give an idea of the importance in budgetary terms of the STI policies of the different governments, a brief overview is provided on the budget outlays for R&D at each of the policy levels (section 3.2.2).

3.2.1 Distribution of Responsibilities in the Belgian STI Policy System

Belgium is a federal country[1] composed of seven autonomous entities: the Federal State, three regions (Flemish Region, Walloon Region and Brussels-Capital Region) and three communities (Flemish Community, French-speaking Community and the German-speaking Community). In practice, the Flemish region and the Flemish Community merged to form a single government, parliament and administration: the Flemish Authority.

Each entity elects its own government and parliament and establishes all regulations and institutions necessary to ensure effective government within its realm of responsibilities. Each 'federated' entity and the Federal State have exclusive powers in a number of research areas.

The *Federal State* is competent for the scientific research necessary for it to perform its own general competences, including scientific research aimed at the execution of international or supranational agreements; space research within an international framework; networks of data exchange on a national or international basis (Belnet), the federal scientific institutes, and – within the framework of cooperation agreements with the communities and/or the regions – programs and actions requiring homogeneous execution at national or international level; the maintenance of a permanent inventory of the country's scientific potential; and Belgian participation in activities of international research bodies. The Federal Government can also take any action in areas belonging to the competences of the federated entities, if acting on the basis of an opinion expressed by the Federal Council for Science Policy. These actions must, furthermore, either be related to an international agreement or refer to actions and programs going beyond the interests of one community or one region. In addition, the Federal Government retains responsibility for a number of other key fields of policy with an influence on STI performance, notably tax and social security (and hence the possibility to provide incentives through the tax system), (scientific) visas, intellectual property law, and so on.

The *communities* act in fields pertaining to the needs and rights of individual citizens; notably primary, secondary and higher education, scientific research and culture. The concept of 'community' refers to persons that make up a community and the bond that unifies them, namely their language and culture. The communities are competent in the following areas: research related to education, culture and other individual matters, such as health policy, and personal assistance. This covers research in these areas as well as research conducted by organizations of the sectors concerned, namely universities and other higher education institutes. It can be said that communities have the main responsibility for fundamental research in universities and applied research in higher education establishments, including international activities of these institutions. They are also in charge of popularization and communication of science.

The creation of the three *regions* responded to the need to develop socioeconomic policies adapted to the specific needs of each territory. The regions have the main responsibility for economically oriented research, technological development and innovation promotion. Regional support and subsidies are the main instruments to enhance the development of new products and processes in SMEs, technology transfer, public research organizations, venture capital, and science parks and incubation centers (supporting start-ups).

The distribution of responsibilities in STI across the various authorities in Belgium is based on fields of competences, rather than on the actors. This is illustrated by the case of universities, major players in the Belgian research system. Whereas the communities are competent for research at universities and other tertiary higher education institutions (HEI, namely 'Hogeschool' in the Flemish system and 'Hautes Ecoles' in the French community) and administer the basic allocations to these organizations, the Federal Government and the regions can also fund projects of HEI for STI activities in their own realm of competences. In practice, this means that universities may receive funding from the Federal Government, regions or communities (according to their location and their linguistic regime), but for different purposes and with different conditions attached to the finances received.

Increasingly, the core of STI policy is interlinked with other policy areas with an influence on innovation in the broader sense. This concerns regional competences in terms of economic policy (under which fall, for example, start-up promotion and risk capital provision) and environmental policy (with the push to promote green or 'eco-innovation'), or federal competences such as fiscal policy (for example tax breaks for R&D activities) or social security (for example issues related to the social security regime of researchers), and so on. In such areas policy initiatives and instruments are developed that may in some cases have a major impact on STI, and this requires, increasingly, consultation amongst the Belgian authorities to ensure an optimal outcome in terms of research and innovation potential.

The distribution of STI competences across all Belgian authorities, as described above, goes hand-in-hand with the need for coordination in

Table 3.1   GBAORD *(including tax credits), million euros, current prices, by authority*

	1998	2009 (previsional)
Flemish Community	518	1147
Federal Authority (including tax credit for R&D)	460	963
French Community	203	291
Walloon Region	104	331
Region of Brussels-Capital	11	29
TOTAL	1296	2761

Source: Federal Cooperation Commission, CFS/STAT.

a number of areas on either a permanent or ad hoc basis. Coordination and consultation between the various components of the Belgian state is organized through a committee embracing these authorities and providing room for dialogue on all matters requiring concerted action at national level. The Inter-Ministerial Conference on Science Policy (CIPS-ICWB) is the coordination instrument between the Federal State, the communities and the regions, composed of those members of respective governments having responsibilities in science policy matters.[2]

3.2.2   Government Budget Outlays for R&D of the Different Authorities in Belgium

Government budget outlays for R&D (GBAORD) give an idea of the financial support in terms of R&D of the different governments in Belgium. The GBAORD indicator is not based on real expenditure on scientific and technological activities but on the budget allocations of the aforementioned authorities, and this irrespective of where the money is spent, thus whether or not it is within the public sector or within the national territory. The GBAORD tells us something about the theoretical destination of the investment. It shows trends in the financial involvement and attitude of the public authorities over time towards investment in research and development.

Based on the results presented in Table 3.1 it turns out that over the period 1998–2009 there has been a substantial increase in government budget outlays for R&D, for each of the governments. In terms of percentages per government, in the year 2009, the Flemish Community represents 41.5 per cent, the Federal Authority 35 per cent[3], the French Community and Walloon Region taken together account for 22.5 per cent, and the Region of Brussels-Capital represents about 1 per cent. In budgetary

Table 3.2   GBAORD (excluding tax credits) by socioeconomic objectives, 2008

1. Exploration and earth exploitation	1.0%	9. Education	0.3%
2. Environment	2.1%	10. Culture, recreation, religion and mass media	2.0%
3. Exploration and exploitation of space	11.8%	11. Political and social systems/ structures/processes	3.1%
4. Transport, telecommunication and other infrastructures	1.9%	12. General advancement of knowledge: R&D financed from General University Funds (GUF)	15.7%
5. Energy	1.5%		
6. Industrial production and technology	33.7%	13. General advancement of knowledge: not GUF	23.5%
7. Health	2.0%	14. Defence	0.2%
8. Agriculture	1.3%	(Other civil research)	0.0%

Source: Federal Cooperation Commission, CFS/STAT.

terms there are three socioeconomic objectives that have substantial funding: 'general advancement of knowledge', 'industrial production and technology', and 'exploration and exploitation of space' (see Table 3.2).

3.2.3   General Orientations for STI Policies of the Different Authorities in Belgium

3.2.3.1   General orientations of STI policies of the Federal Government

The Federal Government is entitled to support scientific and research activities and can develop its own strategy and instruments for science policy in its fields of responsibility granted by the Constitution. At federal level, science policy remains an important department both in terms of its missions as well as by the number of people employed directly or indirectly through the funding programs supported. With a budget in excess of half a billion euros (in GBAORD terms) and more than 5000 people employed, the federal authorities fund a number of specific programs and institutions. A majority of the federal R&D budget is allocated for participation in international scientific and industrial research initiatives (European Space Agency (ESA), Airbus, etc.) and, hence, contributes to reinforcing Belgium's position in the European Research Area (ERA).

Over the last decade, the main driving forces of the Federal Science Policy have been twofold. First, the pursuit of the Federal Science Policy, per se, is based on the implementation of its research programs (notably in the field of climate and sustainable development), stimulation of public and private R&D through tax and social security measures, supporting research infrastructures of national interest, and through a small number of 'flagship' initiatives including the pursuit of Belgian space policy, 'sustainable' nuclear energy (the MYRHHA project) and Belgian polar research. Second, the federal authorities have sought to support the integration of Belgian scientists in the ERA and thereby contribute to the Lisbon Agenda and, in the future, to the ERA 2020 strategy.

For both strands of action, the federal authorities cooperate, or as indicated in the Belgian Report on Science, Technology and Innovation 2010, orchestrate policy, with the other Belgian authorities to ensure that the interests of all actors in the Belgian research and innovation system are taken into account (for example in the field of space research or tax measures), and that Belgium's contribution to meeting EU objectives related to STI is made in a concerted manner.

The Federal Government's science policy seeks to strengthen and promote the Belgian research potential at national and international levels; to foster scientific cooperation between the universities and research centers of the north and south of the country; to support the development of Belgian research in fields such as space and aeronautics; and to promote centers of expertise and Belgium's outstanding scientific heritage and cultural collections at international level.

Table 3.3 presents the budget detail for the main actor at the Federal level (the Federal Science Policy) with inclusion of the tax credits for R&D. In 2009 and 2010, despite the difficult economic context, the federal budget for science policy has been further reinforced (especially tax credits increased – estimated at 470 million euros in 2009), reflecting the efforts

Table 3.3   Budget detail for Federal Science Policy and tax credits for research, 2008

Action lines	Budget 2008
International R&D funding	
Space research	€257.2m
Other international research (+ research infrastructures)	€82.8m
National R&D	
Federal scientific institutions and research organizations	€117.6m
Research programs and grants (+ €31.6m for IUAP)	€100.1m
Other federal actions	€35.3m
Tax credits for research(ers)	€284.5m

Source: CFS/STAT. Data computation: Federal Science Policy and Ministry of Finance.

made in 2009 to consolidate and maintain the commitment to supporting R&D.

3.2.3.2   General orientations of STI policies of the Flemish Government

At the time of the second constitutional reform in 1980, the Flemish authorities merged the community and newly established regional institutions. A single Flemish Parliament, Flemish Government, official consultative bodies and an administration, supported by specific agencies, oversee both community and regional competencies. The Flemish Parliament debates and legitimates all official legal decisions pertaining to both community and regional competence, whilst the Flemish Government is charged with policy execution.

In line with the rapid evolution and profound transformation towards a knowledge-based economy and society, the Flemish Government regards research and innovation as a necessity for the wealth and well-being of Flanders. Since the 1990s, the Government, in consultation with the social partners, has developed a broad-based strategy on STI.

A number of broader based multi-annual strategic plans and targets have been agreed upon by a wide group of stakeholders from government, civil society and industry. These plans set out a wide range of targets across a range of policy fields, amongst which STI is assigned a clear priority. The most recent plan is 'Vlaanderen in Actie' (ViA, Flanders in Action) and the related Pact 2020. ViA aims to drive Flanders into the top five EU regions by 2020 and identifies some strategic breakthroughs to reach this goal, crucial for the future wealth and well-being of all in Flanders. The six breakthroughs are: Open Entrepreneur, Learning Fleming, Medical Centre Flanders, Green City District, Smart Logistics Europe, and Powerful Government. Research, science and innovation play a transversal role across these various themes, and policy initiatives taken in these areas are expected to match the overall goals of the ViA framework. The importance of STI in ViA is reflected by the target to spend 3 per cent of GDP on R&D by 2014. The six 'breakthroughs' of ViA are translated into 20 targets in Pact 2020 (www.flandersinaction.be). Apart from the 3 per cent Barcelona target, these include that:

> Flanders will progress towards a competitive and multi-faceted knowledge economy distinguished by the generation of sustainable prosperity and welfare. In terms of prosperity and welfare, and qua investments, it will rank among the top five knowledge-intensive European regions . . . innovation will be more widely and better distributed across all sectors, types of businesses, and segments of society.

The strategic targets for STI are listed in the 2009–2014 policy note of the Flemish minister for scientific research and innovation and include:

from idea to economic commercialization, market results and societal impact; more creative and innovative entrepreneurship; focus on economic clusters, thematic spearheads and large projects; Flanders as an international player (for example fully-fledged partner in the European research and innovation area); strengthen excellence and dynamism of cutting-edge, non-oriented research as a foundation for innovation; increase opportunities for research talent; more streamlined and output-driven research policy; a top research infrastructure.

Finally, a basis for policy priorities (linked to ViA and Pact 2020) is proposed by the Flemish Science and Innovation Policy Council from 2006, describing six strategic clusters: (i) Transportation – Logistics – Services – Supply chain management; (ii) ICT and Services in Healthcare (e-health); (iii) Healthcare; (iv) New Materials – Nanotechnology – Manufacturing industry; (v) ICT for socioeconomic innovation; and (vi) Energy and Environment.

Aside from the business sector, research and innovation is mainly conducted by two kinds of actors: the six universities of the Flemish Community: the Katholieke Universiteit Leuven (KULeuven), Universiteit Gent (UGent), Universiteit Antwerpen (UA), Vrije Universiteit Brussel (VUB), Universiteit Hasselt (UHasselt), and the Hogeschool-Universiteit Brussel (HUB-KUBrussel); the six public research organizations active in specific areas (IMEC, VIB, VITO, IBBT, SIM, CMI). The other actors that either conduct or are involved in research and innovation are some of the 22 'Hogescholen' (university colleges), the centers of excellence, the scientific institutes, the policy research centers, and organizations such as the ITG, VLIZ, NERF, MIP2, Vlerick School and UAMS.

3.2.3.3 General orientations of STI policies of the Walloon Region and the French-speaking Community

In constitutional terms, the Walloon Region and the French Community are distinct entities and therefore have their own government and administrations. However, with each progressive constitutional reform, cooperation has become more intense. Since 2009, a single Minister-President has presided over the two governments and several other ministers have portfolios for both regional and community affairs. The aim is to improve the level of coherence of government action in a series of policy fields. This is, notably, the case for scientific research, which is the responsibility of a single minister for both regional and community aspects. In theory, individual ministers from either government are autonomously responsible for funding research in their specific fields of competence such as agriculture, environment, energy and health. In practice, there is a high degree of coordination of STI policy – within the government and cross-departmentally at administration level – in order to ensure a coherent use of public funds.

The socioeconomic priorities of the policy strategy have been translated into an operational plan called the Marshall Plan 2.Green (Plan Marshall 2.Vert). This plan is a continuation and a reinforcement of the previous plan that was, adopted in 2005 and implemented during the period 2006–2009. The addition of 'Green' underlines the new orientations to better integrate 'sustainable development' as a cross-cutting priority.

The first Walloon 'Marshall Plan' focused an additional budgetary appropriation of €1bn on five priorities: the development of five competitive clusters; the stimulation of the creation of activities; the reduction of taxation on business; the reinforcement of research and innovation support; vocational training and the mobility of workers. The Marshall Plan 2.Green will invest a further €1.6bn over five years (2009–2014) in the following six priorities: (i) develop human capital; (ii) continue the policy of pôles de compétitivité and business networks; (iii) strengthen scientific research as an engine of the future; (iv) create a favorable framework for creating business and quality jobs; (v) develop 'employment–environment' alliances; (vi) increase employment and infrastructure in the sector of personal services.

The third priority area of the new plan incorporates the main actions to be pursued during the 2009–2014 period as regards STI policy. The Walloon Region and the French-speaking Community are planning to sustain the trend of (re)investment in research and innovation, which began in 2005. These efforts are designed to meet the target set within the framework of the Lisbon European Council, and reiterated in the European Commission's Europe 2020 strategy, to invest at least 3 per cent of GDP in R&D. Funds from both authorities will be invested in the implementation of a joint research strategy, which also involves the Brussels-Capital Region, and focuses on strategic cross-cutting themes. Additionally, both authorities intend to pursue the efforts undertaken since 2005, namely: (i) reinforcing investment in basic research by the French community through the implementation of the second development plan of the National Scientific Research Fund; (ii) the continuation of STI programs started within the first Walloon Marshall Plan: programs of excellence, mobilizing programs, support of research projects of pôles de compétitivité, research commercialization through the creation of spin-offs; and (iii) a continued support for partnerships between university academies and research actors and industry.

The Walloon Region and the French-speaking Community also intend to work together to: (i) offer an attractive career to researchers; (ii) better integrate French-speaking researchers in international networks; (iii) reinforce activities for science awareness in order to encourage young people to pursue scientific and technical careers; (iv) implement a technology assessment process as a tool for decision-making in various areas of public action.

The integration of research and innovation in business strategies is a Walloon priority, and is also continued through the new Marshall Plan, mainly via: (1) measures to improve support for spin-offs; (2) calls for specific projects dedicated to technological innovation partnerships, with a view to encourage partnerships between companies and between research institutions and industry, outside the framework of pôles de compétitivité and (3) support to 'proof of concept' strategies via the dedicated teams within universities supporting research commercialization and via technology incubators. Other measures, forming part of the priority areas 2 and 6 of the Marshall Plan 2.Green, aim at supporting research and innovation in the specific field of the environment, with the creation of a sixth competitive cluster dedicated to 'green' technologies, the creation of a centre of excellence in the field of sustainable development and funding of research programs in areas such as renewable energy, sustainable construction and smart technologies for the management of the electricity network.

3.2.3.4 General orientations of STI policies of the Brussels-Capital Region

Created in 1989, Brussels-Capital is a relatively young region, and during the first decade, the region 'sub-contracted' most of the policy related to research to the Federal authorities. However, over the course of the last decade, it has developed a comprehensive system of encouragement, support and follow-up of research and innovation in Brussels.

To understand the specific orientations of the regional STI policy, it is necessary to take account of some specific features of the 'capital of Europe'. In a very small territory Brussels hosts many universities and colleges of higher education and a number of top-level university hospitals. The region is multilingual and hosts many important international, national and regional representative bodies, policy think-tanks and, of course, the EU institution. With 13 000 employees (of whom approximately 9000 are researchers), the research sector is a significant part of the economy. Moreover, the highly developed, service-driven, economic structure of the Brussels-Capital Region makes a strategy founded on innovation and research, as proposed by the 'Lisbon Strategy', relevant even if Brussels's urban characteristics impose certain trade-offs. Brussels has a significantly large concentration of companies active in research, totaling more than 10 per cent of private employment in Brussels, and a very significant presence of students in higher education. Brussels is characterized by a service economy that forms a base for capitalizing on the knowledge economy. The regional science policy is increasingly structured but suffers from the constraints of resources and the territory of a city-region. The specificities of Brussels as regards multiple players, their proximity, international exposure, the role of capital and the open regional economy, place it in a position from which it can take advantage of the process of open innovation. Also, both the physical and the knowledge infrastructure of the region are an important attraction for large multinational R&D performing enterprises which – for reasons of cost and availability of land – tend to locate at its borders (Teirlinck, 2009).

Initiated since the early 2000s with the creation of the Science Policy Council in 2000 and the adoption of the ordinance of 21 February 2002 on the encouragement and the funding of scientific research and technological innovation, then by the development of the Institute for the Encouragement of Scientific Research and Innovation of Brussels (ISRIB) in 2003, this support has been strengthened considerably, as regards both budgetary resources and programs and regulatory framework.

A first attempt to structure a regional research and innovation policy was made when the government launched, in the context of a broader 2005 agreement called Contract for Economy & Employment (C2E/CET – 2005: *Contrat pour l'Economie et l'Emploi/Contract Economie en Tewerkstelling*), a Regional Plan for Innovation (PRI/GPI: *Plan Régional pour l'Innovation/Gewestelijk Plan voor Innovatie*).

The representatives of the social partners, the academic community and government parties signed the PRI/GPI on 18 December 2006. The aim was to implement a set of coherent measures intended to improve the capacity for innovation of the Brussels-Capital Region. The six strategic targets of the PRI/GPI are:

- Promote the three sectors that bear the most innovation: ICT, health and environment. It is a matter of strengthening the 'clustering' approach in these sectors;
- Increase the rate of innovation through the implementation of specific programs;
- Stimulate the use of innovation through marketing research results and assistance to small enterprises so that they assimilate and use innovations;
- Foster the internationalization of innovation;
- Attract and anchor innovative activities;
- Create an environment that favors innovation.

BOX 3.1   REVISED OR NEW PLANS FOR STI POLICY IN BELGIUM – 2010

Federal Belgian policy focuses on reducing costs of researchers' employment, stimulating the creation and development of SMEs and supporting R&D efforts towards the 3 per cent of GDP Lisbon target.

The Flemish policy focuses on the 3 per cent targets boosting investments in higher education institutions, boosting creativity and innovative capacity, putting more attention on spearheads and output of research, encouraging students to study sciences and giving researchers better prospects. Flanders also foresees a simplification of the set of innovation policy instruments.

Wallonia's strategy focuses on boosting business R&D and linking universities to industry, consolidating clusters, especially in environmental technologies, strengthening human capital and vocational training and giving a stronger focus on sustainable development.

Brussels Capital Region focuses on regional clusters and plans to increase regional R&D capacities up to the 3 per cent target by focusing on ICT, health and environment.

These objectives were made operational through the introduction of new instruments of support and the consolidation of existing instruments. Moreover, the strategy is focused through the selection of ICT, health and environment as the three priority sectors on which the resources available to the institutions responsible for research support were focused. These sectors were selected because of the identified potential as regards research, innovative content, growth and job creation in Brussels.

Given the growing awareness of the importance of research and innovation for the regional economy and the acceptance that the regional authorities should act as a motor, the government has progressively devoted an increasingly greater budgetary share to research and innovation. This trend has been evident since 2004, witnessed by a significant growth in the regional budget devoted to research, increasing from €22m in 2004 to over €37m in 2009, representing an increase of more than 50 per cent. However, as highlighted in section 3.2.2, with a share of only about 1 per cent of total budget outlays for R&D of all governments in Belgium, the Brussels-Capital region remains a relatively small R&D spender.

3.3   A SNAPSHOT ON STI STATISTICS FOCUSED ON BELGIUM

Monitoring through statistics and indicators has become a crucial element in (evidence-based) policy setting. The Lisbon strategy, aimed at converting the European Union (EU) into the most dynamic and competitive knowledge-based economy in the world by 2010, capable of sustainable economic growth with more and better jobs and greater social cohesion, as well as respect for the environment, makes use of statistical targets to monitor progress towards this goal. The Lisbon strategy also acknowledged innovation to be a key driver in the process.

This section presents a snapshot on STI indicators for Belgium, based on the key dimensions of science, technology and innovation. These dimensions involve *enablers*, which are considered drivers of science, technology and innovation; *facilitators* linking business activities to the outside world; and *results* related to the performance of the knowledge-based economy. The presentation of indicators grouped into several dimensions as presented in Figure 3.1 is not to be understood as an assertion that the innovation process is linear, because many feedback mechanisms and interactions exist (Kline and Rosenberg, 1986). In what follows, attention will be paid to main indicators related to these key dimensions. Belgium will be compared with its main commercial partners, EU27, and Japan and the US. For more detailed information on STI indicators we refer to *Key Data on Science, Technology and Innovation Belgium 2010* (Belgian Science Policy Office, 2010a) and for a more global view on indicators we refer to 'OECD STI Outlook' (OECD, 2009c).

3.3.1   Enablers

3.3.1.1   Human resources for S&T
In knowledge-based economies, where ideas and knowledge are central factors in the innovation and growth process, countries must maintain their stock of human capital and educational level. Moreover, the availability of a skilled labor force is an essential condition for competitiveness. In order to achieve optimal use of human capital, there is a need to anticipate shortfalls in the supply of skilled persons and to provide training opportunities throughout a person's professional career.

Human resources in science and technology are so-called input variables. These people and their training are indispensable ingredients for fostering economic growth and enhancing competitiveness and the general future well-being of a nation.

The first and main source of human resources in science and technology

Enablers: drivers of science, technology and innovation (3.1)
Human resources – education, skills and training (3.1.1)
R&D activities – investments and personnel efforts by enterprises, governments, higher education and private non-profit organizations (3.1.2)

Facilitators: linking business to the outside world (3.2)
International linkages – technology balance of payments, high-tech exports, foreign direct investments (3.2.1)
Research productivity – intellectual property rights (patents), publications (bibliometrics) (3.2.2)

Results: performance of the knowledge-based economy (3.3)
Innovative activities in firms – process and product innovation, marketing and organizational innovation, cooperation on innovation, turnover due to new products (3.3.1)
Entrepreneurship – venture capital, firm dynamics (3.3.2)

Note: There is an ongoing discussion on the indicators to be included in the European Innovation Scoreboard in view of the ERA Vision 2020.

Source: Adapted from the European Commission Innovation Scoreboard.

Figure 3.1 Dimensions of science, technology and innovation

(HRST) is, of course, the education system. Some professions are also regarded as belonging to the HRST category, more particularly researchers and engineers.[4]

Compared to the reference countries, Belgium invests most in education as a share of GDP, followed directly by France and the United States (Table 3.4). In Belgium, about 32 per cent of the population aged 25 to 64 years attained a tertiary education, which is 8 percentage points above the EU average. However, in terms of tertiary graduates in S&T, with about 22 per thousand of the population aged 20–29, Belgium is performing below the EU average. In the Netherlands the situation is even worse.

In a knowledge-based economy not only is it important to have a sufficiently large human capital stock of scientists and engineers, it is also important to create opportunities for people so they can constantly refine their skills to keep in touch with the latest developments in science and

Innovation and creativity

Table 3.4   Public expenditure on education and human resources for S&T

	Public expenditure on education as % of GDP[1]	% of population with tertiary education[2]	Tertiary graduates in S&T[3]	S&E degrees at first stage university level[4]	Participation in lifelong learning[5]	Share of foreign doctoral students[6]
	2006	2007	2007	2006	2008	2006
Belgium	6.00	32	21.8	14.0	6.8	31.0
Germany	4.40	24	27.2	11.4	7.9	–
France	5.58	27	25.7	20.7	7.3	35.8
The Netherlands	5.46	31	14.5	8.9	17	–
UK	5.48	32	22.5	17.5	19.9	42.7
EU27	5.04	24	22.1	–	9.5	–
USA	5.51	40	14.7	10.1	–	26.3
Japan	3.47	41	24.1	14.4	–	16.8

Notes:
1. Source: Eurostat, 2009.
2. Source: OECD (2009b). Note: Data expressed as a percentage of the 25–64 age class.
3. Source: Eurostat, 2009. Note: data expressed per 1000 of population aged 20–29.
4. Source: OECD (2009b). Note: data expressed as a percentage of all new degrees at first stage university level.
5. Source: Eurostat, 2009. Note: data expressed as a percentage of the 25–64 age class.
6. Source: OECD (2009b), Education database, 2009. Notes: data expressed as a percentage of total doctoral enrolment in host country. Foreign doctoral students include foreign students from non-OECD countries.

technology. A possible indicator for measuring this is the participation of a population in lifelong learning activities. Belgium and its neighboring countries, Germany and France, show figures that indicate a rather low participation in lifelong learning. This conclusion is especially strong in comparison with countries like the Netherlands and the United Kingdom, where more than 15 per cent of the population indicate they have received education or training in the four weeks preceding the survey.

The creation of knowledge has become an international activity. The community of knowledge workers no longer consists of individuals working independently of one another. Cooperation between researchers with different backgrounds is becoming more and more the prevailing standard. Also, the physical boundaries that hindered a smooth and efficient exchange of information are disappearing at an unrelenting rate, thanks to new developments in information and communication technology. All of this is reflected by the fact that an increasing number of doctoral students stay for a certain period at a research institute abroad. The United Kingdom attracts the largest share of foreign students in the European Union.

3.3.1.2   R&D activities

The EU Lisbon strategy for growth and jobs was launched in 2000 as a response to globalization. One key area was 'more research, development and innovation'. In 2002 at the Barcelona Summit, the goal was set to invest 3 per cent of GDP in research by 2010 in Europe. The Barcelona target also specified the appropriate split of the financing of R&D between public and private sectors (one third public versus two-thirds private). In its 'Europe 2020 – A strategy for smart, sustainable and inclusive growth' (3 March 2010) communiqué, the European Commission proposed to keep the 3 per cent target while developing an indicator which would reflect R&D and innovation intensity. At the Spring European Council of 25–26 March 2010, the European Council adopted the proposal of the European Commission to improve the conditions for research and development, in particular with the aim of bringing combined public and private investment levels in this sector to 3 per cent of GDP. GERD (Gross Expenditures on Research and Development) covers all financial outlays that private and public sectors made on behalf of R&D activities, and so this indicator is widely used to measure the knowledge intensity of a society as a whole (for definitions on R&D indicators we refer to the OECD Frascati Manual (OECD, 2002). The GERD/GDP ratio, expressing the R&D intensity of a country, is regarded as the main indicator for learning about the state of innovation of an economy.

Belgium's R&D intensity is 0.13 percentage points higher than the EU27 average (Table 3.5). Japan and the United States perform a great deal better. As such, the R&D gap (which was at the basis of the set-up of the Barcelona 3 per cent target) tends to remain. Despite some progress on R&D investments, Belgium and other European countries have stagnated in terms of R&D intensity, which shows that growth in these European countries has not been driven by science and technology alone, but also by other factors. Another hypothesis is that research has been executed in a more efficient way, thanks to phenomena like 'open innovation', the merging of technologies, and the concentration of research in fewer labs.

Table 3.5 also illustrates the R&D activities by sector of performance and by source of financing of the R&D activities. The GERD in Belgium is highly influenced by the two main R&D performers, that is the business enterprise sector and the higher education sector. Their respective

Table 3.5 R&D intensity (1999–2007), and by sector of performance and source of funds

	GERD as % of GDP		R&D intensity by sector of performance, 2007				R&D intensity by source of funds, 2007			
	1999	2007	Business Enterprise	Higher education	Government	Private non-Profit	Business Enterprise	Government	Other national sources	Abroad
Belgium	1.94	1.90	1.32	0.40	0.15	0.02	1.16	0.42	0.07	0.25
Germany	2.40	2.53	1.77	0.41	0.35	0.00	1.72	0.70	0.01	0.10
France	2.16	2.04	1.29	0.40	0.32	0.02	1.06	0.78	0.04	0.15
The Netherlands	1.96	1.71	0.97	0.52	0.22	0.00	–	–	–	–
UK	1.82	1.82	1.15	0.47	0.16	0.04	0.85	0.55	0.10	0.32
EU27	1.72	1.77	1.12	0.4	0.23	0.02	0.97	0.6	0.04	0.16
USA	2.64	2.66	1.92	0.35	0.29	0.10	1.76	0.75	0.15	–
Japan	3.02	3.44	2.68	0.43	0.27	0.06	2.67	0.54	0.22	0.01

Source: OECD (2009a).

R&D intensity is 1.32 per cent and 0.40 per cent in 2007. Both sectors represent 69.5 per cent and 21.1 per cent respectively of the national total R&D expenditure. Like the more 'research-intensive' countries such as the US, Japan and Germany, more than two-thirds of R&D expenditures are performed in the business sector in Belgium. Regarding the financing of R&D, government, business enterprise and abroad together finance more than 95 per cent of R&D expenditures (this is the case in most countries). Despite an increase in public budgets for R&D since 2000, the 1 per cent public funding target remains way out of reach in Belgium (0.54 per cent in 2007) and this goes for the other European countries as well. The same comment can be made with regard to the 2 per cent private funding target (1.36 per cent in 2007). The private funding in Belgium represents more than two-thirds of the GERD funding.

An important aspect to be taken into account when considering business R&D in Belgium is the concentration of R&D in multinational enterprises (Teirlinck, 2009). For the business sector, big R&D-intensive multinationals (foreign-controlled affiliates and parent companies) play an important role and the share of industrial R&D realized under foreign control is approximately 60 per cent.

When internationally benchmarking R&D expenditures, the sector structure of an economy needs to be taken into account. For Belgium, in spite of the increasing weight of services (75 per cent of Belgium's total value-added in 2007), the R&D expenditures incurred in the business sector in 2007 were essentially distributed in the manufacturing industry (76.3 per cent), with a dominant position of (high-tech manufacturing) pharmaceuticals representing close to 30 per cent of all R&D expenditures in the business enterprise sector (Table 3.6).

In terms of regional distribution (Nomenclature of Territorial Units for Statistics – NUTS) the R&D intramural expenditures can be divided into three regional levels (NUTS1): the Brussels-Capital Region, the Flemish Region and the Walloon Region. Figure 3.2 informs us about two issues: the geographical concentration of research in Belgium over the three regions, on the one hand, and the importance of each of the four performing sectors in each region on the other. These data only deal with performance of R&D, not the funding.

3.3.1.3 Government Budget Appropriations of Outlays on R&D (GBAORD)

As highlighted before, the GBAORD is based on the budget programs of the various federal, regional and community authorities. Some of these are linked to scientific policy and others to budgets assigned to scientific and technological activities.

Table 3.6   *Business enterprise intramural R&D expenditure (BERD) in*
             Belgium per industry

	1999	2007
Manufacturing industries	81.9	76.4
High-tech	36.5	42.4
Aircraft and spacecraft	1.4	1.9
Office, accounting and computing machinery	0.2	0.6
Radio, television and communication equipment		
and apparatus	15.9	9.0
Pharmaceuticals	17.8	28.3
Medical, precision, optical, watches and clocks		
instruments	1.2	2.6
Medium high-tech	29.1	20.2
Motor vehicles, trailers and semi-trailers	3.8	2.8
Electrical machinery and apparatus n.e.c.	2.4	2.9
Chemicals and chemical products (less		
pharmaceuticals)	18.1	8.8
Machinery and equipment n.e.c.	4.8	5.7
Medium low-tech	5.4	4.8
Low-tech	10.9	9.0
Other industries	3.2	3.2
Services	14.9	20.4
High-tech	7.2	9.6
Computer and related activities	6.2	6.0
Research and development	0.3	0.0
Telecommunications	0.7	3.6
Medium-tech	6.0	8.3
Low-tech	1.7	2.5
Total BERD	100.0	100.0

Source: Federal Cooperation Commission, CFS/STAT.

For international comparisons, it is worth mentioning that the weight of the socioeconomic objective 'defense' in the total GBAORD can be quite important in some countries (in 2008: US: 56 per cent; France: 27 per cent; UK: 21 per cent). The GBAORD indicator reveals that the authorities in Belgium have not been the best public investors in R&D in Europe (see Table 3.7). However, there is a tendency for Belgium to genuinely catch up with the European average. As noted before, the exclusion of tax credits for R&D and more specifically the large differences in importance of tax credits for R&D in different countries bias international comparisons excluding this policy measure.

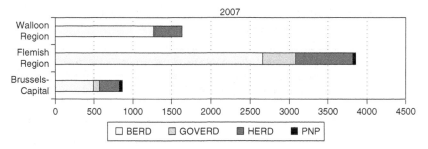

Notes: BERD: business expenditures on R&D; GOVERD: Government expenditure on R&D; HERD: Higher Education Expenditure on R&D; PNP: Private non-profit.

Source: Federal Cooperation Commission, CFS/STAT.

Figure 3.2 Intramural R&D expenditures: regional data for all sectors, 2007

Table 3.7 GBAORD in percentage of GDP (without tax credits)

	1999	2008		1999	2008
Belgium	0.58	0.68	UK	0.67	0.64
Germany	0.81	0.79	EU27	0.71	0.72
France	0.94	0.75	USA	0.83	0.99
The Netherlands	0.78	0.70	Japan	0.63	0.70

Source: OECD (2009a); data of EU27: Eurostat (Science, technology and innovation database).

3.3.2 Facilitators

3.3.2.1 International linkages
The Technology Balance of Payments (TBP) registers the commercial transactions related to international technology transfers. It consists of money paid or received for the acquisition and use of patents, licenses, trademarks, designs, know-how and closely-related technical services (including technical assistance) and for industrial R&D carried out abroad, and so on.

The degree of internationalization of the diffusion of a country's technology can be expressed by looking at the share of the national technology receipts and payments in the national GERD. These shares are among the highest in Belgium and can be related to the relatively high presence of foreign-controlled affiliates. A higher 'technology receipts/R&D expenditure' ratio could also mean that the R&D effort is contributing

Table 3.8   Technology balance of payments – receipts and payments as percentage of GERD

	Technology receipts in % of GERD[1]		Technology payments in % of GERD[1]		Average publication output[2] (per 10 000 inhabitants)	Number of USPTO patent applications (filing year)[3] (per million inhabitants)	
	1999	2007	1999	2007	2004–2008	1999	2007
Belgium	84.8	79.4	77.2	91.3	13.0	117.8	166.3
Germany	25.2	53.2	33.5	47.2	9.4	206.8	287.0
France	8.8	–	10.1	–	8.8	103.1	126.2
The Netherlands	–	–	–	–	15.0	130.2	241.0
UK	65.0	68.1	33.6	35.2	13.2	118.4	150.3
EU27	–	–	–	–	7.4	88.8	122.4
USA	16.2	22.2	5.3	13.1	9.9	536.4	799.9
Japan	6.4	14.0	2.7	4.0	6.1	377.5	616.7

Sources:
1.   OECD (2009a).
2.   Web of Science, Eurostat, US Census Bureau, Statistics Bureau, ECOOM.
3.   OECD (2009a).

to substantial technology-exporting capacity. And when the 'technology payments/R&D expenditure' ratio is high, it implies a development strategy based on imports of foreign technology rather than the use of native technology.

The largest economies such as the US and Japan have lower shares. Their domestic R&D effort, to a large extent, satisfies their country's technology requirements. Larger European economies such as Germany and the United Kingdom have intermediate ratios.

Eye-catching for Belgium is the appearance of a TBP deficit in 2007, after a long period with a favorable balance. The recent deficit of TBP in Belgium mainly comes from capital accounts and some current accounts such as royalties and technical services. Presenting the data per sector makes it possible to identify the sectors contributing the most to this kind of transaction, and thus the areas in which Belgium is specialized when it comes to the trade of technology. The totals of the payments and the receipts of TBP by categories of TBP operations are shown in Table 3.8.

3.3.2.2   Research productivity
Scientometric indicators have become a standard tool of evaluation and analysis in science policy and research management. These indicators are

supposed to represent objective measures of productivity and impact, provided the underlying data sets form sufficiently large and statistically representative samples. Scientometric indicators have therefore long since become widely accepted measures of research performance at the national level.

Table 3.8 presents the average publication output per 10000 inhabitants for the period 2004–2008. The UK, the Netherlands and Belgium represent the highest standard in the set. In these countries, more than ten papers per 10000 inhabitants have been published. These countries lie distinctly above both the European and American standard. The last two EU enlargements in 2004 and 2007 have somewhat lowered the publication 'density' with respect to the EU15. The data reflect a large variation of this indicator within the European Union.

Regarding patents, the number of patents by Belgian inventors at the USPTO has increased from 118 to 166 per million inhabitants since 1999; this is well above the EU average but quite behind Germany, the Netherlands and especially the US and Japan. This gap could be attributed to different business strategies, to the fact that many important research-active companies are foreign owned or are at least multinational companies, and thus pursue an international strategy regarding where and how to patent. Benchmarking Belgium with the rest of Europe or the US regarding ICT or biotechnology patents, shows a comparatively better position for Belgium when it comes to biotechnology.

3.3.3 Results

3.3.3.1 Innovation activities in firms

Innovation is a much broader concept than R&D. It is about the implementation, not only of new products and processes, but also of organizational and marketing novelties. R&D is merely one of several inputs into a whole, larger, system, called the *innovation system*. In the same vein, patents or other IPRs are only some of the many outputs of this system. This systemic view considers innovation to be a complex process involving various actors in a dynamic of mutual interaction. 'Innovation' is to be seen both as a process and as the output of this process. Some remarks can be formulated.

First, there has been a broadening of the very concept of innovation. Innovation is no longer to be regarded in its narrow 'technological' sense. Nowadays, it also concerns making use of new organizational models for introducing innovative marketing methods. These two latter dimensions are jointly described as 'non-technological innovation'. Non-technological innovation is in most countries almost as important as, if

*Table 3.9   Technological and non-technological innovators and turnover
             from innovation, 2002–2004*

	Firms having introduced an innovation (in % of all firms) – period 2002–2004		Share of turnover from product innovations (% of total turnover) in 2004	
	Technological innovators	Non-technological innovators	Manufacturing	Services
Belgium	48.2	46.6	17.8	10.4
Germany	56.2	61.1	26.1	11.8
France	31.6	42.5	17.1	7.5
The Netherlands	32.4	31.5	13.9	5.2
UK	38.7	37.5	18.5	12.8
EU27	36.5*	40.7*	18.9	10.4
Japan	21.6	55.8	4.8	4.8

Note: * Except Latvia, Slovenia, Finland, Sweden and the United Kingdom.

Sources: Federal Cooperation Commission, CFS/STAT, CIS4; Eurostat (NewCronos database), and OECD (2009d) 'Innovation in firms: a microeconomic perspective'.

not more important than, technological innovation. Moreover, technological and non-technological innovation show up as natural complements, as the introduction of new products and processes often involves the introduction of new business models. This calls for policies aimed at targeting non-technological innovation as well.

Second, as far as technological innovation is concerned, it has been realized that R&D is not the only way to acquire knowledge. Knowledge can also be 'insourced' from outside the firm's boundaries. Conversely, internally-generated knowledge may be 'exported' to the outside world. Specifically, there are a significant proportion of such non-R&D technological innovators (Table 3.9).

Third, there is increasing awareness of the importance of innovation, in both technological and non-technological dimensions, for the services sector as well. Firms in the services sector earn a non-negligible part of their turnover from their product innovations. This suggests that wider policy attention is being paid to innovation in the services sector and to the services sector needs.

Fourth, paralleling the importance of non-R&D technological innovators and of well-functioning knowledge transmission mechanisms, light needs to be shed on the 'emergence' of the 'open innovation' paradigm. Open innovation refers to the fact that firms increasingly tend both to use

Table 3.10   Formal cooperation agreements in innovation, 2002–2004

	Manufacturing	Services		Manufacturing	Services
Belgium	22.0	14.9	UK	12.9	13.4
Germany	14.2	7.0	European		
France	14.1	11.7	Union	10.5	9.6
The Netherlands	18.4	10.0	Japan	8.4	6.2

Sources: Federal Cooperation Commission, CFS/STAT, CIS4; Eurostat (NewCronos database); OECD (2009d) 'Innovation in firms: a microeconomic perspective'.

external knowledge for their innovation activities, and to allow the outside world to access their internal knowledge. One way to access or transmit knowledge is through formal cooperation agreements. Such agreements are pervasive, both across countries and across sectors, especially in Belgium (see Table 3.10). Formal cooperations are in general somewhat more widespread in the manufacturing than in the services sector. The most commonly used cooperation partners are to be found within the business relations: suppliers and clients. By contrast, universities and public research institutes are not used as often as cooperation partners, so that greater efforts might be made to increase their attractiveness. Finally, given the increased internationalization of R&D, one should notice the importance of international cooperations. Another way to access or generate knowledge is through informal cooperations, that is accessing publicly-available knowledge. The most commonly encountered sources are, again, clients and suppliers.

A company may also have expenditures on R&D either within the unit (intramural) or outside it (extramural). To a growing extent R&D is being bought (or sub-contracted). Extramural expenditures are the sums that a unit, organization or sector reports having paid or that they have committed to pay to another unit, organization or sector for the perform-ance of R&D during a specific period. This includes acquisition of R&D performed by other units, and grants given to others for performing R&D (Figure 3.3).

The most important effects of innovation are market oriented, concern-ing the product range, the market share, the entry on new markets, or the quality of products (see Table 3.11). On the other hand, it is worth noticing that meeting regulations or reducing environmental impacts show up as some of the less frequent effects. Turning to the principal hampering factors, the costs of innovation, followed by a lack of internal finance to support these costs, are the most frequent hampering factors (see Table 3.12). Lack of competition ('market dominated by established

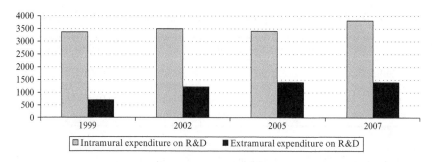

Source: Federal Cooperation Commission, CFS/STAT.

Figure 3.3　*Intramural and extramural R&D expenditures, in million constant euros, 1999–2007*

enterprises'), lack of qualified personnel, and risk aversion ('uncertain demand for innovation') also seem to be frequently-encountered important hampering factors.

3.3.3.2　Entrepreneurship

Under the heading of 'entrepreneurship' we deal with venture capital investment and firm dynamics. *Venture capital investment* can be defined as private equity for investment in companies. It is provided by special-

Table 3.11　*Effects of innovation in Belgium, 2002–2004*

% of firms with technological innovation activities rating the selected effect as 'highly important'	Manufacturing	Services
Improved quality of goods or services	46.1	47.5
Increased range of goods or services	31.7	38
Entered new markets or increased market share	30.5	36.1
Increased capacity of production or service provision	28.1	22.9
Improved flexibility of production or service provision	27.7	20.9
Reduced labor costs per unit output	17.5	15.6
Reduced environmental impacts or improved health and safety	16.7	9.2
Met regulatory requirements	14.1	14.5
Reduced materials and energy per unit output	9.0	8.6

Source: Federal Cooperation Commission, CFS/STAT, CIS4.

Table 3.12   Hampering factors for innovation in Belgium, 2002–2004

% of all firms rating the selected hampering factor as 'highly important'	Manufacturing	Services
Innovation costs too high	19.4	15.4
Lack of internal funds	19.1	13.5
Market dominated by established enterprises	13.9	13.9
Lack of qualified personnel	13.6	9.7
Uncertain demand for innovations	12	10
Lack of finance from external sources	11.4	8.4
Difficulty in finding cooperation partners	7.2	5.7
Lack of information on markets	4.2	5.2
Lack of information on technology	4.3	1.9

Source: Federal Cooperation Commission, CFS/STAT, CIS4.

ized financial firms acting as intermediaries between primary sources of finance (such as pension funds or banks) and firms (formal venture capital). It is also provided by so-called 'business angels' (usually wealthy individuals experienced in business and finance who invest directly in firms). Management buy-outs, management buy-ins and venture purchase of quoted shares are excluded.

In general, data on venture capital is broken down into two investment stages. First, the early stage consists of seed capital and start-up funding. Seed capital is provided to research, assess and develop an initial concept. Start-up financing is provided for product development and initial marketing. Second, expansion and replacement financing is provided for the growth and expansion of a company that is breaking even or trading profitably. Based on the data for Belgium, the problem is not so much the provision of early-stage venture capital but rather the financing of expansion and replacement activities.

Regarding *firm dynamics*, early-stage entrepreneurial activity (TEA) is one of the principal indicators of entrepreneurship. It focuses predominantly on the early stages of entrepreneurship as it looks at the percentage of the 18–64 population who are either nascent entrepreneurs or owner-managers of a new firm. This indicator is published in the Global Entrepreneurship Monitor (GEM), which is a worldwide research consortium. These indicators are based on over 180 000 interviews conducted in 54 countries during May and October of 2009. The relative focus on entrepreneurship in innovation-driven economies lies on dynamics – the creation of new firms and the replacement of less efficient ones – and on promoting new products and entering new markets.

Nascent entrepreneurs are those actively involved in setting up a business they will own or co-own, referring to a business that has not paid salaries, wages, or any other payments to the owners for more than three months. The indicator is expressed as a percentage of the 18–64 population. Young ownership rates point to those people who are currently an owner-manager of a new business. It refers to an ongoing business that has paid salaries, wages, or any other payments to the owners for more than three months, but not more than 42 months. The indicator is expressed as a percentage of the 18–64 population. Nascent entrepreneurs and young ownership together add up to early-stage entrepreneurial activity.

The established business ownership rate refers to the percentage of the 18–64 population who are currently owner-managers of an established business. This refers to owning and managing an ongoing business that has paid salaries, wages, or any other payments to the owners for more than 42 months. The business discontinuation rate points to the percentage of the 18–64 population who have, in the past 12 months, discontinued a business, either by selling, closing, or discontinuing an owner/management relationship with the business. This indicator is not to be equated with the business failure rates.

Belgium performs quite weakly with regard to entrepreneurial activity and established business ownership and discontinuation. Again, the relatively high presence of large multinational companies influences these data. Anyhow, the data presented here question the conclusion of the European Commission (European Commission, 2009a) that 'For Belgium, one of the innovation followers, innovation performance is above the EU27 average but the rate of improvement is below that of the EU27. Relative strengths, compared to the country's average performance, are in Linkages & entrepreneurship, Innovators and Economic effects. Relative weaknesses are in Firm investments and Throughputs'. This can be explained by the fact that the EU took its conclusions solely based on venture capital provision and innovation statistics. As is shown in Table 3.13, this picture is incomplete.

3.3.3.3 Macroeconomic effects

Gross domestic product (GDP) is often used as a measure of economic activity. It is defined as the value of all goods and services produced in a country or region less the value of any goods or services used in their creation. The volume index of GDP per capita in purchasing power standards (PPS) is expressed in relation to the European Union (EU27) average set to equal 100 (see Table 3.14). If the index of a country is higher than 100, this country's level of GDP per head is higher than the EU average, and

Table 3.13   Venture capital investments and firm dynamics

	Venture Capital investments as % of GDP, 2008		Entrepreneurial activity, 2009			Established business ownership and discontinuation rate, 2009	
	Early stage	Expansion & replace-ment	Early stage	Nascent firms	Young firms	Established: ownership	Established: discontinu-ation
Belgium	0.029	0.075	3.5	2.0	1.6	2.5	1.3
Spain	0.009	0.094	5.1	2.3	2.8	6.4	2.0
Hungary	0.002	0.030	9.1	5.4	3.7	6.7	3.2
Germany	0.019	0.050	4.1	2.2	2.1	5.1	1.8
France	0.023	0.102	4.3	3.1	1.4	3.2	1.9
Netherlands	0.038	0.084	7.2	3.1	4.1	8.1	2.5
UK	0.040	0.304	5.7	2.7	3.2	6.1	2.1
EU27	0.022	0.109	–	–	–	–	–
USA	0.048	0.150	8.0	4.9	3.2	5.9	3.4
Japan	–	–	3.3	1.9	1.3	7.8	1.4

Note: Venture capital investment is expressed as a percentage of GDP at market prices to account for the size of the economy.

Source: Global Entrepreneurship Monitor, 2010; Eurostat, 2009, Structural Indicators.

Table 3.14   Macroeconomic performance indicators, Belgium internationally benchmarked, 1999–2008

	GDP per capita in PPS		Labor productivity per person employed**		Employment rate*	
	1999	2008	2000	2008	1999	2008
Belgium	123.0	115.1	136.6	125.5	59.3	62.4
Germany	122.1	115.6	108.0	107.0	65.2	70.7
France	114.7	108.0	125.1	121.6	60.9	64.9
Netherlands	130.8	134.0	114.4	114.5	71.7	77.2
UK	117.8	116.2	110.8	110.0	71.0	71.5
EU27	100.0	100.0	100.0	100.0	61.8	65.9
USA	162.6	154.7	141.8	144.9	73.9	70.9
Japan	117.7	110.7	98.8	99.7	68.9	70.7

Notes: * In percentage of the 15–64 age group. ** Basic figures are expressed in PPS, i.e. a common currency that eliminates the differences in price levels between countries allowing meaningful volume comparisons of GDP between countries. Note that 'persons employed' does not distinguish between full-time and part-time employment. Break in series in 2005.

Source: Eurostat, 2009, Structural Indicators; Eurostat, Community Labour Force Survey.

vice versa. Basic figures are expressed in PPS, that is a common currency that eliminates the differences in price levels between countries, allowing meaningful volume comparisons of GDP between countries. This index is intended for cross-country comparisons rather than for temporal comparisons. GDP per capita in Belgium is well above the EU average and comparable with the main trade partners and Japan. However, it is lagging behind the Netherlands and especially the US.

The labor productivity per person employed is calculated as the GDP in purchasing power standards (PPS) per person employed relative to the EU27. GDP per person employed is intended to give an overall impression of the productivity of national economies expressed in relation to the European Union (EU27) average. If the index of a country is higher than 100, this country's level of GDP per person employed is higher than the EU average, and vice versa.

The employment rate is calculated by dividing the number of persons aged 15 to 64 in employment by the total population of the same age group. The employment rate is low in Belgium, and the gap with the main trade partners is not reducing.

A last set of macroeconomic indicators relate to the sector structure of the Belgian economy (see Table 3.15). In this respect, the share of high and medium-high technology manufacturing sectors and of knowledge-intensive service sectors as a share of total employment are presented. For the former there is a decrease over the period 1999–2008 (note that only Germany forms an exception to this, which explains part of the differences of STI policy making – OECD (2010)).

The share of exports of high-technology products in the total exports is calculated as the share of exports of all high-technology products of total exports. Belgium performs very weakly in this regard. The opposite is true for foreign direct investment intensity (an indicator of market integration).

The index measures the intensity of investment integration within the international economy. The direct investment refers to the international investment made by a resident entity (direct investor) to acquire a lasting interest in an entity operating in an economy other than that of the investor (direct investment enterprise). Direct investment involves both the initial transactions between the two entities and all subsequent capital transactions between them and among affiliated enterprises, both incorporated and unincorporated. Data are expressed as a percentage of GDP to remove the effect of differences in the size of the economies of the reporting countries.

Table 3.15   Characteristics of the sector structure: Belgium in an
international context, 1999–2008

	Share of high and medium-high technology manufacturing sectors in total employment[a]		Share of knowledge-intensive service sectors in total employment[a]		High-tech exports[b]		Foreign direct investment intensity[c]	
	1999	2008	1999	2008	1999	2006	1999	2008
Belgium	7.2	6.3	36.0	38.5	7.9	6.6	–	22.1
Germany	10.9	10.9	29.9	35.3	14.2	14.1	3.8	2.4
France	7.2	6.1	34.7	37.0	24.0	17.9	5.9	5.2
Netherlands	4.7	3.4	39.1	42.7	21.9	18.3	12.0	0.7
UK	7.6	4.9	39.5	42.7	27.3	26.5	9.6	4.7
EU27	–	6.7	–	33.0	20.4	16.6	–	2.2
USA	–	–	–	–	30.1	26.1	2.6	–
Japan	–	–	–	–	25.1	20.0	0.4	–

Notes:
a.   High and medium-high technology manufacturing: pharmaceuticals; computers; optics; electronics; chemicals; electrical equipment; machinery and equipment; motor vehicles, trailers and semi-trailers; other transport equipment. Data on EU27 are from 2007.
b.   High-technology products are defined as the sum of the following products: aerospace, computers, office machinery, electronics, instruments, pharmaceuticals, electrical machinery and armaments. The total exports for the EU do not include the intra-EU trade.
c.   Average value of inward and outward FDI flows divided by GDP.

Source: Eurostat, Community Labour Force Survey; Eurostat, Structural indicators.

3.4   SOME CRITICAL REMARKS AND PERSPECTIVES FOR STI POLICY MAKING IN BELGIUM

3.4.1   Some Critical Remarks

As in most of the other EU Member States, Belgium translated the 3 per cent Lisbon objective into a national objective and, since the start of the Lisbon agenda, a broad range of initiatives at different government levels have been taken. In section 3.2 the policy commitment to an upward trend in public investment in RTDI by each of the governments in Belgium was highlighted. However, the Erawatch Country Report[5] for Belgium

(European Commission, 2009b) suggests that in terms of resource mobilization, and despite the commitment of the public authorities at federal and regional level to meet the 3 per cent GERD/GDP target, research intensity in the economy in recent years has been declining or stable.

To reach the Lisbon objective, additional appropriations for research funding have been made by all authorities. However, in terms of resource mobilization, the main challenges include: (i) justifying resource provision for research activities; (ii) securing long-term investment in research; (iii) dealing with barriers to private R&D investment (with particular attention to the risk of relocation of R&D activities of the key foreign investors); (iv) providing qualified human resources (including salary conditions).

Seen from a European Commission perspective (European Commission, 2009b), most policy making in Belgium is done through a bottom-up process where interest groups lobby for increased support for one or more areas related to scientific research and its commercial exploitation. Unfortunately, over the last decade this has been done without a clear understanding about the knowledge demand needs (why, in what fields, for whom and to what end is one seeking to increase knowledge production) and in a context of weak assessment of the outputs and results of research programs.

On the knowledge side, the industrial specialization versus the scientific specialization allied to the low internal capabilities of most SMEs to absorb knowledge hamper knowledge circulation. Moreover, in terms of demand there is little focus on society-driven research; in terms of production a main policy-related risk is the non-attractive salaries for researchers and fragmentation of the system; and in terms of circulation there is a challenge for ongoing underinvestment in training and technology diffusion (European Commission, 2009b).

The European Innovation Scoreboard (EIS)[6] 2009 (European Commission, 2009c) positions Belgium amongst the group of innovation followers (along with Austria, Cyprus, Estonia, France, Ireland, Luxembourg, the Netherlands and Slovenia) with innovation performance below those of the 'innovation leaders' (Denmark, Finland, Germany, Sweden and the UK) but close to or above that of the EU27 average. The EIS also calculated growth in innovation performance using data over a five-year period (2004–2008), based on absolute changes in the indicators. Belgium's rate of improvement is slightly below the EU27 average and behind that of innovation leaders such as Finland and Germany. The EIS 2009 identifies Belgium's relative strengths, compared to the country's average performance, in 'Linkages & Entrepreneurship' and 'Innovators and Economic effects', while relative weaknesses are in 'Firm Investments'. Over the past five years, strong growth has been witnessed in terms of 'Venture Capital' (17.8 per cent). Performance in 'Firm investments' and 'Innovators' has worsened, in particular due to a decrease in non-R&D innovation expenditures (–8.5 per cent).

Considering the effect of the financial crisis between late 2008 and early 2009 on innovation in Belgium, the results from the Innobarometer 2009 (European Commission, 2009a) are encouraging. As a direct effect of the crisis, 23 per cent of EU27 innovators decreased their innovation expenditures; however, Belgian innovative firms had one of the lowest percentages (15 per cent), while only 14 per cent of Belgian innovating firms, the lowest national figure in the EU27, thought their innovation expenditures would decrease in 2009 as compared to 2008, compared to 29 per cent for the EU27.

However, a closer look at the indicators as presented in section 3.3 revealed that some of these 'general tendency' conclusions based on the EIS sometimes hide negative or positive underlying tendencies. For example, despite the overall good performance in terms of 'venture capital' and 'entrepreneurship', a relatively weak performance for Belgium can be noted in terms of venture capital for expansion and replacement, as well as in terms of firm renewal and entrepreneurial activity. These findings are closely related to high innovation costs, lack of internal funds, and a market dominated by established enterprises. These factors are considered the most important hampering factors for innovation in Belgium. Moreover, the presented STI performances cannot be seen independently of the sector structure of the Belgian economy which is highly dominated (especially in terms of R&D expenditures and patent activity) by large multinational enterprises. These examples show that STI (composite) indicators should be considered with caution.

Finally, the indicators actually applied in the European Innovation Scoreboard (and in many other STI data reports like, for example, the Belgian Report on STI Indicators 2010) are to a large extent driven by data availability rather than data necessity to properly address (i) the policy context which is oriented towards smart, sustainable and inclusive growth as well as (ii) the increasingly international context of STI. These elements are briefly reflected on in the next section on perspectives for STI policy making in Belgium.

3.4.2 Perspectives for STI Policy Making in Belgium

Regarding its STI policy, the small open Belgian economy is highly sensitive to international trends in STI (policies). Over recent years, science, technology and innovation have witnessed important changes with major implications for STI policies. On a biannual basis, the OECD 'STI

Outlook' describes important 'global' trends in STI policy. We pick up two important trends highlighted in the last STI report (OECD, 2009c) which are of particular importance for Belgium: the accelerated internationalization of STI, which is closely related to the paradigm of 'open innovation', and the societal challenges for STI (policy). Both issues have major implications for the reflection on more appropriate STI indicators.

The first trend is the *accelerated internationalization of STI* and the intertwining of regional and national innovation systems and the emergence of international systems (like the EU) presenting a new context for STI policy making. Despite the Lisbon Strategy, Europe has been unable to reduce its (business) R&D deficit within the triad, and is challenged by newly emerging economies such as China and India (European Commission, 2007a). Over the last few decades, policy responses in Europe to reduce the R&D deficit were mainly characterized by a domestic focus. However, this territorially based view is not completely in line with the ideas suggested by innovation system(s) thinking to integrate regional, national, EU innovation networks into broader (global) ones. Policy making in Belgium has been largely inspired by EU policy making and for a small open economy the global context is even more important.

The domestic focus of STI policies ignores the reality of a changing landscape for R&D in which Europe will take a less dominant position and in which R&D activities of business enterprises (in particular those of multinational enterprises) are increasingly footloose and beyond policy makers' control. European-based companies have indeed good reasons to move parts of their R&D capacities abroad, ranging from nearness to foreign local markets to the need to be exposed to new ideas and intellectual resources. Despite the fact that beneficial returns from inward foreign direct investment (FDI) in R&D are not automatic and that outward FDI in R&D should not be considered a priori as being negative, actual policy measures towards FDI in R&D in the EU member states are largely biased towards the attraction of inward FDI and do not target the valorization of outward FDI, and, in more general terms, of knowledge developed outside Europe (Teirlinck, 2009). The ignorance of opportunities of outward FDI in R&D is also recognized by the 'Expert Group Knowledge for Growth' (European Commission, 2006), highlighting the need for policy makers in Europe to give greater consideration to how Europe can take advantage of foreign knowledge, located both at home and abroad. A similar remark can be made regarding open innovation or knowledge exchange across national borders. Here as well no arguments exist for policy makers to (try to) restrict policy measures to their own territory, as is actually the case (at EU level: see European Commission (2007a and 2007b); for policy making in Belgium, see Soete (2007)).

At present there are serious biases in data collection in favor of 'inward' STI flows and their effects. The measurement and effects of (cross-border) 'outward' STI flows are somewhat ignored. Also, some aspects of open innovation, for example the outsourcing of R&D and its effects on the internal R&D, are underinvestigated (Teirlinck et al., 2010). Therefore, policy makers should stimulate further efforts to measure and collect internationally comparable data on cross-border R&D and (open) innovation, and to investigate the implications for the domestic R&D and innovation base.

However, the increasingly open and international context for research and innovation should be addressed from the perspective of regional specificities. In this respect, looking below the national level, the European Commission's (2009c) EIS Regional Innovation Scoreboard 2009 report places all three Belgian regions in the group of 'medium-high innovators' (Flanders having shifted from high to medium-high between 2004 and 2006 data sets studied in the report). However, while on a European-level benchmarking exercise the three regions perform relatively similarly, regional strengths and weaknesses are somewhat different, conforming to the socioeconomic profile, the sectoral specialization of the economies, the specialization of the research base, the (un)employment rate, entrepreneurial activity rates and propensity to innovate, and so on. For instance, the highly urbanized Brussels-Capital region is strongly service sector dominated, while the Flemish region economy is more highly industrialized, in terms of the share of manufacturing in regional value-added, than either of the two other regions. In particular, Flanders has a much higher share of employment in high-tech manufacturing than the other two regions. The 'Key STI data' report (Belgian Science Policy Office, 2010a) highlights a number of these regional differences. For instance, there is a relative concentration of research activities in Flanders (61 per cent of intramural R&D expenditures in 2007, 64 per cent in 2002) even if Wallonia has improved its share in recent years (26 per cent compared to 23 per cent, and indeed has the highest R&D/GDP share of the Belgian regions), notably thanks to an improved position in terms of BERD.

Therefore, for a small open economy such as Belgium and its regions, increased internationalization of STI and more 'open innovation' tendencies deserve to be met through adapted policy measures. The strength of Belgium's decentralized organization is that each region is taking the measures that best suit their needs. In order to formulate adequate policies, a thorough appreciation of the relevant statistics and indicators, and the implications they bring in their wake, is instrumental. Interesting areas to consider are responding tendencies towards (i) a distributed innovation process in which networking has become a vital issue; (ii) a need to complement outsourced R&D with in-house knowledge generation; (iii) an optimizing strategy for raising the efficiency of R&D activities because of increased risk and cost issues; (iv) an internationalization of R&D activities and concomitant spatial division of labor; and (v) a conversion towards R&D activities directed at the knowledge-intensive services sectors (Howells, 2008).

The second and more recent trend relates to *STI strategies increasingly driven by social and to some extent global challenges* such as climate change, energy security, health and quality of life. Most recent trends point to a 'greening' of national research and innovation policies since increasingly countries tend to include environmental issues, climate change and energy in their national STI policy strategic priorities. Of course, this may not ignore the fact that improving national competitiveness (mainly in terms of raising productivity growth, jobs, and living standards) remains a common goal of national/regional plans or strategies for STI. This has important implications for the governance of STI, which still largely remains a key issue on national agendas but is now challenged to extend across international cooperation in STI needed to address global challenges.

But also at national or regional level these changes imply enhanced cooperation across ministerial or departmental functions to strengthen linkages between science policy and other policy departments as well as higher involvement of societal stakeholders in STI policy making. The governance structures for STI policy making are increasingly organized as a multi-layered matrix with both bottom-up and top-down flows in the advisory and decision-making processes in which ministries, advisory bodies and a range of different actors are involved. The focus on interactions and interdependencies between different policies is commonly referred to as the broader 'policy mix' (Nauwelaers, 2009). Despite the trend towards broadening of innovation policy to meet societal challenges (as reflected in the Marshall Plan 2.Green; in Vlaanderen in Actie 2020; and in the Regional Innovation Plan Brussels) and to ensure that all policy measures are being brought into play to strengthen the national innovation system, there is clearly room for improvement. Despite the fact that the actual discussion needs to be to link STI policy with other policy domains like environment, health, energy supply, safety . . . in Belgium, even within STI policy making, policies at different government levels are not always seen in relation to each other. A good example of this is the introduction – by the federal government – of the tax credits for R&D personnel (in private enterprises, in public research organizations and universities, and involved

---

BOX 3.2   THE LOGIC MODEL FOR POLICY INTERVENTION

Regardless of its nature (policy, program, measure, project), a public intervention can be analyzed as a set of financial, organizational and human resources mobilized to achieve, in a given period of time, an objective or set of objectives, with the aim of solving or overcoming a problem or difficulty affecting targeted groups.

Logic models are models that help identify and set out the relationship between the socioeconomic needs to be addressed by the intervention and its objectives, inputs, processes, outputs and outcomes, which include results (immediate changes that arise for direct addressees at the end of their participation in a public intervention) and impacts (longer-term effects of the intervention).

---

in private–public cooperation in R&D) and the many initiatives at the level of the regions in terms of R&D subsidies which envisage – at least to some extent – similar outcomes/impacts. But even at the level of separate governments, policy instruments are not always designed in a complementary way. Due to over-fragmentation of the research system there is a challenge to ensure synergies and cooperation between research funding instruments at different levels (for the Flemish Region: see Soete, 2007).

Moreover, the economic crisis and the government budget constraints force STI policies to pay considerably more attention to the outcomes and impacts of public spending on research and innovation. Therefore, policy makers should stimulate (data collection and analysis) efforts to better assess the (socio-) economic impacts of STI policy measures. As noted in the OECD STI Outlook (OECD, 2009c) this requires adapted reflections on STI indicators (for example not simply counting bibliometrics or patents, but relating these to – at least for Europe – the Europe 2020 strategy for green, inclusive and smart innovation). In this respect, the current European Innovation Scoreboard (focusing on traditional input–output STI indicators) is at odds with the policy objectives. Therefore indicators should more adequately follow the policy intervention logic model (see Box 3.2) and take into account the longer-term impacts of STI policies.

The building blocks of logic models are presented in Figure 3.4 (European Commission, 2004, pp. 71–2, and OECD, 2002) and include:

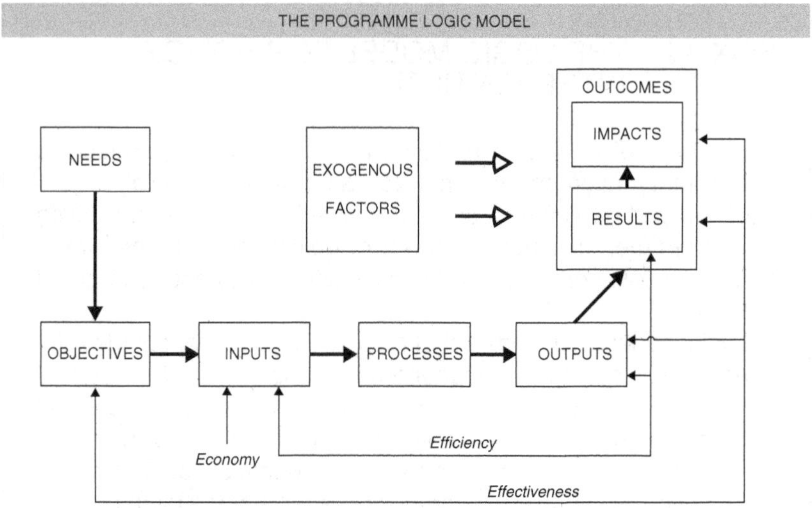

THE PROGRAMME LOGIC MODEL

Source: European Commission (2004, p. 72).

Figure 3.4   The logic model

- *Needs:* Needs are problems or difficulties affecting concerned groups, which the public intervention aims to solve or overcome.
- *Objectives:* Objectives are initial statements of the outcomes intended to be achieved by an intervention. A distinction should be made between global, intermediate, immediate and operational objectives.
- *Inputs* are financial, human, and material resources that are mobilized for the implementation of an intervention.
- *Processes* are procedures and activities employed to convert inputs into outputs (for example procedures for delivering subventions or selecting projects for financing). The concept also covers the generation of management information and its use by managers.
- *Outputs* are what are produced or accomplished with the resources allocated to an intervention (for example R&D grants distributed to firms).
- *Outcomes* are changes that arise from the implementation of an intervention and which normally relate to the objectives of this intervention. Outcomes include results and impacts. Outcomes may be expected or unexpected, positive or negative (for example R&D tax incentives attracting investors to a region but causing 'hollowing-out' of the local research capabilities).

- *Results* are the immediate changes that arise for direct addressees at the end of their participation in an intervention (for example increased R&D investment due to R&D grants).
- *Impacts* are longer-term socioeconomic consequences that can be observed after a certain period after the completion of an intervention, which may affect either direct addressees of the intervention or indirect addressees falling outside the boundary of the intervention, who may be winners or losers. It is important to note the broad scope ('socioeconomic', direct and indirect, positive and negative) and time dimension ('longer term', 'observed after a certain period after the completion of an intervention') of 'impacts'.

Indicators are of key importance for evidence-based policy making. Therefore, a great deal of attention is paid to measuring the effects of RTDI investment. Though they are not the only tool for capturing such effects, policy makers attach great importance to them, and they often attain higher visibility in the policy debate than qualitative impact statements. As far as indicators measuring the effects of RTDI investment are concerned, a clear distinction needs to be made between output indicators, result indicators and impact indicators. Impact indicators clearly concern the measurement of the long-term, broad socioeconomic impacts of RTDI investment. The main challenge when dealing with indicators is to identify the good conditions and practices regarding the design and use of indicators to assess the impact of public RTDI financing and as such to make impact assessment a more useful tool for policy making in the field of RTDI.

Because of the emphasis in RTDI investment effect measurement so far on outputs and results rather than impacts, until now RTDI-related indicator work has focused mainly on developing and collecting R&D input and output indicators, which analysts then tried to relate to each other. This is problematic since econometric analysis of the relationship between R&D and outcomes is typically based on a linear conception of innovation and the idea that innovation starts with basic research, followed by applied research and development and ends with the production and diffusion of new products and processes in the economy. However, it is widely acknowledged that innovation is more complex, with multiple feedback loops between stages and actors, and innovation results from the interplay of public and private RTDI investment, commercial interests and many other factors. Even more important, however, is the fact that, since many of the impacts of RTDI only emerge over time, these kinds of indicators and these types of analyses ignore the long-term benefits of public funding for RTDI for a country's economy and society.

Moreover, a potential paradox can result from the use of indicators as impact proxy for a policy measure. The use of indicators improves the short-term 'impact' of a measure (obviously since it is the goal) but sometimes it may also change the global logic/economy of a measure/policy. Indeed, in spite of being an advanced and partial interim measure of the intended objectives of a measure (with the logic model behind), indicators tend to be confused with these objectives themselves. Then, the building and the use of indicators contaminates the logic model. The bias (small in the beginning) may become stronger with time. As a consequence, intended objectives (economical and societal) can remain largely unachieved and impacts can be lower than they could have been in the long term.

In Belgium (as in most other EU Member States), for about a decade, impact assessment exercises of public funding for RTDI have occurred on an ad hoc basis mainly depending on the government level and on the level of the ministerial department/agency (Delanghe and Teirlinck, 2009). Also there is no systematic reflection regarding making a better causal link between indicators and policy objectives. Therefore, there is clearly room for improvement in this area.

NOTES

1. Five main constitutional reforms, which took place in 1970, 1980, 1988/89, 1993 and 2001, have progressively put in place the legal framework and the institutions necessary for the establishment of a Federal State. The last institutional reform in 2001 concerned the devolution of competence for foreign trade, agriculture and development to the regions.
2. The CIPS-ICWB has established two permanent administrative sub-committees, attended by representatives from each authority: the International Co-operation Commission (CIS) for international matters, and the Federal Co-operation Commission (CFS) for national matters. Examples of matters dealt with by these committees are the permanent inventory of scientific potential in Belgium, or the positioning of Belgium in the EU's Seventh Framework Programme for Research and Technological Development (FP7).
3. It has to be noted that R&D tax credits are not integrated into the GBAORD as tax credits deal with forgone revenues for the government. As such they are less visible in STI statistics. However, the recent tax credits change the numbers and the respective weight of each of the Belgian authorities in the total public effort regarding research funding. The Ministry of Finance estimates the forgone revenues for 2009 due to the main R&D tax credits at a total of 470 million euros. This comes very close to the GBAORD for the Federal authorities, which is slightly above 500 million euros. The OECD is working on an indicator showing the indirect government support for research (through tax credits) in comparison with GBAORD for OECD countries. However, many methodological issues remain to be solved in order to measure tax credits adequately.
4. The OECD has published a 'Manual on the measurement of human resources devoted to S&T' to harmonize the collection of these data (OECD, 1995).
5. The Erawatch Country Reports intend to provide an evidence-based and horizontally – among the EU Member States – comparable assessment of strengths and weaknesses and policy related opportunities and risks for each of the Member States.

6. All EIS reports mentioned can be downloaded at: http://www.proinno-europe.eu/projects/homepage/public/1435.

REFERENCES

Belgian Science Policy Office (2010a), *Key Data on Science, Technology and Innovation Belgium 2010*, Brussels: Belgian Science Policy Office.
Belgian Science Policy Office (2010b), *Belgian Report on Science and Technology 2010*, Brussels: Belgian Science Policy Office.
Casey, T. and I. Collins (2004), 'The monitoring & impact assessment indicators study: the MIP's study', The Netherlands: *Technopolis*.
Delanghe, H. and P. Teirlinck (2009), 'Optimising the policy mix by the development of a common methodology for the assessment of (socio-)economic impacts of RTDI public funding', DSTI/STP/TIP 18, Paris: OECD.
European Commission (2004), *Evaluating EU Activities: A Practical Guide for the Commission Services*, Luxembourg: European Commission.
European Commission (2006), 'Globalization of R&D: linking better the European economy to "foreign" sources of knowledge and making EU a more attractive place for R&D investment', Expert Group Knowledge for Growth, Brussels: European Commission.
European Commission (2007a), *Europe in the Global Research Landscape*, Brussels: European Commission.
European Commission (2007b), 'Green paper: the European Research Area: new Perspective', Brussels: European Commission.
European Commission (2009a), 'Innobarometer 2009', Flash EB Series no. 267, Brussels: European Commission.
European Commission (2009b), 'Erawatch Country Report: Analysis of policy mixes to foster R&D investment and to contribute to the ERA: Belgium', Luxembourg: European Commission.
European Commission (2009c), 'European Innovation Scoreboard' available at: http://www.proinno-europe.eu/projects/home page/public/1435.
Eurostat (2009), http://epp.eurostat.ec.europa.eu/portal/page/portal/eurostat/home.
Howells, J. (2008), 'New directions in RD: current and prospective challenges', *R&D Management*, **38**, 241–52.
Kline, S.J. and N. Rosenberg (1986), 'An overview of innovation', in R. Landau and N. Rosenberg (eds), *The Positive Sum Strategy: Harnessing Technology for Economic Growth*, Washington, DC: National Academy Press, pp. 275–305.
Nauwelaers, C. (2009), 'Policy mixes for R&D in Europe', a study commissioned by the European Commission, Directorate General for Research, Brussels: European Commission.
OECD (2002), *Frascati Manual*, Paris: OECD.
OECD (1995), 'The measurement of scientific and technological activities: manual on the measurement of human resources devoted to S&T – Canberra Manual', Paris: OECD.
OECD (2009a), *Main Science and Technology Indicators 2009-2*, Paris: OECD.
OECD (2009b), *Education at a Glance 2009: OECD Indicators*, Paris: OECD.
OECD (2009c), *STI Outlook*, Paris: OECD.
OECD (2009d), 'Innovation in firms: a microeconomic perspective', Paris: OECD.

OECD (2010), *Main Trends in Science, Technology and Innovation Policy*, DSTI/ STP 10, Paris: OECD.

Reid, A. and N. Bruno (2010), 'Institutions and competences for STI in Belgium', in Belgian Science Policy Office (ed.), *Belgian Report on Science and Technology 2010*, p. 13.

Soete, L. (2007), 'Eindrapport: Expertgroep voor de Doorlichting van het Vlaams Innovatie-Instrumentarium', available at: http://www.iwt.be/sites/default/files/eindrap_doorlichting_innovatie_instrumentarium.pdf.

Teirlinck, P. (2009), 'Foreign direct investment in business R&D in Belgium in comparison with other EU member states: statistical overview and policy-making', Brussels: Belgian Science Policy, Research Studies 10.

Teirlinck, P., M. Dumont and A. Spithoven (2010), 'Corporate decision-making in R&D outsourcing and the impact on internal R&D employment intensity', *Industrial and Corporate Change*, March.

4. A longitudinal perspective on research and innovation in Belgium

**Filip De Beule, Dieter Somers and
Ilke Van Beveren**

4.1 INTRODUCTION

This chapter aims to discuss the innovation performance of firms located in Belgium by using three successive waves of the Community Innovation Survey (CIS) for Belgium. Since the data in each wave are representative for the full population of firms employing at least ten people, both in terms of firm size distribution, sector of activity and region, the data allow us to compare firms' innovative performance over time and across regions and sectors.

As will be discussed in greater detail below, the CIS data are part of a harmonized framework, coordinated by Eurostat.[1] The survey has been sent out every two to four years since the mid-1990s. The representative nature of the data allows us to compare the innovative performance of firms in different regions and sectors and with different ownership status. Apart from data on firms' innovative performance (for example product and process innovation), the data contain information on a number of other firm-level characteristics, such as group membership, innovation funding, innovative inputs (R&D), cooperation and knowledge sources that can be accessed by firms.

Although the CIS data for Belgium have been used in a growing number of publications in recent years (for example Blechinger et al., 1998; Brouwer and Kleinknecht, 1999; De Beule and Van Beveren, 2012; Mohnen and Hoareau, 2003; Tether et al., 2001), most of these studies analyze the CIS data with a specific research question in mind. For instance, Czarnitzki et al. (2011) use the CIS data for Flanders to analyze the role of financing constraints in firms' innovative performance and Van Beveren and Vandenbussche (2010) investigate the relationship between firm-level exports and innovative performance. The current chapter aims to approach the data in a much more encompassing way, by focusing on differences between firms in terms of their innovative performance according to their sector of activity, region and ownership. In doing so, we aim to uncover salient facts emerging from the data, which could be a starting point of future research. Moreover, our analysis can potentially uncover important facts relevant to policy makers.

This chapter is structured as follows. Section 4.2 discusses the Community Innovation Survey set-up and data in greater detail. Section 4.3 compares the innovative performance of firms by region, sector of activity and ownership. Finally, in section 4.4 we discuss potential implications of our findings.

4.2   COMMUNITY INNOVATION SURVEY

The firm-level innovation data used in this chapter are taken from the Community Innovation Survey for Belgium and are obtained through the Belgian Science Policy.[2] The CIS survey is organized every two to four years. Qualitative questions refer to a three-year period (for example has your enterprise introduced a product innovation between 1998 and 2000), while quantitative questions always pertain to the last year of the period (for example internal R&D spending in 2000). Sampling in the CIS survey for Belgium is based on the full population of firms in all business sectors, with at least ten employees (Teirlinck, 2005).[3] Since sampling for the CIS survey occurs independently for each wave and firms are not required to report (that is participation in the survey is voluntary), firms that have participated in the survey for a particular wave are not necessarily part of subsequent or earlier waves. The final CIS data are representative in terms of firm size distribution (number of employees, divided into five size classes), region (three main regions of Belgium) and sector (NACE two-digit sector).

The CIS survey can be divided into three parts. In the first part, firms are asked to answer some general questions (for example size of the firm, ownership status and trade status). In the second part, firms are asked to report whether they have introduced a product[4] and/or process[5] innovation, and whether they had an ongoing or abandoned innovation project[6] during the previous three years (current year also counts). The third part of the survey only needs to be completed by firms that have responded positively to at least one of the questions in part 2. Part 3 contains detailed questions related to firms' innovation activities and expenditures, their sources of information and their types of collaboration.

As stated earlier, this study builds on the results of three successive Belgian CIS waves (CIS3, CIS4 and CIS5). The first survey holds information for the period from 1998 to 2000. The second survey consists of data from 2002 to 2004. Finally, the third survey provides information from 2004 to 2006. Our initial dataset consists of 7894 observations. After removing observations of firms with missing information on key variables, we end up with 7865 observations. The first survey consists of 1287 firms; the second survey comprises 3307 companies; and finally, the last survey comprises 3271 enterprises. As firms are randomly sampled from the population, firms can participate in each wave of the survey.

4.3 ANALYSIS OF THE CIS DATA FOR BELGIUM

4.3.1 Comparison by Region

This section makes a distinction between firms from the Flemish region, the Walloon region and Brussels. From Table 4.1, we can observe that 3102 firms are located in the Flemish region, while 1631 and 1219 firms are situated in the Walloon region and Brussels respectively. Table 4.1 also indicates that 37 per cent of all firms in Brussels are part of foreign multinationals, while only 24 per cent and 28 per cent of all firms in the Walloon region and the Flemish region are part of a foreign multinational.

From Table 4.2, we can observe that firms from the Flemish region (Flanders) have the largest firm size. Regarding funding, the table shows that only about 8 per cent of all firms in Brussels reported having received funding from local, national or EU governments. This percentage is significantly larger in the Flemish region and the Walloon region (Wallonia), where around 15 per cent and 16 per cent of the firms received funding. This can be explained by the fact that there are relatively more foreign multinationals located in Brussels and, in general, those firms receive less funding (Ebersberger et al., 2005).

When we take a look at the innovation characteristics in Table 4.2, the figures suggest that the Flemish region is the most innovative region of the

Table 4.1 Number of firms by geographical region and ownership structure

	Brussels	Flemish region	Walloon region	Total
Standalone firms	523	1470	864	2857
Foreign multinationals	456	869	390	1715
Belgian groups	240	763	377	1380
Total	1219	3102	1631	5952

Table 4.2   *Descriptive statistics of key variables by geographical region*

Variables	Brussels (BR)	Flanders (FL)	Wallonia (WL)	Total	Significance		
					BR–FL	BR–WL	FL–WL
Number	1219	3102	1631	5952			
Firm size (employment)	37.75	48.72	38.94	43.44	***		***
Funding[d][1]	0.079	0.151	0.163	0.140	***	***	
Innovative firms[d][2]	0.438	0.571	0.431	0.508	***		***
Firms performing internal R&D[d]	0.227	0.351	0.260	0.304	***	**	***
R&D intensity (Internal R&D/turnover)	0.015	0.016	0.017	0.016			
Share of innovative products in turnover	0.065	0.091	0.063	0.077	***		***
Share of brand new products in turnover	0.059	0.080	0.057	0.068	***		***
Product Innovation[d]	0.305	0.405	0.289	0.351	***		***
Process Innovation[d]	0.291	0.397	0.278	0.339	***		***
Product & Process Innovation[d]	0.200	0.280	0.184	0.232	***		***
Products new to market and firm[d]	0.264	0.320	0.243	0.286	***		***

Collaboration[d]	0.165	0.248	0.152	0.200	***	***
Collaboration within own enterprise group[d 3]	0.527	0.514	0.457	0.513		
Collaboration with external parties[d 3]	0.841	0.866	0.862	0.864		
Collaboration with institutions[d 3]	0.606	0.743	0.642	0.700	***	***
Importance of knowledge sources[4]						
Importance of internal sources	2.102	2.186	2.052	2.127		***
Importance of market sources	1.290	1.505	1.313	1.417	***	***
Importance of institutional sources	0.574	0.693	0.568	0.641	***	***
Importance of other sources	1.027	1.259	1.039	1.160	***	***

Notes:

Significance levels: *** $p < 0.01$; ** $p < 0.05$; * $p < 0.10$.

All values reported refer to sample means of each variable.

d. Dummy variable

1. Dummy that indicates whether the firm has received regional, national or EU-level innovation subsidies.
2. Dummy that indicates whether the enterprise has performed some innovative activities during the previous two years.
3. Dummy that indicates the type of collaboration partner.
4. Variable that takes a value between 0 and 3, whereby 0 indicates that this source is not used and 3 indicates that this source is very important.

three. The figures show that 58 per cent of all firms in the Flemish region performed some innovative activities,[7] compared to only 43 per cent in the Walloon region and 44 per cent in Brussels. All other figures, related to internal R&D, R&D intensity, share of new products in turnover, product and or process innovation, and collaboration confirm that firms in the Flemish region are, on average, more innovative than those of the other regions. The largest difference between the three regions can be found in the percentage of firms that reported having introduced a product innovation. This percentage is 41 per cent in the Flemish region, 29 per cent in Brussels and 31 per cent in the Walloon region. Another outcome of the study is that the innovation performance of firms located in Brussels is not significantly different from firms located in the Walloon region. This is surprising, as the Walloon region is considered the least developed region of Belgium (Capron, 2001).

Possible explanations might be related to external economies of agglomeration or urbanization. Marshallian agglomeration spillovers within specific industries might make more clustered firms within specific regions more innovative, while Jacobian urbanization spillovers within specific regions might improve firms' innovativeness more in general. Evidence for Belgium (De Beule and Van Beveren, 2012) has shown, on the one hand, that firms enjoy a significantly positive impact from increased sectoral concentration. Controlling for research and development intensity, export intensity, foreign ownership, funding, size and age, own sector employment concentrations are shown to be a significant conduit in the innovation and renewal process of firms' product portfolio. On the other hand, firms also seem to enjoy a significantly positive impact on their innovativeness from urbanization economies. Given that Flanders scores better on both accounts, it is not surprising to find greater innovativeness as compared to Brussels and especially Wallonia. Furthermore, although Brussels has a large contingent of multinational firms, most of these firms are linked to services, such as coordination centers, headquarters and financial intermediaries. As such, the sector distribution of firms clearly also has an impact on the innovativeness of firms.

However, a more detailed analysis of innovators in particular has shown that while, on the one hand, firms sometimes prefer higher agglomeration and urbanization areas; they sometimes prefer to stay out of competitors' way. For instance, De Beule and Van Beveren (2012) demonstrate for Belgium that the most innovative firms are not inclined to invest in agglomerated or urbanized centers. This is in line with recent research that shows that industry leaders are reluctant to locate near competitors (Shaver and Flyer, 2000). These results suggest that firms with the best technologies will gain little, yet competitively suffer when their technologies, employees, and access to supporting industries spill over to competitors. Therefore, these firms have little motivation to cluster geographically despite the existence of agglomeration economies. Conversely, firms with the weakest technologies have little to lose and a lot to gain; therefore, these firms are motivated to cluster geographically.

4.3.2 Comparison by Sector of Activity

This section makes a distinction between low-tech manufacturing and high-tech manufacturing, low-tech service and high-tech service sectors. To group the firms into these sectors, we used an existing classification from Eurostat (2008). The results from the survey show that most firms in Belgium are active in the low-tech sector, with 1811 firms active in low-tech manufacturing and 1822 firms active in the low-tech service sector. Furthermore, there were 810 and 1156 firms active in the high-tech manufacturing and the high-tech service sector respectively. The rest category[8] consisted of 353 companies.

Table 4.3 and 4.4 show that manufacturing firms are on average larger than service firms, with high-tech manufacturers having the largest size. Regarding funding, we can observe that manufacturing firms obtain more public funding than service firms. In addition, the tables show that high-tech manufacturers and high-tech service firms receive significantly more funding than their low-tech counterparts. Because these differences are quite large, we can safely say that governmental authorities are favoring these high-tech industries. Governments are favoring these high-tech industries because it is believed that they offer the highest prospects for development (Christensen, 2010). Studies have shown, however, that they only provide a marginal contribution to Western economies, while low-tech sectors remain a very important factor in the contribution to GDP (Hirsch-Kreinsen, 2008; Hirsch-Kreinsen et al., 2003). A recent study by De Beule and Van Beveren (2009) has found that high-tech industries only accounted for around 5 per cent of total employment or net value-added. These findings suggest that governmental authorities might be excessively focused on these high-tech sectors.

When we take another look at Tables 4.3 and 4.4, we notice that manufacturing firms are more innovative than service firms. The tables, for instance, show that 69 per cent of high-tech manufacturing firms and 56 per cent of low-tech manufacturing firms reported having performed innovative activities, while this percentage is 56 per cent for high-tech service firms and only 36 per cent for low-tech service firms. The percentage of firms that reported having performed internal R&D and products and/or process innovations is also higher for manufacturing firms. In addition,

Table 4.3   Descriptive statistics of key variables of manufacturing firms

Variables	Low-tech Man	High-tech Man	Total
Number	1811	810	2621
Firm size (employment) ***	46.70	57.86	49.89
Funding[d][1] ***	0.167	0.251	0.193
Innovative firms[d][2] ***	0.560	0.685	0.599
Firms performing internal R&D[d] ***	0.335	0.505	0.385
R&D intensity (Internal R&D/turnover) ***	0.006	0.024	0.012
Share of innovative products in turnover ***	0.068	0.134	0.089
Share of brand new products in turnover ***	0.062	0.119	0.079
Product Innovation[d] ***	0.366	0.541	0.42
Process Innovation[d]	0.405	0.436	0.414
Product & Process Innovation[d] ***	0.270	0.336	0.29
Products new to market and firm[d] ***	0.303	0.453	0.349
Collaboration[d] ***	0.219	0.332	0.254
Collaboration within own enterprise group[d][3] ***	0.427	0.606	0.499
Collaboration with external parties[d][3]	0.843	0.859	0.850
Collaboration with institutions[d][3]	0.702	0.732	0.714
Importance of knowledge sources[4]			
Importance of internal sources ***	2.059	2.344	2.16
Importance of market sources	1.469	1.514	1.485
Importance of institutional sources ***	0.623	0.768	0.675
Importance of other sources	1.222	1.257	1.235

Notes:
All values reported refer to sample means of each variable.
d. Dummy variable.
1. Dummy that indicates whether the firm has received regional, national or EU-level innovation subsidies.
2. Dummy that indicates whether the enterprise has performed some innovative activities during the preceding three years (current year included).
3. Dummy that indicates the type of collaboration partner.
4. Variable that takes a value between 0 and 3, whereby 0 indicates that this source is not used and 3 indicates that this source is very important.
Significance levels are based on regressions with size, sector and regions as independent variables. Significance levels: *** $p < 0.01$; ** $p < 0.05$; * $p < 0.10$.

manufacturing firms are more likely to collaborate. These results tend to confirm previous findings (Tether et al., 2001). These differences shown above might, however, also be due to the different innovation orientation between manufacturing and service firms. Service firms tend to place a greater emphasis on the improvement of their skills and organizational

Table 4.4   Descriptive statistics of key variables of service firms

Variables	Low-tech Services	High-tech Services	Total
Number	1822	1156	2978
Firm size (employment) ***	35.17	41.95	37.67
Funding[d][1] ***	0.053	0.169	0.098
Innovative firms[d][2] ***	0.361	0.562	0.439
Firms performing internal R&D[d] ***	0.138	0.392	0.237
R&D intensity (Internal R&D/turnover) ***	0.003	0.048	0.02
Share of innovative products in turnover ***	0.043	0.112	0.070
Share of brand new products in turnover ***	0.038	0.1	0.063
Product Innovation[d] ***	0.212	0.439	0.301
Process Innovation[d] ***	0.246	0.347	0.286
Product & Process Innovation[d] ***	0.137	0.271	0.189
Products new to market and firm[d] ***	0.170	0.353	0.241
Collaboration[d] ***	0.108	0.252	0.164
Collaboration within own enterprise group[d][3]	0.5	0.512	0.507
Collaboration with external parties[d][3]	0.898	0.874	0.883
Collaboration with institutions[d][3] ***	0.592	0.72	0.667
Importance of knowledge sources[4]			
Importance of internal sources ***	2.015	2.26	2.137
Importance of market sources ***	1.275	1.415	1.345
Importance of institutional sources ***	0.464	0.759	0.606
Importance of other sources ***	0.973	1.176	1.074

Notes:
All values reported refer to sample means of each variable.
d. Dummy variable.
1. Dummy that indicates whether the firm has received regional, national or EU-level innovation subsidies.
2. Dummy that indicates whether the enterprise has performed some innovative activities during the preceding three years (current year included).
3. Dummy that indicates the type of collaboration partner.
4. Variable that takes a value between 0 and 3, whereby 0 indicates that this source is not used and 3 indicates that this source is very important.
Significance levels are based on regressions with size, sector and regions as independent variables. Significance levels: *** $p < 0.01$; ** $p < 0.05$; * $p < 0.10$.

practices, which are pervasive across the economy, but are often neglected by manufacturing firms (Tether, 2005). Because the CIS does not capture these innovation types, it is underestimating the true innovation performance of service firms.

When we compare high-tech manufacturing firms with low-tech

manufacturing firms and high-tech service firms with low-tech service firms, we can notice that the high-tech firms significantly outperform their low-tech counterparts. However, this difference might be partly caused by their higher funding opportunities, since access to finance positively affects firms' ability to innovate and commercialize their innovations (Aharonson et al., 2008; Almus and Czarnitzki, 2003; Czarnitzki and Fier, 2002; Czarnitzki and Licht, 2006).

4.3.3   Comparison by Group Affiliation

In this section, we make a distinction between stand-alone firms, firms that are part of a foreign multinational and firms that are part of a Belgian group. Table 4.5 shows that our dataset consists of 2852 stand-alone firms, 1712 firms that are part of foreign multinationals and 1388 firms that belong to Belgian groups.

Previous studies have shown that R&D activities are mostly being carried out at the headquarters location (Castellani and Zanfei, 2003; Markusen, 2004; Patel and Pavitt, 1991). This could lead to the hypothesis that foreign-owned firms could have a lower level of innovation activities than domestic-owned firms. However, several recent studies (Castellani and Zanfei, 2006; Criscuolo et al., 2005; and Frenz and Ietto-Gillies, 2007) provide empirical evidence that firms that are active on international markets are more innovative than their national counterparts, even after controlling for size and sector distribution. Specifically, Frenz and Ietto-Gillies (2007) argue that group membership is an important determinant of the propensity to innovate. Furthermore, they have found that firms which are part of a multinational corporation have a higher innovation performance than those belonging to a domestic corporation. A further analysis of these multinationals has shown that it is the degree of multi-nationality that influences the innovation performance (Frenz et al., 2005; Frenz and Ietto-Gillies, 2007). These results suggest that the degree of multinationality is positively related to firms' innovation performance, as it increases the number of product and process innovations and R&D expenditures. It appears that enterprises can learn from being part of a network and source knowledge from their internal linkages. Table 4.5 confirms that foreign multinationals and Belgian groups rely significantly more on internal knowledge sources compared to Belgian stand-alone firms.

The results in Table 4.5 confirm that group membership increases the propensity to innovate, as Belgian groups and foreign multinationals have a higher propensity to innovate than stand-alone firms. The table shows that almost 60 per cent of all firms that belong to a group reported having

Table 4.5 *Descriptive statistics of key variables by group affiliation*

Variables	Stand-alone firms (SA)	Foreign multi-nationals (FM)	Belgian groups (BG)	Total	Significance		
					SA–FM	SA–BG	FM–BG
Number	2852	1712	1388	5952			
Firm size (employment)	26.94	75.41	58.14	43.33	***	***	***
Funding[d1]	0.134	0.117	0.182	0.14	***	***	***
Innovative firms[d2]	0.435	0.585	0.561	0.508	**	***	
Firms performing internal R&D[d]	0.237	0.341	0.387	0.302	***	***	***
R&D intensity (Internal R&D/turnover)	0.014	0.016	0.019	0.01			
Share of innovative products in turnover	0.065	0.092	0.082	0.077			
Share of brand new products in turnover	0.057	0.083	0.075	0.069			
Product Innovation[d]	0.279	0.436	0.401	0.353	***	***	
Process Innovation[d]	0.288	0.394	0.392	0.342		**	**
Product & Process Innovation[d]	0.185	0.287	0.28	0.236	***	***	*
Products new to market and firm[d]	0.224	0.357	0.326	0.286	***	***	

95

Table 4.5 (continued)

Variables	Stand-alone firms (SA)	Foreign multi-nationals (FM)	Belgian groups (BG)	Total	Significance		
					SA–FM	SA–BG	FM–BG
Collaboration[d]	0.134	0.255	0.275	0.202	***	***	***
Collaboration within own enterprise group[d,3]	0.115	0.764	0.634	0.517	***	***	***
Collaboration with external parties[d,3]	0.848	0.863	0.874	0.862			
Collaboration with institutions[d,3]	0.682	0.709	0.709	0.701	**		
Importance of knowledge sources[4]							
Importance of internal sources	1.832	2.404	2.28	2.14	***	***	**
Importance of market sources	1.365	1.435	1.52	1.428		**	***
Importance of institutional sources	0.544	0.697	0.742	0.646	***	**	**
Importance of other sources	1.125	1.099	1.313	1.164	***	*	***

Notes:
All values reported refer to sample means of each variable.
d. Dummy variable.
1. Dummy that indicates whether the firm has received regional, national or EU-level innovation subsidies.
2. Dummy that indicates whether the enterprise has performed some innovative activities during the previous two years.
3. Dummy that indicates the type of collaboration partner.
4. Variable that takes a value of between 0 and 3, whereby 0 indicates that this source is not used and 3 indicates that this source is very important.
Significance levels are based on regressions with size, sector and group affiliation as independent variables. Significance levels: *** $p < 0.01$; ** $p < 0.05$; * $p < 0.10$.

performed innovative activities, while only 44 per cent of the stand-alone firms were innovative. Some might argue that these firms are more likely to perform innovative activities because they are also typically larger (as confirmed in the table) and some studies have argued that larger firms innovate more (Damanpour, 1992; Veugelers and Cassiman, 1999). However, this finding is contradicted by other studies that also took other factors into account such as the market structure (Acs and Audretsch, 1988; Cohen and Levin, 1989; Syrneonidis, 1996).

Furthermore, from the table we can conclude that these companies are significantly more likely to perform internal R&D activities. We can observe that 39 per cent of the foreign multinationals and 34 per cent of the Belgian groups performed internal R&D, while only 24 per cent of all stand-alone firms reported to have internal R&D activities. Concerning R&D intensity and share of innovative products in turnover, we again can observe that foreign multinationals and Belgian groups perform significantly better. Next, when we turn to the percentage of firms that reported having introduced a product and/or process innovation, this percentage is once more significantly larger for those companies belonging to a group. These differences are the most pronounced in the percentage of firms that reported having introduced a product innovation.

Given that many of the statistics reported in Table 4.5 show that Belgian groups are not statistically different from foreign multinationals in terms of their innovative effort and performance, and because existing empirical studies suggest that innovation performance is largely explained by multinationality, this might be an indication that Belgian groups exhibit the same degree of multinationality as foreign multinationals. This assumption seems acceptable, since Belgium only has a small market size, which encourages firms to move abroad. Unfortunately, the surveys are not able to capture the degree of multinationality of these firms, that is firms are only asked to report whether they belong to a group and where the headquarters of that group is located. As a result, we do not observe to what extent groups with Belgian headquarters are truly multinational firms, with foreign affiliates abroad. Therefore, we are not able to assess the relationship between the degree of multinationality of these firms and their innovative performance.

The figures regarding collaboration also show that foreign multinationals and Belgian groups reported to have collaborated more often than stand-alone firms. The results in Table 4.5 show that of these companies that collaborated, more than 63 per cent collaborated within the own enterprise (76.4 per cent and 63.4 per cent respectively). This can be seen as an advantage of being part of an enterprise group, as it gives the firms a better access to knowledge sources within the internal network. It is also not surprising that foreign multinationals and Belgian groups attach a greater importance to internal knowledge sources as it reflects their larger knowledge base and financial sources. In addition, foreign multinationals and Belgian groups consider institutional sources as more important. This can be explained by the finding that larger and more R&D-intensive firms are more likely to source knowledge from universities and government labs (Mohnen and Hoareau, 2003; Veugelers, 1997).

4.4   CONCLUSION

Although innovation is obviously the result of a firm's development efforts – as R&D intensity is shown to be the single most important determinant of firm innovativeness – knowledge externalities from outside the firm can play a crucial role in firms' innovative performance (Johansson and Forslund, 2008). Our analysis of Belgian firms, based on the Community Innovation Survey data for three successive waves, suggests that firms in Flanders enjoy a location premium, given that they are shown to demonstrate more innovativeness across the board. On the one hand, firms seem to enjoy a significantly positive impact from increased sectoral concentration. On the other hand, firms also seem to enjoy a significantly positive impact on their innovativeness from urbanization economies (De Beule and Van Beveren, 2012).

When we compare high-tech manufacturing firms with low-tech manufacturing firms and high-tech service firms with low-tech service firms, we notice that the high-tech firms significantly outperform their low-tech counterparts in terms of innovative activities. However, further results suggest that this difference can potentially be explained by the higher average funding opportunities for high-tech firms. Furthermore, other results (De Beule and Van Beveren, 2012) with regard to sectoral differences have shown that, after controlling for funding, and so on, low-tech manufacturing and service sectors benefit from localization economies in their innovation process, while medium- and high-tech sectors do not. This is in line with recent research that has increasingly shown the sustained competitiveness and innovativeness of low-tech sectors in high-wage European countries (Maskell, 1998; Hirsch-Kreinsen, 2008; Christensen, 2010; Hansen and Winther, 2011). High knowledge-intensive service firms, on the other hand, seem to benefit most from urbanization economies in the form of heterogeneity across sectors within their region.

Our comparison of the ownership and innovative characteristics of firms shows that not only is most research and development carried out by either foreign subsidiaries in Belgium or Belgian multinational groups, but also innovative performance is much higher for companies that are part of multinational groups, either foreign or Belgian. The figures regarding collaboration also show that foreign multinationals and Belgian groups reported to have collaborated more often than stand-alone firms.

These findings have implications both for firms and for policy makers. For firms, this means that research and development could be put to better use, as the return on investment in innovation – that is expenditure on research and development – is potentially more productive in regions with relatively more sectoral agglomeration. These regionally agglomerated sectors accumulate sources of spillovers, which in turn attract innovators and support innovation. This is, however, more so for low-tech manufacturing and service industries than for high-tech industries. Yet, high knowledge-intensive service firms also seem to be able to benefit from larger, more diverse regions in their innovation process. Given that these industries are still predominant in Belgium, much progress can be made.

For policy makers, this implies that agglomeration can be an important channel in the overall promotion of innovation. Policy focus is, however, often on high-technology industries and not on low-tech sectors. Funding at regional, national and European level, for instance, is currently mostly awarded to firms in less-agglomerated, high-tech manufacturing industries and least to firms in low-tech service and manufacturing industries. Although it is encouraging to see that R&D funding has a significantly positive effect on product innovation and renewal (except for high-tech manufacturing industries), our results suggest that funding could be used more effectively and efficiently in more agglomerated and low-tech industries, in particular (De Beule and Van Beveren, 2012).

This, in turn, suggests that Belgian (regional) innovation policy, which currently invests relatively more effort into the fast and effective development of high-tech industries, should not overlook the stimulus of innovation in low-tech sectors, especially given its importance in terms of employment and value-added. The results indicate that policies should focus more on the innovation of (medium) low-tech industries, although perhaps not at the expense of high-tech sectors.

Finally, given that subsidiaries of foreign – as well as Belgian – multinationals outperform purely domestic companies, companies as well as governments should take steps towards increasing the internationalization of firms in order to improve their innovativeness.

NOTES

1. Data are collected by national (or even regional in the case of Belgium) statistical authorities and assembled and aggregated at the European level by Eurostat.

2. Although the Community Innovation Survey is EU-based (hence comparable data are available for all EU countries), firm-level data are confidential and can only be obtained through the National Statistical Office. We are thankful to Manu Monard and the CFS-STAT Commission for granting us access to the data (onsite) and for their hospitality during visits there.
3. This cut-off can differ in different European countries.
4. A product innovation is defined as 'the market introduction of a new good or service or a significantly improved good or service with respect to its capabilities, such as improved software, user friendliness, components or sub-systems.
5. A process innovation is defined as 'the implementation of a new or significantly improved production process, distribution method, or support activity for goods or services.
6. Ongoing or abandoned innovation projects are innovation activities to develop product or process innovations that were abandoned in the last three years (current year included) or are still ongoing. These innovation activities include 'the acquisition of machinery, equipment, software and licenses; engineering and development work, training, marketing and R&D when they are specifically undertaken to develop and/or implement a product or process innovation.'
7. Firms have performed some innovative activities, if they introduced a product or process innovation in the preceding three years (current year included), or if they have some ongoing or abandoned innovation projects.
8. This rest category includes the NACE 2 codes 10, 14, 24, 40, 41 and 45.

REFERENCES

Acs, Z.J. and D.B. Audretsch (1988), 'Innovation in large and small firms: an empirical analysis', *The American Economic Review*, **78**(4), 678–90.
Aharonson, B.S., J.A.C. Baum and A. Plunket (2008), 'Inventive and uninventive clusters: the case of Canadian biotechnology', *Research Policy*, **37**(6–7), 1108–31.
Almus, M. and D. Czarnitzki (2003), 'The effects of public R&D subsidies on firms' innovation activities: the case of Eastern Germany', *Journal of Business & Economic Statistics*, **21**(2), 226–37.
Blechinger, D., A. Kleinknecht, G. Licht and F.I. Pfeiffer (1998), 'The impact of innovation on employment in Europe: an analysis using CIS data', ZEW Discussion Paper 98-02, ZEW.
Brouwer, E. and A. Kleinknecht (1999), 'Innovative output, and a firms' propensity to patent. An exploration of CIS micro data', *Research Policy*, **28**(6), 615–24.
Capron, H. (2001), 'Transition towards the knowledge-based economy: growth potential and learning regions', in *The Belgian Innovation System: Lessons and Challenges*, Belgian Federal Office for Scientific Technical and Cultural Affairs, pp. 193–220.
Castellani, D. and A. Zanfei (2003), 'Innovation, foreign ownership and multinationality. An empirical analysis on Italian manufacturing firms', Working Paper, University of Urbino, available at: http://www.econ.uniurb.it/siepi/dec03/papers/castellani.pdf.
Castellani, D. and A. Zanfei (2006), *Multinational Firms, Innovation and Productivity*, Cheltenham, UK and Northampton, MA, USA: Edward Elgar Publishing.
Christensen, J.L. (2010), 'Low-tech, high-performing clusters in knowledge-based

economies', paper presented at 'Opening up innovation: strategy, organization and technology', DRUID Summer Conference, San Sebastien, Spain, 13–14 July 2009.

Cohen, W.M. and R.C. Levin (1989), 'Empirical studies of innovation and market structure', *Handbook of Industrial Organization*, **2**, 1059–107.

Criscuolo, C., J. Haskel and M. Slaughter (2005), 'Why are some firms more innovative? Knowledge inputs, knowledge stocks and the role of global engagement', *NBER Working Paper Series*, 11479.

Czarnitzki, D. and A. Fier (2002), 'Do innovation subsidies crowd out private investment?: Evidence from the German service sector', *Applied Economics Quarterly*, **48**(1), 1–25.

Czarnitzki, D. and G. Licht (2006), 'Additionality of public R&D grants in a transition economy', *Economics of Transition*, **14**(1), 101.

Czarnitzki, D., H. Hottenrott and S. Thorwarth (2011), 'Industrial research versus development investment: the implications of financial constraints', *Cambridge Journal of Economics*, **35**(3), 527–44.

Damanpour, F. (1992), 'Organizational size and innovation', *Organization Studies*, **13**(3), 375.

De Beule, F. and I. Van Beveren (2009), 'Belgium's diamond of competitiveness: a comparison between foreign and domestic companies', in D. Van Den Bulcke, A. Verbeke and W. Yuan (eds), *Handbook On Small Nations in The Global Economy: The Contribution of Multinational Enterprises to National Economic Success*, Cheltenham, UK and Northampton, MA, USA: Edward Elgar Publishing, pp. 30–49.

De Beule, F. and I. Van Beveren (2012), 'Does firm agglomeration drive product innovation and renewal? An application for Belgium', *Journal of Economic and Social Geography*, **103**(4), 457–72.

Ebersberger, B., H. Lööf and J. Oksanen (2005), 'Does foreign ownership matter for the *innovation activities of firms in Finland*', VTT Working Papers 26, VTT Technical Research Centre of Finland, Espoo.

Eurostat (2008), *Sector classification according to technology intensity and knowledge intensity*, Eurostat, Luxembourg, available at: http://epp.eurostat. ec.europa.eu/cache/ITY_SDDS/Annexes/htec_esms_an2.pdf.

Frenz, M. and G. Ietto-Gillies (2007), 'Does multinationality affect the propensity to innovate? An analysis of the third UK Community Innovation Survey', *International Review of Applied Economics*, **21**(1), 99–117.

Frenz, M., C. Girardone and G. Ietto-Gillies (2005), 'Multinationality matters in innovation: the case of the UK financial services', *Industry & Innovation*, **12**(1), 65–92.

Hansen, T. and L. Winther (2011), 'Innovation, regional development and relations between high- and low-tech industries', *European Urban and Regional Studies*, **18**(3), 321–39.

Hirsch-Kreinsen, H. (2008), '"Low-Tech" innovations', *Industry & Innovation*, **15**(1), 19–43.

Hirsch-Kreinsen, H., D. Jacobson, S. Laestadius and K. Smith (2003), 'Low tech industries and the knowledge economy: state of the art and research challenges', Working Paper 10, Department of Industrial Economics and Management, Royal Institute of Technology (KTH), Stockholm.

Johansson, B. and U. Forstund (2008), 'The analysis of location, colocation and urbanization economies', in C. Karlsson (ed.), *Handbook of Research on*

Cluster Theory, Cheltenham, UK and Northampton, MA, USA: Edward Elgar Publishing.

Markusen, J.R. (2004), *Multinational Firms and the Theory of International Trade*. Cambridge, MA: MIT Press Books.

Maskell, P. (1998), 'Low-tech competitive advantages and the role of proximity: the Danish wooden furniture industry', *European Urban and Regional Studies*, 5(2), 99–118.

Mohnen, P. and C. Hoareau (2003), 'What type of enterprise forges close links with universities and government labs? Evidence from CIS 2', *Managerial and Decision Economics*, 24(2–3), 133–45.

Patel, P. and K. Pavitt (1991), 'Large firms in the production of the world's technology: an important case of "non-globalisation"', *Journal of International Business Studies*, 22, 1–21.

Shaver, J. and F. Flyer (2000), 'Agglomeration economies, firm heterogeneity, and foreign direct investment in the United States', *Strategic Management Journal*, 21(12), 1175–93.

Syrneonidis, G. (1996), 'Innovation, firm size and market structure: Schumpeterian hypotheses and some new themes', *OECD Economic Studies*, 27, 35–70.

Teirlinck, P. (2005), 'Report CIS 4', *Belgian Science Policy*.

Tether, B.S. (2005), 'Do services innovate (differently)? Insights from the European Innobarometer Survey', *Industry & Innovation*, 12(2), 153–84.

Tether, B.S., I. Miles, K. Blind, C. Hipp, N. de Liso and G. Cainelli (2001), 'Innovation in services: an analysis of CIS-2 data on innovation in the service sector', a report for the European Commission DG12, CRIC, University of Manchester.

Van Beveren, I. and H. Vandenbussche (2010), 'Product and process innovation and firms' decision to export', *Journal of Economic Policy Reform*, 13(1), 3–24.

Veugelers, R. (1997), 'Internal R&D expenditures and external technology sourcing', *Research Policy*, 26(3), 303–15.

Veugelers, R. and B. Cassiman (1999), 'Make and buy in innovation strategies: evidence from Belgian manufacturing firms', *Research Policy*, 28(1), 63–80.

5. Which Portuguese firms are more innovative? The importance of multinationals and exporters

Armando Silva, Oscar Afonso and Ana Paula Africano

5.1 INTRODUCTION

Since different countries perform differently with respect to innovation ability, and given that countries' performances mainly reflect firms' innovation abilities, several related questions arise: (1) which countries are most innovative? (2) which firms are most innovative? (3) is there any connection between firms´ innovativeness and their level of global engagement?

The firm's innovation level is related to: (1) firms' specific aspects (for example, size, managerial initiative or managerial risk assumption); (2) time-specific factors; (3) technological characteristics of the sectors that firms belong to; (4) market concentration level; and (5) market orientation (for example, domestic or international).

Some models (for example, Jones, 2002) assume that the stock of knowledge is a public good, equally and freely available to all firms worldwide; in contrast, Grossman and Helpman (1991) and Parente and Prescott (1994) present models in which firms have to face costs and difficulties in adopting new technological knowledge. Such barriers differ across time and countries, suggesting that external trade may influence firms´ ability to adopt and adapt existing technological knowledge. Nowadays it is common to accept that the existing stock of knowledge is quite differently appropriated and benefited from by various firms.

According to this line of reasoning, the more globally engaged firms could obtain larger stocks of ideas through their foreign sources such as international suppliers, customers or, in the case of multinationals, through their internal worldwide pool of information. In addition, higher exposure to foreign markets could reduce costs associated with the adoption of new technologies. Lederman (2009) calls this the Global

Engagement hypothesis, according to which 'importing' foreign know-how (through licensing), foreign investment or exporting activities are positively correlated with innovation, and especially product innovation. This hypothesis also assumes that trade protectionism raises the costs of global engagement, adding difficulty to innovation. Additionally, it assumes that the density of knowledge available to local firms spurs innovation, and that the more globally engaged firms have a higher knowledge density available to work with.

The existence of a positive relationship between the level and the growth of technological knowledge and foreign exposure has been documented in several papers, using firm-level data (for example, Alvarez and Robertson, 2004 or Cassiman and Veugelers, 1999). There is general agreement that this positive connection results from the highly competitive pressure of international markets, which require firms' constant technological updating and adaptation. Nevertheless, Silva and Leitão (2007) found that Portuguese industrial firms with high export intensity were less capable of innovating. They explained that the majority of high export-intensive firms belonged to clothing and footwear industries and worked on an outsourcing basis, adopting a low-price strategy which did not rely on product innovation.

Criscuolo et al. (2005) for UK firms and Wagner (2008) for German firms developed a new approach to testing the global engagement hypothesis. These authors used the Knowledge Production Function (KPF) as a theoretical framework to evaluate the innovation versus international engagement connection. This methodology assumes that knowledge outputs result from the combination of knowledge inputs and flow of ideas coming from the existing knowledge stock. This framework is superior to other approaches to the extent that it allows us to estimate several versions of the KPF. It is thereby possible to evaluate which factors really matter in regard to the innovative performance of firms.

In line with Criscuolo et al. (2005) and Wagner (2008), this chapter aims to test the global engagement hypothesis for Portuguese firms using the KPF approach. By considering the Community Innovation Survey (CIS) as a database for the period 2002–04, we follow primarily Criscuolo et al. (2005). Our analysis yields a set of results that indicate a confirmation of the above hypothesis. We find that the most internationally engaged firms report much more knowledge output, whatever measure is used.

Moreover, the use of suitable econometric models allowed us to understand that much of the higher knowledge output created in globally engaged Portuguese firms was the product of: (1) higher levels of knowledge inputs; (2) higher levels of informational flows used; (3) greater efficiency in their use. Our findings also provide evidence that existing knowledge is not uniformly accessible to Portuguese firms.

The chapter is organized as follows. Section 5.2 describes the theoretical foundations of KPF that support our empirical studies and reviews the empirical studies on the subject. Section 5.3 presents the main statistics for CIS 4 in Portugal, highlighting the actual differences between purely domestic and globalized firms. Section 5.4 discusses the main econometric and estimation issues. Section 5.5 presents estimation results. Section 5.6 performs an exercise of innovation accounting using the estimates obtained and the actual differences in data. Section 5.7 concludes the chapter.

5.2 INNOVATION FACTORS AND EMPIRICAL LITERATURE

5.2.1 International Factors of Innovation: Theory and Modeling Approach

In line with Coe and Helpman (1995), we know that the benefits of innovation are much more evenly distributed than the expenditures on innovative R&D. This is a sign of the importance of global technological diffusion. Technological knowledge can be diffused internationally in several ways: Foreign Direct Investment (FDI), labor mobility, communication patterns and imitation. In the latter case, international trade is the vehicle through which diffusion occurs.

Based on Grossman and Helpman (1991) and Parente and Prescott (1994), our assumptions is that firms face barriers to adopting foreign technological knowledge. These authors argued that the reduction of the differences among different countries' economic growth relies on the ability to reduce barriers to the adoption of technology, and they assume that greater trade openness favors the weakening of the resistance to such technology adoption. It is also assumed that barriers are reduced by FDI. Additional channels to technological diffusion are imports of intermediate inputs, incorporating new technological knowledge, and exports, which increase the firms' markets and thus expand firms' returns on innovative efforts.

In a certain sense, innovation is 'a collective learning process' (Silva and Leitão, 2009) in which organizational and environmental factors affect a firm's specific innovative ability. This so-called 'systematic approach' to the innovation process allows a new vision for: (1) the role performed by external partners; and (2) the importance of the information flows that disseminate knowledge within the system.

On the other hand, the fact that different firms produce different amounts of new knowledge has opened the possibility of using KPF in a very similar way to a production function for goods and services (for example, Geroski, 1990; Love and Roper, 1999; Roper et al., 2008). In the KPF framework, production of new output knowledge relies on the competitive environment in which each firm acts and also on the assumption that new knowledge depends on two types of inputs: innovation input activities such as R&D activities (which allow the emergence of knowledge) and the flow of ideas from the existing knowledge stock.

Using the approach followed by Criscuolo et al. (2005), which is in line with Griliches (1979) and Romer (1990), we can write the KPF in the simpler Cobb–Douglas form:

$$\Delta K_i = H_i^{\lambda} K_i^{\varphi}. \tag{5.1}$$

The creation of new ideas, the change of the knowledge stock (ΔK_i) depends on the investment in the process of knowledge creation (H), human capital or R&D activities, and on the existing knowledge stock, K, from which ideas can be generated through the knowledge information flows. Parameters λ and φ represent, respectively, the elasticity of new idea creation on knowledge investment and from the existing knowledge stock. Subscripting K in (5.1) means that firms have different access to the existing knowledge stock, since each existing idea might not be equally crucial to all firms. Besides, as firms can learn from their internal knowledge stock and from external sources, it is essential to identify distinct channels through which they can be encouraged to innovate.

Following Criscuolo et al. (2005) and Wagner (2008), a new KPF version is presented:

$$\Delta K_i = f(H_i, K_{ii}, K_{i\_i}, X_i) \tag{5.2}$$

This version of the KPF assumes that changes in the knowledge stock (ΔK_i) depend on: (i) H: the investment in the process of knowledge creation (R&D activities or other non-R&D investments); (ii) X_i: a vector of other determinants such as size, industry or sector; (iii) K_{ii}: the flow of ideas to firm i from within; (iv) K_{i_i}: the flow of ideas to firm i from outside the firm. In this case, K is thus decomposed into two different components.

Woerter and Roper (2008), discussing the importance of market-demand factors versus supply-side factors (firms' capability of innovation), also presented a similar KPF using:

$$I_{it} = \phi_0 + \phi_1 XMG_{it-j} + \phi_2 HMG_{it-j} + \phi_3 K_{it} + \phi_4 RI_{it} + \phi_5 IND_i$$

$$+ \phi_6 TDUM_t + v_i + \varepsilon_{it} \qquad (5.3)$$

In (5.3), the independent variables are, respectively, export-market growth, XMG, home-market growth, HMG, the availability of existing knowledge stock, K, firms' internal resources, RI, industry resources, IND, which may affect post-innovation returns and control dummy variables, $TDUM$. All these variables explain firms' innovation output (I).

5.2.2 Empirical Studies on Innovation and Foreign Exposure

There are several empirical papers that study the specific connection between the level of global engagement of firms and their innovative performance. Using logit models for Brazilian firms, Braga and Willmore (1991) found that the probability of firms innovating was increased both by their foreign property and by their exporter orientation. In another study of the choice between internal and external technology acquisition for Belgian firms, Cassiman and Veugelers (1999) found, using logit models, that 'All else equal, a firm that exports 10 per cent more of its production has a 3.74 per cent higher probability of being an innovating firm.' (p. 71). Also using logit models, Alvarez and Robertson (2004) found that Chilean and Mexican exporting firms had a higher probability of process, packing, product and organizational administration innovations (the exceptions being innovations in product designs and in the purchase of foreign licenses). They also showed that those effects were not linear and relied on export destination, as exports to more developed markets were associated with a higher probability of innovating.

Using KPF and CIS data for the UK firms, Criscuolo et al. (2005) found, through probit (and Tobit) models, that globally engaged firms did generate more innovative outputs. Moreover, they also found that higher innovative capacity was related to greater use of knowledge inputs and especially to higher learning from more knowledge sources. Wagner (2008) also uses KPF for German firms and confirms the previous results, reinforcing the thesis that the importance of the knowledge sources varies with the type of innovation performed.

5.3 DATA ISSUES ON INNOVATION IN PORTUGUESE FIRMS: SUMMARY STATISTICS

According to the Summary Innovation Index for 2006 and 2009, Portugal is classified as a moderate innovator country, given that its innovation level is still lower than the EU average but its innovation growth is three times higher than the EU average, making it a growth leader among the moderate innovator group. The Portuguese CIS is part of a European Union-wide survey which reports firms' answers to: output of innovation efforts (in product, process, organizational and marketing innovations), inputs of innovation, sources of information-knowledge for innovation efforts, partnerships between firms and other institutions, obstacles to innovation and effects of innovation. It is a voluntary postal survey and covers the manufacturing and the service sectors. The CIS follows the OECD and EUROSTAT (2005) Oslo Manual, which guides each national survey.

We use the fourth survey carried out in Portugal (CIS 4), conducted in 2005. The survey questioned 7370 firms (representative of a population of 27797 firms) about their innovative activity in the period 2002–04; 74.3 per cent of those firms answered.

In 2006, 40 per cent of Portuguese firms surveyed had innovation activities on products or processes; this percentage is higher than the EU average (33 per cent) but still far below German and Swiss firms' performances (53 per cent). If we also include innovations in organizational and marketing levels, this number reaches 62 per cent. The percentage of innovative firms increases in line with the size of firms.[1] Since the specific number of employees per firm is not available – the data only includes size categories of firms[2] – we chose, as a proxy, an ordinal variable with the existing four dimensions to measure the size of firms.

Given data availability, we created four levels for global engagement of Portuguese firms:[3] (i) Global Multinationals (*GM*), which are subsidiaries[4] (of foreign firms) located in Portugal and which export – this being the group of most globalized firms in the data; (ii) Internal Multinationals (*IM*), which are subsidiaries of foreign firms located in Portugal but which do not export; (iii) Exporters (*EXP*), which do not belong to foreign groups and which export; and, (iv) Purely Domestic (*DOM*), which neither export nor are part of a multinational. Our CIS 4 benchmark sample has 4815 firms: 353 *GM* (7.3 per cent of the sample), 131 *IM* (2.7 per cent), 1904 *EXP* (39.6 per cent) and 2427 *DOM* firms (50.4 per cent).

Table 5.1 shows that there are clear basic differences in overall performance across these four groups: average 'size' (measured by classes of employment level), average output growth (2002–04) and average output level (2004) are highest for *GM*, followed by *IM* and *EXP*, all far above the *DOM* firms. Given the limitations of the data employed we are not able to compute 'labor productivity of firms' as we have no access to the exact number of workers. We can, nevertheless, divide each of the four groups' average turnover by each firm's group labor dimension (average size) and obtain a proxy for labor efficiency. The global results follow the same

Table 5.1   Summary statistics on overall performance

Sub-sample	Average size	Average output (thousands of €)	Average output growth 2002–04 (%)	Output/Size (thousands of €)
GM	3.03	67 424	15.45	22 252
EXP	2.46	23 848	11.40	9 694
IM	2.80	59 653	13.29	21 305
DOM	2.22	12 453	−16.28	5 609
All	2.39	22 301	2.65	9 331

Source: Authors' calculations.

pattern: *GM* and *IM* have 'labor productivity' levels four times higher than *DOM* firms; *EXP* almost doubles the performance of *DOM* firms.

There is also heterogeneity in the distribution of each type of firm through the 35 different two-digit codes of economic activity. *GM* firms are mainly involved in wholesale retail, services to firms and manufacture of vehicles, trailers and semi-trailers. *EXP* firms are involved in the afore-mentioned sectors and also in textile manufacturing, manufacture of wearing apparel and fur dressing and dyeing. More than half of *IM* firms are involved in services to other firms, including insurance companies.

5.3.1   Knowledge Output

In line with Pavitt (1982), the use of several knowledge output measures occurs due to the assumption that there is no single measure to fully assess innovation activities. Table 5.2 shows the higher knowledge output level of the more internationally engaged firms in comparison to the poorer performance of *DOM*. Whatever measure is used, *IM* firms are better than *DOM* firms; *EXP* are better than *IM* and *DOM* firms, and *GM* are the best of all.

'Innovation of Product or Process'[5] is an indicator that assumes the value of 1 if a firm undertakes any product or process innovation (excluding purely organizational innovations).[6] According to the third Oslo Manual of OECD and Eurostat (2005), the definition of innovation refers to new products or services for each firm, but not necessarily to the market. *DOM* firms report only half the innovations undertaken by *GM* and only two-thirds of those produced by *EXP*. When we split innovation into innovation in products and innovation in processes, the greater differences between domestic and more globally engaged firms are observed with respect to products. In fact, *DOM* firms present almost twice as many process innovations in comparison with their own product innovations.

Table 5.2   Knowledge outputs (mean values)

Sub-sample	Innovation product or process	Product innovation	Process innovation	IPPOM	Novel sales (thousands of €)
GM	66%	48%	60%	83%	7570
EXP	50%	33%	41%	69%	2164
IM	48%	31%	37%	77%	2442
DOM	33%	17%	29%	53%	878
All	43%	27%	36%	62%	1921

Notes: Values are the percentages of firms that report that type of innovation in comparison with all the firms of the group.

Source: Authors' calculations.

If we add Organizational Innovation (as a result of strategic decisions of each firm) and Innovation of Marketing (design, distribution, pricing and promotion) to the previous components, we obtain the second and largest knowledge output measure.[7] By aggregating the queries concerning firms' Innovation on Product, Process, Organization and Marketing (*IPPOM*), differences between groups are reduced and *IM* becomes the second most innovative group, overcoming *EXP*.

Finally, knowledge output is measured by 'Novel Sales' (sales of new and improved products; the novelty of the product refers to new to the firm or new to the market – domestic or global – with which the firm operates). Only 25 per cent of sample firms reported Novel Sales. *DOM* firms present an output that is a ninth of *GM*'s and a third of *EXP*'s performance.

5.3.2   Knowledge Input

Concerning knowledge inputs, the same patterns of differentials are observed: more globally engaged firms use more inputs in producing new ideas. Knowledge inputs are captured either by R&D expenses or by non-R&D expenses. *Intramural R&D Expenses* refers to the creative work of personnel guiding the knowledge increase and to investment spending on buildings and specific equipment for R&D activities. *Extramural R&D Expenses* refers to the acquisition of R&D from either public or private institutions. *Non-R&D Expenses* may include the acquisition of equipment, machinery, software and hardware specifically to produce new products or services, and also expenses for other forms of external knowledge – buying or licensing of patents or rights.

Table 5.3 Knowledge inputs (mean values)

Sub-sample	Intramural R&D (1000s of €)	Extra mural R&D (1000s of €)	Non R&D expenses (1000s of €)	Total innovation expenses (1000s of €)	Innovation effort intensity (%)	Personnel training (% of firms)
GM	163	94	607	864	1.28%	57.5%
EXP	63	21	260	344	1.44%	33.6%
IM	20	8	274	302	0.50%	40.5%
DOM	23	6	102	131	1.05%	25.7%
All	49	18	207	274	1.22%	32.8%

Notes: *Innovation effort intensity* means the ratio of total innovation expenses to turnover. *Personnel Training* is the binary dummy variable equal to 1 if, as defined by CIS 4, the employees receive internal or external training specifically oriented to the development and introduction of new products or processes or of highly improved ones.

Source: Authors' calculations.

As reported in Table 5.3, for *Intramural R&D expenses*, *GM* presents a seven times higher level and *EXP* a three times higher level than *DOM* firms. The differences for *Extramural R&D* are even more pronounced. In *Total Innovation Expenses* the differences between the groups of firms are quite similar.[8]

Given the possibility that the superiority of more global firms may reflect their greater size, we also study the behavior of 'Innovation Effort Intensity', which represents the share of *Total Innovation Expenses* in each firm's turnover. In contrast with previous results, we find that on the one hand *EXP* firms show the highest innovation effort intensity, while on the other hand *DOM* firms present an unexpectedly high value compared to *IM* and *GM* firms. This may result as both *GM* and *IM* firms may rely on their parent firms' innovation efforts.

In the light of the unavailability of data on R&D personnel, we used the percentage of firms of each group that reported internal or external personnel training specifically oriented to the development and introduction of new products or processes. More than 50 per cent of all *GM* firms report having achieved that type of personnel training, but only a quarter of *DOM* firms report implementing personnel training for innovation.

5.3.3 Sources of Knowledge Information

Given the fact that not all the variation in knowledge outputs can be accounted for by variation in knowledge inputs, it is important to study how and where firms acquire information on knowledge improvements, and how important those sources are. In CIS 4, each innovative firm was asked to report where any valuable information for innovation came from and how important it was: high (code 3), medium (code 2), low (code 1), null (code 0).

Table 5.4 shows the mean values of these answers, considering the information origin: Internal to firms (including information internal to the firm or to the group), from Suppliers and Clients ('vertical type'), from Universities and Polytechnics and other interface organizations, from Government laboratories and institutions, from Competitors, from 'free access sources' including information obtained from Conferences, Scientific publications, Professional meetings and finally from Private consulting.

In general, *GM* learn twice as much and *EXP* learn 1.8 as much as *DOM* firms. The difference is even more evident in learning from universities and government institutions. On the other hand, *DOM* firms find their highest level of learning in clients and suppliers and their lowest level in such 'formal sources' as government and universities.

5.3.4 Overall Knowledge Statistics

The four groups of firms differ in all three areas of KPFs: knowledge outputs, knowledge inputs and access to flows from existing knowledge. The data in Table 5.5 also show that more globally engaged firms have higher 'knowledge output productivity'.

Using 'Novel Sales per intramural R&D expenses', *GM* displays an 'innovation productivity' four times as great as *DOM* firms, which represents twice the level of *EXP*. This suggests that innovation resources may display different levels of efficiency depending on firms' global engagement levels.

CIS also allows us to ascertain whether a firm participates in active innovation projects with other firms or non-commercial institutions. Firms were also encouraged to state which collaboration partner was the most crucial from a list of other firms in the group, suppliers, clients, competitors, private consultants, universities and polytechnics, government laboratories and public R&D institutions. This questionnaire was answered by 528 firms. Suppliers (25 per cent of all answers), other firms of the same group (23 per cent) and clients (18 per cent) were the sources of cooperation most cited. Looking at the partnerships formed by *EXP*, the most crucial partners were clients and suppliers, each indicating 23 per cent of all cooperation agreements. This could mean that exporting firms learn more in knowledge terms from clients and suppliers.

On the other hand, it was possible to recognize that the lack of information was the main obstacle firms faced concerning innovation ability.

Table 5.4 Knowledge flows (mean values), values in units

Sub-sample	Internal	Suppliers	Clients	Universities	Government	Competitors	Conferences	Scientific	Professional	Consultants	All sources
GM	0.88	1.13	0.98	0.73	0.66	1.18	1.26	1.14	1.14	0.90	1.00
EXP	0.76	0.89	0.85	0.59	0.53	0.64	0.90	0.95	0.90	0.63	0.90
IM	0.62	0.87	0.82	0.39	0.38	0.82	0.69	0.75	0.72	0.53	0.67
DOM	0.53	0.61	0.59	0.29	0.25	0.61	0.61	0.60	0.55	0.38	0.50
All	0.65	0.77	0.73	0.44	0.40	0.79	0.77	0.79	0.74	0.52	0.59

Notes: Each variable is a categorical indicator of how important a different knowledge source is to the firm's innovation activity. Each of them takes four possible values: 0, 1, 2, 3; higher values have greater importance as an information source. For each cell, there is the mean of each sub-sample. 'All sources' represent the average of all types of sources. In the table we report the mean values for each group of firms.

Source: Authors' calculations.

Table 5.5   Knowledge output productivity

Sub-sample	Novel sales per intramural R&D expenses (€)	Novel sales per total innovation expenses (€)
GM	56	9
EXP	26	6
IM	44	8
DOM	14	6
All	23	7

Source: Authors' calculations.

The shortage of market information, the lack of innovation partnerships and scarcity of skilled personnel were also handicaps impeding more innovation. As regards the usefulness of innovation as perceived by the respondents, by far the largest proportion of answers identified labor cost reduction and higher flexibility in production as the most important effects, thus suggesting the possibility of productivity improvements.

5.4   ESTIMATION ISSUES AND ECONOMETRIC STRATEGIES

At the estimation level, given the different nature of the two measures of knowledge output, different econometric estimators were required. *Innovation – Product or Process* is a binary variable assuming only 0 or 1 values, but *Novel Sales* is a continuous non-negative variable, although frequently assuming 0 values.

For the binary variable *Innovation – Product or Process* we estimate several KPF versions using probits (and also logits, but these are not reported). We report the marginal effects on the dependent variable, at the mean values of the regressors, and we also present the standard errors of marginal effects. The aim is to report the *ceteris paribus* effect of a unit increase in the independent variable on the probability that the dependent variable equals 1.

Endogeneity may be important in these estimations. Some regressors, namely those connected with knowledge inputs, may be correlated with the regression error term; in fact, some unobserved determinants of innovation success can also 'affect' knowledge-level inputs. This can result from certain unobserved firm fixed effects, such as a highly-valued R&D culture or a high propensity for new ideas and organizational changes. It can also arise from time-varying effects, for example a high (but short-run) firm managerial talent or a country-favorable innovation policy. In order to minimize those handicaps, we use a common set of control variables for all estimations: in particular, industry and service dummies, size (measured by the same categories of level of employment) and public support for firms' innovation.[9] Furthermore, our global-engagement regressors have the advantage that they may proxy for unobserved firms' effects such as their managerial ability.

We could not employ other recommended strategies to deal with endogeneity, such as instrumental variables or panel data methods, due to limitations of data availability (for example, R&D personnel, skill level of the personnel) and the fact that other CIS data waves were not available.[10] As we will see later on, variables connected to endogeneity are not central in our analysis and therefore this potential problem will not affect our main conclusions.

With regard to the second innovation measure, *Novel Sales*, given the fact that this variable, while being a continuous non-negative, equals 0 for many firms, we estimate KPF using the Tobit model. As in many censored regression models, a change in a certain independent variable has two kinds of effects: a change in the mean of the dependent variable, given that it is already observed, and also a change in the probability of the dependent variables being observed (given the fact that it has not been yet). In order to obtain the marginal effects of interest, we use the McDonald and Moffitt (1980) decomposition to report marginal effects conditional on positive Novel Sales; that is, the former kind of effect. In order to perform it in *Stata*10, we followed Cong (2001) and Kang (2007).

Estimation of KPF raises some measurement issues: possible measurement errors in regress and (output knowledge) and regressors (input and knowledge flows) may arise; the answers to the survey may be question and context dependent. Nevertheless, our data give us the possibility of controlling for many possible biases from the omission of relevant variables in KPF specification.

5.5 ESTIMATION RESULTS

Tables 5.6 and 5.7 report the estimates of two KPF versions that are associated with the two different measures of knowledge output that we use: *Innovation – Product or Process* and *Novel Sales*, respectively. For each version of KPF function we estimate three different specifications, always reporting marginal effects of the regressors on the dependent variable. In all specifications the variable *DOM* is excluded as a regressor, since those firms are our reference group in all analyses.

Table 5.6   Estimates of KPF for 'Innovation – Product or Process'

	(1)	(2)	(3)
GM	0.250	0.0770	0.181**
	(0.0290)	(0.0310)	(0.0570)
EXP	0.138	0.059	0.045*
	(0.0160)	(0.0230)	(0.0290)
IM	0.096**	0.0280+	0.148*
	(0.0480)	(0.0260)	(0.0680)
Total Expenses in Innovation		0.0012	0.0003**
(thousands €)		(0.0001)	(0.0001)
Internal Info.			0.294
			(0.0030)
Clients Info.			0.102
			(0.0260)
Supply Info.			0.231
			(0.0250)
Size	0.073	0.009*	0.014+
	(0.0110)	(0.00680)	(0.0200)
Public Support	0.476	0.170	0.004+
	(0.0600)	(0.0640)	(0.0440)
Wald chi^2	269	211	1240
Prob > Chi^2	0.0000	0.0000	0.0000

Notes:
Each column is a differently estimated specification, and each line reports the marginal effects for that regressor as estimated by probit. Robust standard errors appear below the coefficients' estimates. We compute the estimation of marginal effects at the mean values of the regressors. All specifications include an additional (not reported) control variable: two digit industry/service dummies.
* and ** mean statistical significance at 10% and 5%, respectively.
+ means not statistically significant: if nothing is mentioned, all estimates are statistically significant at the 1% level.
Excluding regression (1), we also use as accessory variable the square of the input variable; results, available upon request, show that general conclusions are not changed.

Source: Authors' calculations.

Regression 1 uses as independent variables the three global engagement levels: *GM, EXP, IM*. Next, we consider as additional independent variable *Total Innovation Expenses* in regression 2.

Finally, regression 3 includes ten additional independent variables that capture knowledge information flows (although we only report the three most important: internal, clients and supplier). To help control cross-firm differences that may impact on a firm's innovative performance, all regressions include as control variables: public support to firms innovation; 35 two-digit industry or service dummies and four classes of firm size.

5.5.1 Estimates of KPF for 'Innovation – Product or Process'

Table 5.6 reports the estimates for the three different specifications used to study the Knowledge Production Function for *Innovation – Product* or *Process*.

In column 1, the estimates show that all globalization indicators are positive and statistically significant, and their values suggest that the more globalized firms have a higher probability to innovate than the less globalized ones. We detect that *GM* are 25 percentage points (p.p.) more likely to innovate than the omitted *DOM* firms. For exporters, the advantage over *DOM* is 14 p.p.

In column 2 we add the knowledge input indicator, *Total Innovation Expenses*. It is positive and statistically significant. Coefficients of the global engagement indicators are reduced by two-thirds: *Total Expenses in Innovation* is significant in explaining innovation.

Column 3 reports the regressions that include the ten variables capturing knowledge information flows, although we only report the three most important. Overall, the estimates confirm the hypothesis that knowledge information flows contribute positively to the innovation output. Seven in ten sources of knowledge information considered are statistically significant, with special relevance for internal sources, suppliers and clients. The coefficients of international engagement are now even smaller than in regression 2. Overall, all these regression results confirm both the global engagement hypothesis and the importance of the two control variables: *Public Support* and *Size*.

5.5.2 Estimates of KPF for 'Novel Sales'

Table 5.7 reports the estimates for the three different specifications used to study the Knowledge Production Function for *Novel Sales*.

In regression 1 the three globalization indicators are positive and statistically significant, and their values reveal that the more globalized firms generate more *Novel Sales* than the less globalized ones. The estimates show that, conditional on *Novel Sales* being non-zero, the change of a *DOM* firm to a *GM* firm generated, *ceteris paribus* and on average, a surplus of 7 million euros of *Novel Sales*. For exporters this advantage is of 3 million euros.

In column 2 we add *Total Innovation Expenses*. It is positive and statistically significant. Finally, in regression 3 the coefficients of all knowledge

Table 5.7   Estimates of knowledge production function for 'Novel Sales'

	(1)	(2)	(3)
GM	6.902.512	6.631.781	3.809.126
	(1.211.844)	(1.149.034)	(763.328)
EXP	3.224.619	3.164.698	1.434.692
	(757.447)	(754.729)	(461.351)
IM	2.571.090**	2.547.325**	1.900.967**
	(1.141.183)	(1.131.200)	(955.296)
Total Innovation Expenses		260**	160**
(thousands €)		(0.100)	(0.070)
Internal Info			1.066.805
			(288.922)
Clients Info			326.482*
			(199.005)
Supply Info			1.244.162
			(283.883)
Size	1.665.308	1.572.377	795.797
	(413.614)	(405.027)	(261.044)
Public Support	2.982.656	2.710.994	679.145**
	(518.280)	(503.339)	(289.464)
F-statistics	7	6	4
Prob > chi^2	0.0000	0.0000	0.0000

Notes: Each column is a differently estimated specification; each line reports the marginal effects for that regressor as estimated by Tobit. For each specification we present the marginal effects conditional on non-zero values for Novel Sales. As already mentioned in comments after Table 5.2, censored firms are 75 per cent of our sample. See also notes to Table 5.6.

Source: Authors' calculations.

information flow variables are statistically significant (although we only report the three most important) and they have a positive impact on *Novel Sales*, with the exception of private consulting and government information. The global engagement indicators fall by 25 per cent to 50 per cent once the knowledge informational flow variables are introduced. The most relevant informational flows are suppliers, internal information and scientific sources. Free sources are also vital. The impact of clients is smaller than that found in previous KPF versions.

Bearing in mind estimates in Tables 5.6 and 5.7, we can state that the subsidiaries of multinationals have a higher propensity to innovate than exporters; looking at column 3 in both tables, we can observe that *IM* coefficients are systematically higher than *EXP* coefficients.

Table 5.8   Innovation accounting statistics

	Product or Process Innovation	Novel Sales (thousand €)
Actual difference between GM and DOM firms (Table 5.2)	33 p.p.	6692
Estimated difference between GM and DOM firms (Tables 5.6, 5.7)	25 p.p.	6903
GM Share of Total Innovation expenses	< 1%	1%
GM Share of Knowledge Information-Flows	161%	39%
GM Share left unexplained	75%	56%
Actual difference between EXP and DOM firms (Table 5.2)	17 p.p.	1286
Estimated difference between EXP and DOM firms (Tables 5.6, 5.7 and 5.8)	14 p.p.	3224
EXP Share of Total Innovation Expenses	< 1%	< 1%
EXP Share of Information Flows	159%	39%
EXP Share left unexplained	28%	42%
IM Share of Total Innovation Expenses	Not significant	−0.2%
IM Share of Information Flows	Not significant	37%
IM Share left unexplained	Not significant	67%

Note: The shares do not add up to 100 per cent because the effects associated with control variables are not considered.

Source: Authors' calculations.

5.6   INNOVATION PATTERNS OF GLOBALIZED FIRMS

In this section we try to establish how much of the higher innovation-output level of the more global firms, in comparison with *DOM* firms, is explained by: (1) their greater use of the knowledge input *Total Innovation expenses*; (2) their greater ability to access and use knowledge flows; and (3) their globalized nature, which means the part left unexplained by (1) and (2).[11] Table 5.8 presents general statistics for these issues and for each of the two Innovation output indicators.[12] Appendix B presents the procedures used to compute these values, which are then reported in Table 5.8 (column 1, rows 1 to 3).[13]

When we look at values reported in Table 5.8, several conclusions arise. First, our KPF estimates seem suitable to explain the differences, in actual data, between different groups of firms, given that estimated differences are similar to their actual values.

As regards the innovation accounting of the *Innovation – Product or Process*, similar results for *GM* and *EXP* firms are arrived at. For both groups, the use of knowledge information flows explains most of their superior innovation output. As for *Novel Sales*, both *GM* and *EXP* firms show similar patterns of innovation accounting. Their superior innovation output is due to their use of information flows and globalized nature, in almost equal terms. Given that absorptive capacity of firms, to take advantage of knowledge flows, depends on realized innovation inputs, the importance of innovation expenses may be higher than thought.

5.7   CONCLUDING REMARKS

In line with recent trends in trade literature, for the first time we apply to Portugal a new way to assess connections between innovation performance and international exposure of firms.

This study uses a Knowledge Production Function framework and data from the European Community Innovation Survey, 2002–04, for Portuguese firms, to test those alleged and expected connections, known in the literature as the Global Engagement hypothesis. We argue that the test confirms that hypothesis.

This study shows that Portuguese firms that are more globally engaged have a higher ability to innovate. Moreover, as the level of global engagement rises, that superiority increases – *GM* firms are the best in all knowledge output indicators. These results arise from their higher use of knowledge inputs – *Total Innovation Expenses* – from their greater access to a larger stock of ideas – knowledge information flows – and from their globalized nature. Those results were consistently confirmed in the two knowledge production functions used to test the Global Engagement hypothesis: *Innovation Product or Process* and *Novel Sales*.

This study also finds that the access to knowledge information flows has a systematically higher impact on innovation ability than knowledge inputs, which is in line with previous studies. Moreover, our study reveals that the importance of knowledge information sources varies with both the type of innovation output indicator considered and the level of firms' global engagement. In fact, Portuguese firms access the global knowledge stock through three main channels: internal pool of information (especially for multinational firms), market contacts with clients and suppliers (especially for exporters).

On the other hand, those outcomes have allowed us to verify that existing knowledge stock is not uniformly accessible throughout the world, and that the more engaged firms have both more access to it and a higher capacity for taking advantage of it. This logic is often called the 'paradox of openness' (Laursen and Salter, 2007): on the one hand, the innovation creation requires firms' 'openness', resulting in additional importance for the ability to access and adopt others' ideas – knowledge information flows – and on the other hand, in order to apply and benefit from those innovations, firms also need to obtain returns from their innovative ideas, which in turn requires their own internal effort and appropriability capacity.

We are conscious that there are also other organizational and environmental aspects that the Knowledge Production Function framework does not capture and which may be of importance in explaining the alleged innovation superiority of the most globally engaged firms. Nevertheless, in spite of data limitations and a few methodological handicaps, our findings contribute to a better understanding of the innovation process.

NOTES

1. On average, firms spent about 2 per cent of their global turnover in innovation input. The portion of innovative firms is greater than 75 per cent for R&D services, communications, technical analysis, chemicals and petrol, but in other sectors it is lower than 30 per cent: apparel, textiles and leather industries. Of all innovators, 10 per cent had received public financing or even public subsidies.
2. We were not allowed to access the real number of employees but only the four groups of total firms' employment: group 1 (5 to 9 employees), group 2 (10 to 49), group 3 (50 to 249) and group 4 (more than 250).
3. Data do not allow us to recognize which Portuguese firms have FDI, which would permit a wider analysis of global engagement.
4. In line with Birkinshaw (1997), subsidiaries are identified as operational units controlled by the multinational headquarters and located outside the home country.
5. This is a composite variable that aggregates the answers to product innovation and process innovation.
6. See table in Appendix A for detailed definitions of the variables used and the associated CIS questions.
7. Although not used in the following sections of this chapter.
8. In Portugal, the non-R&D expenses in innovation account for three-quarters of all innovation expenses.
9. We also include, although not reported, a dummy variable for firms that employ Personnel Training specifically oriented to innovation.
10. GPEARI/MCTES withheld data invoking confidentiality issues.
11. Meaning the high efficiency connected with the nature of more globalized firms in translating *Total Innovation expenses* and knowledge information flows into innovation outputs.

12. In these statistics we do not consider the estimates of the usual control variables. For this reason the sum of the shares is not equivalent to 100 per cent.
13. Although not reported, for the sake of brevity, similar procedures and computations are made for *Novel Sales*.

REFERENCES

Alvarez, R. and R. Robertson (2004), 'Exposure to foreign markets and plant-level innovation: evidence from Chile and Mexico', *Journal of International Trade & Economic Development*, **13**(1), 57–87.

Birkinshaw, J. (1997), 'Entrepreneurship in multinational corporations: the characteristics of subsidiary initiatives', *Strategic Management Journal*, **18**(3), 207–29.

Braga, H. and L. Willmore (1991), 'Technological imports and technological effort: an analysis of their determinants in Brazilian firms', *The Journal of Industrial Economics*, **39**(4), 421–32.

Cassiman, B. and R. Veugelers (1999), 'Make and buy in innovation strategies: evidence from Belgian manufacturing firms', *Research Policy*, **28**, 63–80.

Coe, D. and E. Helpman (1995), 'International R&D spillovers', *European Economic Review*, **39**(5), 859–87.

Cong, R. (2001), 'Marginal effects of the Tobit model', *Stata Technical Bulletin*, **10**(56), 27–34.

Criscuolo, C., J. Haskel and M. Slaughter (2005), 'Global engagement and the innovation activities of firms', *NBER Working Paper* 11479.

Geroski, P.A. (1990), 'Innovation, technological opportunity and market structure', *Oxford Economic Papers*, **42**(3), 586–602.

Griliches, Z. (1979), 'Issues in assessing the contribution of R&D to productivity growth', *Bell Journal of Economics*, **10**, 92–116.

Grossman, G. and E. Helpman (1991), *Innovation and Growth in the Global Economy*, Cambridge, MA: The MIT Press.

Kang, J. (2007), 'The usefulness and the uselessness of the decomposition of Tobit coefficients', *Sociological Methods Research*, **35**(4), 572–82.

Jones, C. (2002), 'Sources of US economic growth in a world of ideas', *American Economic Review*, **92**(1), 220–39.

Laursen, K. and A.J. Salter (2007), 'The paradox of openness appropriability and the use of external sources of knowledge for innovation', paper presented at 'Appropriability, proximity, routines and innovation', DRUID Conference 2007, Copenhagen, 18–20 June.

Lederman, D. (2009), 'The business of product innovation. International empirical evidence', *World Bank Policy Research Working Paper* 4840.

Love, J. and S. Roper (1999), 'The determinants of innovation: R&D, technology transfer and networking effects', *Review of Industrial Organization*, **15**(1), 43–64.

McDonald, J.F. and R. Moffitt (1980), 'The uses of Tobit analysis', *Review of Economics and Statistics*, **62**, 318–21.

OECD, Eurostat (2005), *Oslo Manual: Guidelines for Collecting and Interpreting Innovation Data*, Paris: OCED.

Parente, S. and E. Prescott (1994), 'Barriers to technology adoption and development', *Journal of Political Economy*, **102**(2), 298–321.

Pavitt, K. (1982), 'R&D, patenting and innovative activities: a statistical exploration', *Research Policy*, **11**(1), 33–51.

Romer, P. (1990), 'Endogenous technological change', *Journal of Political Economy*, **98**(5), 71–102.

Roper, S., J. Du and J. Love (2008), 'Modelling the innovation value chain', *Research Policy*, **37**, 961–77.

Silva, M.J. and J. Leitão (2007), 'What determines the entrepreneurial innovative capability of Portuguese industrial firms?', *Munich Personal RePEc Archive Paper* no. 5216, October.

Silva, M.J. and J. Leitão (2009), 'Co-operation in innovation practices among firms in Portugal: do external partners stimulate innovative advances?', *International Journal of Entrepreneurship and Small Business (IJESB), Special Issue: Entrepreneurship and Innovation*, **7**(4), 391–403.

Wagner, J. (2008), 'International firms activities and innovation: evidence from knowledge production functions for German firms', *The ICFAI Journal of Knowledge Management*, **2**, 47–62.

Woerter, M. and S. Roper (2008), 'Openness and innovation: home and export demand effects on manufacturing innovation: panel data evidence for Ireland and Switzerland', *KOF Working Paper* no. 210.

APPENDIX A: SURVEY QUESTIONS IN CIS 4

1. Measures of Knowledge Outputs

Variable name	Question in CIS 4
Product Innovation	During the three-year period 2002–04, did your firm introduce any technologically new or significantly improved products (goods or services) which were new to your firm?
Process Innovation	During the three-year period 2002–04, did your firm introduce any technologically new or improved processes for producing or supplying products which were new to your firm?
Novel Sales	Please estimate how your turnover in 2004 was distributed between products (goods or services) introduced during the period 2002–04 which were: New to your firm or to the market your firm belongs to + Significantly improved (% of total turnover)

2. Measures of Knowledge Inputs

Variable name	Question in CIS 4
Intramural R&D	Please tick if there is expenditure in the category [of] Intramural research and experimental development (R&D); [and if so ticked], please estimate innovative expenditure in 2004, including personnel and related investment expenditures (no depreciation)
Extramural R&D	Please tick if there is expenditure in the category [of] Extramural research and experimental development (R&D); [and if so ticked], please estimate innovative expenditure in 2004, excluding machinery, software and other external knowledge
Total Innovation expenses	Please estimate innovative expenditure in 2004, in Intramural R&D, Extramural R&D and other non-R&D as machinery, software and other external knowledge

3. Measures of Knowledge Flows

Variable name	Question in CIS 4: Sources of Information for Innovation Activities
	Please indicate the sources of knowledge or information used in your technological innovation activities, and their importance during the period 2002–04

3. Measures of Knowledge Flows

Internal Information	Self within the firm or from Group. Other firms within the firm group
Vertical Information	Suppliers of equipment, materials, components or software; Clients or customers
Information from competitors	Competitors
Commercial Information	Private consultants and R&D firms
Free Information	Professional conferences, meetings, trade associations fairs, exhibitions
Information from Schools	Universities and Polytechnic schools
Information from Government	Government research organizations and offices

APPENDIX B: INNOVATION ACCOUNTING FOR *GM* FIRMS AND *INNOVATION – PRODUCT OR PROCESS*

	Estimates of KPF (1)	Actual differences between GM and DOM firms (2)	(3) = (1) × (2)	Share (4) = (3): 0.250
Estimated difference between *GMDOM*				0.250
Intramural R&D Expenses (*1000s €*)	0.00001	163−23 = 140	0.00014	0.001
Internal Information	0.287	0.88−0.53 = 0.35	0.10045	0.402
Clients Information	0.100	0.98−0.59 = 0.39	0.039	0.156
Suppliers Information	0.233	1.13−0.61 = 0.52	0.1212	0.485
All knowledge information flows	–		0.406	1.620
GM nature – left unexplained	0.188		0.188	0.752
Total contributions				0.001+1.622+ 0.752 = 2.375

Notes:
This table combines the coefficient estimates of Table 5.8 with differences between the mean values of Tables 5.2, 5.3 and 5.4 to calculate what explains the actual differences in *Innovation – Product or Process* between *GM* firms and purely domestic ones.
The shares do not add up to 100% because the effects associated with control variables are not considered.

6. The effect of export promotion programs on export satisfaction: a study in the Flemish design sector

Ysabel Nauwelaerts and Elena Vijfeyken

6.1 INTRODUCTION

In this chapter we investigate the export performance satisfaction of Flemish creative SMEs from a resource-based view. We focus on the effects of support actions by a governmental organization, taking into account the effects of internal firm resources. The creative industry represents a growing industry in Flanders: the growth rate of employment and added value is double compared to the total industry. Today's consumers are looking for diversification and new impulses which are often provided by the creative industries (Maenhout et al., 2006).

To define the creative industry in Flanders we used the study of Maenhout et al. (2006) that also relies on the definition of the creative industry established by Rutten et al. (2004).

> The creative industry is a specific form of activity that produces products and services which are the result of individual or collective creative labor and entrepreneurship. Content and symbolism are the most important elements of these products and services. They are consumed because they evoke an emotional meaning and an experience. Here the creative industry plays an important role with the development and maintenance of lifestyles and cultural identities in the society (Rutten et al., 2004, pp. 19–20).

On average 10 per cent of the total consumption in 2007 in Flanders originates from products and services like books, music, design, fashion, museums, radio and television. The total household expenditures for food and beverages exceed the expenditures for the creative industry only by about 5 per cent (Statbel, 2009). In addition, creative firms in Flanders are highly oriented to niche products, which are in high demand on international markets. The unique Flemish character of these creative SMEs offers them a strong position on foreign markets.

Flemish exports accounted for 201 billion euros in 2008, representing 80 per cent of total Belgian exports (FIT, 2009). While the creative sector represents only a small part in these total exports, it has an important growth potential (Maenhout et al., 2006; Rutten et al., 2004). However, since most of the creative firms are micro or small firms, they often need to rely on public or private support in their internationalization process.

Research into small firms' exporting has been mainly descriptive, lacking the necessary theoretical underpinnings that could contribute to the substantial export strategy literature (Gemünden, 1991). In addition, it is only in recent years that the empirical datasets have become larger and the methods used have become more sophisticated. Dhanaraj and Beamish (2003), for example, examined 157 firms using structural equation modeling. While previous work on export promotion has implicitly addressed many issues related to firm resources, Dhanaraj and Beamish (2003) argue that the resource-based view can provide a suitable theoretical framework for internationalization models. The ability of smaller firms to become successful international competitors depends upon the resources they possess to invest in potential export opportunities (Anderson and Kheam, 1998; Crick et al., 2001). SMEs frequently lack necessary internal resources, know-how and information about foreign markets (Alvarez, 2004; Ramaswami and Yang, 1990; Wolff and Pett, 2000). Smaller firms can overcome these limitations of inadequate information about foreign markets by choosing partners who possess this knowledge, such as distributors, international trade associations and other types of export intermediaries as well as government services.

The resource-based model used for our study mainly follows Wilkinson and Brouthers (2006), who examined the effectiveness of a set of export promotion services in 105 American SMEs. They demonstrate the linkage between the difficulties experienced by smaller firms on international markets and their ability to overcome these difficulties through the development of internal and external resources. We use the framework of Wilkinson and Brouthers (2006) in the growing creative industry by studying the effects of export promotion programs (EPPs) in Flanders. We investigate the actions supported by the governmental organization 'Flanders Investment and Trade' (FIT)[1] to help and stimulate export activities by Flemish creative SMEs. More precisely, we test the effects of FIT's export-stimulating programs organized in the home and in the host country on the export satisfaction of Flemish creative SMEs. We thereby also take into account the effects of internal firm resources on their export performance satisfaction.

Recent studies found a direct relationship between firm resources and export performance (Bloodgood et al., 1996; Wilkinson and Brouthers,

2006). Inspired by this literature, we consider the following internal resources in our study: reserves in marketing resources, reserves in management and reserves in production capacity. We assume that the level of these internal firm resources is positively associated with firm satisfaction with export performance. The growth of international sales and export intensity are used as control variables. On the side of the external resources, earlier studies on EPPs provided mixed results on the effectiveness of these services: they reported positive effects of EPPs like trade shows on firm performance, but also found that the effectiveness of some EPPs like trade missions varies, depending on the internal and external conditions (Cavusgil and Naor, 1987; Wilkinson and Brouthers, 2000 and 2006). In our study, we take into account EPPs supported by the Flemish governmental organization FIT. We distinguish between, on the one hand, export-stimulating instruments in the export countries such as meeting days organized in the export country or the presence on international fairs with individual Product sample booths, Group booths or Catalogue booths and, on the other hand, export-stimulating instruments organized in the home country such as the invitation of foreign buyers or the organization of 'export days' focusing on specific sectors or export regions. The dependent variable 'export performance satisfaction' is measured by the perception of the manager on his or her export performance.

No previous study has investigated the impact of export promotion programs for a specific sector, certainly not for the creative sector. The existing study of Wilkinson and Brouthers (2006) focuses on the Anglo-Saxon market, while our focus lies on a small regional market, the Flemish region, and a specific sector, the creative sector. From a social-economic view, this is relevant because our results can help export-supporting organizations (like FIT) to allocate their budget efficiently to the various programs. Moreover, this research is interesting for creative companies in general because it shows which EPPs are effective and efficient.

We developed a survey based on an extensive literature review and with the help of FIT. The survey included questions on the internal resources (the firms' reserves of marketing, of management and of production capacity) and also on external resources (that is the various EPPs in the home and host countries). FIT provided us with the email addresses of 1597 creative SMEs. Most of these firms are micro and small firms, active in the furniture and related creative activities in Flanders. Eighty responses were returned, of which only 65 were complete and suitable for testing. The analysis of our findings leads to the following conclusions. On the side of the internal resources, we see different results when we distinguish between the 'purely creative firms', that have their own designer or design department and firms that do not. For the purely creative firms, marketing reserves seem to be positively related to export performance satisfaction, while for the other group it is the extra production capacity which is positively related to export performance satisfaction. These results suggest that extra marketing efforts are particularly effective in promoting and stimulating exports in the creative companies and the design industry. On the side of the external resources, we find that among the EPPs organized in the international export market only the individual Product sample booths at international fairs seem to have a significant positive effect on export performance satisfaction. Other EPPs like catalogue booths or trade missions and export days did not show significant effects on export performance satisfaction. For the EPPs organized in the home country, only the sector-oriented invitations of foreign potential clients focusing on a specific sector seem to have a small, positive, significant effect on export performance satisfaction. All other EPPs organized in cooperation with FIT show no significant effects.

These results are in line with those of Wilkinson and Brouthers (2006) who found that, even after controlling for internal firm resources, the use of trade shows and programs identifying agents and distributors contributes positively to SME satisfaction with export performance. In their study of 2000, they also found that international trade missions and objective market information programs are negatively associated with direct exports. For the creative sector, we can conclude that for EPPs organized in the home countries as well as in the host countries, only those activities that are oriented towards a particular industry or sector seem to be effective. This observation is of great importance in practice, since it indicates that it is important for governmental organizations to focus on sector- or industry-specific actions and instruments. EPPs oriented towards larger markets, covering various industries, seem to lose a large part of their effect.

6.2 CONTRIBUTION TO THE LITERATURE

6.2.1 The Creative Sector

The success of a creative company depends mainly on its creativity (Nauwelaerts and Frank, 2007). Creativity is their unique competitive advantage (Maenhout et al., 2006). It is very important in this sector not only to be creative but always to try to be innovative (Nauwelaerts and Frank, 2007). Financially it is important for the creative company not only to have a healthy financial structure, with enough starting capital and own resources, but also to have a financial structure that is adapted to its strategy, and therefore it needs to be flexible (Nauwelaerts and Frank, 2007).

Most of the companies in the creative sector will strategically focus on niches which are continuously looking for unique and innovating designs. The combination of a niche market together with a flexible organization structure and the production of small volumes represent their success factor. Big companies are mostly uninterested in small volumes and don't possess their specific knowledge, hence they will not represent a threat (Nauwelaerts and Frank, 2007).

Remarkable for creative SMEs is their shortage in financial, administrative and management knowledge, which often leads to cash flow problems. Training can provide a solution. Experience will eventually decrease the chance of cash flow problems when this is combined with frequent participation in interactive networks and workshops. This indicates the need for external experts, advisors or 'outsiders' (Nauwelaerts and Frank, 2007).

Customer relationships and networking with suppliers are important for creative companies. This will make their enterprise more flexible and increase their chance of success. Government institutions, supporting organizations or professional associations can offer a surplus to firms but mostly they are not invoked (Nauwelaerts and Frank, 2007).

6.2.2 Internationalization of SMEs

Many articles focusing on the internationalization of SMEs recognize the importance of positioning themselves in one way or the other with something unique. A successful strategy seems to internationalize through niche markets and work very closely with local partners (Kuivaleinen et al., 2004). The specialization in relatively unexploited markets where competition intensity is low generates growth chances and helps to avoid sharp competition with multinational corporations. These so-called 'unique competitive advantages' can be realized by focusing on innovation, unique competences or creativity or through unique partnerships. Working closely with local partners or 'outsiders' may lead to a network of partners (Rugman and D'Cruz, 2000). Also management makes the difference in the internationalization process. Management determines whether an SME internationalizes, at what rate and how efficient and successful this will be. Entrepreneurship is more about intuition than about knowledge and experience (Etemad, 2004). This is an advantage for the creative sector, which often doesn't possess the required business skills, but which has the will to internationalize (Nauwelaerts and Frank, 2007) and possess the required innovative and creative capabilities. Innovation and creativity clearly seem to increase the export performances of a country (DiPietro and Anoruo, 2006).

Organizations supporting internationalization in Belgium are divided into different federal and regional organizations. Some organizations only support one aspect of internationalization (such as export or foreign investment), while others support the whole subset of internationalization activities. This support can vary from purely offering information up to giving substantial financial support (Onkelinx and Sleuwaegen, 2009). Lederman et al. (2010) have proven that export-supporting organizations can contribute effectively to the export performances of a country. The organizations are mainly important because they help to overcome trade barriers and avoid asymmetric information.

Somehow, support delivered by this type of supporting organization does not always seem to be adapted to the needs of SMEs. Onkelinx and Sleuwaegen (2009) found that SMEs mainly need information about foreign markets and the identification of foreign partners. Concerning the identification of foreign partners in particular there appears to be a gap between the support offered by 'outsiders' and the support needed by the SMEs. Hollaender et al., (2010) also observed an important gap between the demand and supply of support in internationalization activities of Flemish furniture designers.

Niche SMEs mainly require information about the legislation in foreign markets, the identification of foreign partners and general information about foreign markets. SMEs in niche markets have to be supported twice as much by the development or adjustments to their products for export markets than SMEs in mass markets. Furthermore, they need to develop their international business skills while SMEs in mass markets don't seem to have this need (Onkelinx and Sleuwaegen, 2009). Hence it is important that these organizations or outsiders take this into account when contacting these types of firms and want to support them with their internationalization.

Onkelinx and Sleuwaegen (2008) argued that government support is very important for the internationalization of an SME, but the success of the internationalization is even more dependent on the entrepreneur itself. SMEs need to see the possible advantages of internationalization and need to specify these in their strategy. Over the past 20 years trade barriers have been mitigated, but internationalizing is still very difficult for SMEs. The main reason for this is that they only have limited information about foreign markets. When they want information, they trust their network, such as their clients and suppliers. The risks and uncertainties related to internationalizing do not make it any easier.

6.2.3   Export Assistance

An effective export promotion has to respond to the diversity of the international markets today and it has to support selective sectors. Export promotion which is directed to all or too many sectors has proven to be ineffective because the available resources are too widely dispersed (Islam and Cook, 1999; Onkelinx and Sleuwaegen, 2008). SMEs and creative SMEs are frequently shown to be lacking in internal resources, know-how and information about foreign markets. Academics see this as an argument for export promotion programs for SMEs (Alvarez, 2004; Nauwelaerts and Frank, 2007).

The 'resource-based view' assumes also that internal resources of a company strongly affect the profitability of potential export opportunities. Therefore, in several studies, the internal resources are added to the model, next to the external resources. Wilkinson and Brouthers (2006) apply the resource-based view and have proven the impact of internal resources on the export performances of SMEs.

We distinguish several levels of involvement in the export process, going from accidental exports to dedicated export involvement. When a firm evolves in this process, the knowledge of the market improves, the level of involvement increases, and the needs change with respect to the export promotion programs (Gençtürk and Kotabe, 2001).

The export promotion instruments of FIT, organized in the country of exports, can be divided into three types of export promotion instruments (Flanders Investment & Trade, 2010):

1. Identifying agents and distributors
    *   Export days in the host country: For a specific sector, FIT brings interested foreign companies in contact with Flemish providers. On export days in the host country they organize meetings with important buyers.
2. Trade shows
    *   Catalogue booth: Firms don't have to travel to present their products at the show themselves. They only have to hand in their catalogue and FIT will do the rest.
    *   Product sample booth (PSB): The firm sends a representative to the trade show who presents its brochures, products or samples there. A PSB is not an individual stand but the firm can clearly be distinguished from other Flemish enterprises that also use this stand. In addition, the PSB is not very costly for the firm.
    *   Group stands: FIT installs the stand at well-known and promising trade shows and organizes everything from admin-

istration to logistics. The clients only needs to concentrate on their sales.
3. Trade missions
   - Prospection and business trips: The firm travels with a delegation to the target market, where FIT has a customized program worked out to meet interesting people who could be useful for the enterprise.

The export promotion instruments of FIT, taking place in the home country, can be divided into two types of export promotion instruments:

1. Objective market information activities:
   - Seminars: Experts and fellow companies bring trends and actual information about the export market, sector or a theme.
   - Export days in the home country: All Flemish economic representatives (VLEVs) of a certain area travel to Flanders and offer interesting discussions, testimonials, opportunities to network and to discuss projects.
   - Contact days: They offer the opportunity to ask questions about international projects in a specific country to VLEVs or commerce secretaries. There is also the possibility to start a conversation with an expert from your target market.
2. Identifying agents and distributors:
   - Inviting foreign buyers: Foreign buyers are invited to Flanders or a Flemish city where a trade show takes place and are offered the opportunity to present their products or services to the right decision makers.

6.2.3.1 Identifying agents and distributors

Activities of SMEs can be seriously hampered when an inappropriate distributor or agent is selected or when the relationship between them is unstable. Hence it is a big challenge to find the appropriate agent or distributor abroad. Besides that, SMEs are undermined by foreign competition having control over the distribution channel, which will increase costs for newcomers. Wilkinson and Brouthers have proven in their study of 2006 that export programs identifying agents and distributors have a positive impact on export performances of an SME. This is confirmed by research done by Flanders District of Creativity. They concluded that SMEs need to identify foreign partners, which is also true for SMEs in niche markets. But there is a gap between what is offered and what is needed (Onkelinx and Sleuwaegen, 2009). This leads us to the following hypotheses about export days in the host country and inviting foreign buyers:

Hypothesis 1: The use of export days in the host (export) country is positively related to the export performance satisfaction of creative companies.

Hypothesis 2: The invitation of foreign buyers to the home country is positively related to the export performance satisfaction of creative companies.

6.2.3.2   Trade shows

Trade shows allow firms to test the market potential abroad; they make it possible to recruit candidate distributors or to network and they can be used to study the market, by analyzing market opportunities and comparing offers from the competition (Leonidou et al., 2002).

Until now trade shows have only been studied by Wilkinson and Brouthers (2006) on a company level. They concluded that sector-oriented trade shows contribute effectively to export performances of SMEs. Before, it was already proven that trade shows increase direct exports at the country level (Wilkinson and Brouthers, 2000). Moreover they lead to an increase in export sales and awareness of the product (Leonidou et al., 2002). However, they don't contribute significantly to trade relationships in the long term (Alvarez, 2004).

Seringhaus and Rosson (1998 and 2000) investigated the difference between companies that use assistance from international trade shows and those that don't. The independent companies appear to be more effective but have more experience. The assisted companies were also effective but to a lesser extent; they have less experience and make use of export performance organizations. The assisted companies undergo a faster learning process, since they can lean on experienced people. Therefore it's recommended that these organizations focus on small businesses while giving export assistance. FIT focuses only on SMEs.

FIT organizes three different activities at trade shows. The first one, catalogue booths, does not possess the previously mentioned characteristics which are typical for trade shows. There is no personal contact with customers, they can't collect information about the host countries themselves and networking is not possible. This leads to Hypothesis 3:

Hypothesis 3: The use of catalogue booths is not significantly correlated to the export performance satisfaction of creative companies.

Besides catalogue booths, FIT also provides two other support actions: PSBs and group stands. The main difference between these is that participants at a PSB have an equally divided exposition surface and with group stands this is not the case.

The definition used in the literature does overlap here; this brings us to Hypotheses 4 and 5:

Hypothesis 4: The use of product sample booths is positively related to the export performance satisfaction of creative companies.

Hypothesis 5: The use of group stands is positively related to the export performance satisfaction of creative companies.

6.2.3.3 Trade missions

According to Wilkinson and Brouthers (2006), trade missions do not directly contribute to export performances but are interesting for newly exporting companies since they offer them the opportunity to gain experience and gather knowledge. They allow firms to see how business is done abroad, which services and products are available, how accessible potential clients are, and so on. Trade missions will rather increase knowledge and competences of the company about the export market (Wilkinson and Brouthers, 2000) but not the export performances themselves. When they do contribute to sales, this will mainly be due to the long-term relationship that has been established (Spence, 2003). Alvarez (2004), however, observes that there is no significant relationship between trade missions and trade relations in the long term. Furthermore the study of Moini (1998) ranks trade missions as the least effective of 16 export promotion instruments in terms of received and expected advantages. Beeman et al. (2007) analyzed 180 enterprises and their use of trade missions between 1995 and 2004. Yet their results show an increase in employment. Employment can also be used as a good parameter for overall business performances. The rise was greater for small and medium businesses.

Despite some contradictions in the literature, we expect, like most research results including those of Wilkinson and Brouthers (2006), no significant relationship, leading us to Hypothesis 6 for prospection and business trips:

Hypothesis 6: The use of trade missions, prospection and business trips is not significantly correlated to the export performance satisfaction of creative SMEs.

6.2.3.4 Objective market information activities in the home country

Seminars, export days in the home country and contact days offer clients information about a specific sector or country. Previous studies (Wilkinson and Brouthers, 2000 and Simpson and Kujawa, 1974) concluded that this kind of information has a negative influence on direct exports of a state, because the client is not able or willing to analyze the given information. This will occur particularly in the creative sector, because the majority of creative firms do not have a sufficiently economic background to evaluate this information. The negative association can also be explained by the states spending more money on trade shows than on market information activities, resulting in a negative impact of market information activities. This leads us to the following hypothesis:

Hypothesis 7: The use of seminars, export days in the home country and contact days is not significantly correlated to the export performance satisfaction of creative companies.

6.3 METHODOLOGY

We developed a survey based on an extensive literature review, focusing on the work of Wilkinson and Brouthers (2006) and with the help of FIT. FIT provided us with the email addresses of 1597 creative SMEs. Most of these firms are micro and small firms, active in the furniture and related creative activities in Flanders.

To increase the response rate, a second mailing took place, which was followed by phone calls. Eighty responses were returned, of which only 65 were complete and suitable after data cleaning. The response rate is therefore relatively low, at 5 per cent. This is 9 per cent lower than the strongly comparable study of Wilkinson and Brouthers (2006), but still acceptable because 51 of the 65 respondents have a managerial function in the company.

The short period between sending the survey and collecting the data, together with the fact that small companies typically don't have time to answer the survey, could be an explanation for the low response rate.

With a linear multiple regression analysis we try to determine to what extent export performance satisfaction is influenced by various EPPs in the home and host countries on the one hand and influenced by internal resources on the other hand.

6.3.1 Dependent Variable: Export Performance Satisfaction

To measure 'export performance satisfaction' we used more subjective information, namely the perceptions of the managers concerning their export performance. There are three good reasons for using these perceptual measures. First of all, SMEs are often reluctant or unable to give 'hard' financial data. Secondly, objective financial data is not available for all SMEs in our population. This makes it impossible to check whether the given answers are correct. And last, even when we are able to access accurate financial data it is hard to interpret them (Robertson and Chetty, 2000). Geringer and Herbert (1991) demonstrate that there is a strong correlation between perceptual measures and objective financial data. The use of a subjective measure will increase the response rate.

Previous studies used the following perceptual measures to determine export performance satisfaction: (1) sales growth in foreign markets; (2) overseas market share; (3) number of countries exporting to; and (4) overall export performance (Julien and Ramangalahy, 2003; Leonidou et al., 2002; Robertson and Chetty, 2000; Wilkinson and Brouthers, 2006). Respondents were asked to rate these four measures on a five-point Likert scale (1 = very satisfied; 5 = very dissatisfied).

The Cronbach's alpha test was 0.907, which indicates a strong correlation between the four perceptual measures. The correlation matrix also shows correlation. Therefore we can convert the four measures into one variable, 'Export performance satisfaction' (Robertson and Chetty, 2006; Wilkinson and Brouthers, 2006).

6.3.2   Independent Variables

Three models were estimated. In the first model, all export promotion programs are included. In the second and third we only included, respectively, EPPs that took place in the home country and those that took place in the host country. The EPPs are measured by asking how often the instrument was used by the SME during the last (previous) five years (from 2005) (Wilkinson and Brouthers, 2006).

Since the export performance satisfaction is not only influenced by these EPPs but also by other external and internal resources, according to the resource-based view, we also take into account a set of control variables and internal resources. These variables have proven their relationship to the export success of SMEs in previous studies (Alvarez, 2004; Gençtürk and Kotabe, 2001; Leonidou, 2004; Leonidou et al., 2002; Wilkinson and Brouthers, 2006).

Wilkinson and Brouthers (2006) used 'Firms' reserves of marketing', 'Firms' reserves of management', 'Firms' reserves of production capacity', 'Foreign turnover', 'Export intensity' and 'Export barriers'.

The first three variables, 'Firms' reserves of marketing', 'Firms' reserves of management' and 'Firms' reserves of production capacity', are included as 'internal resources' in our models. They are measured by asking to what extent the firm has enough capacity in those three areas.

We selected these variables on the basis of the following literature. Yang et al. 1992 (in Wilkinson and Brouthers, 2006) investigated whether a firm was likely to export based on the availability of unused internal resources such as marketing staff, production capacity and management time. Wilkinson and Brouthers (2006) investigated whether these three variables would increase export, and found a positive impact. The positive impact of marketing reserves on exports was confirmed in various studies (Alvarez, 2004; Leonidou, 2004; Leonidou et al., 2002; Wilkinson and Brouthers, 2006).

'Growth in foreign turnover', measures how strongly their exports increase yearly on average over the last five years (in percentages).

'Export intensity' of an SME consists of five levels: accidental export, exploratory export, experimental export, active export and dedicated export (Cavusgil et al., 2008). As an SME moves up to a higher export-level, it will deliver better performances in terms of sales and profitability (Gençtürk and Kotabe, 2001). The more a company advances, the better its export performances are. We asked our respondents on which level they are situated and in order to exclude misunderstandings, we added a clear definition of each level, which can be found in Appendix 2.

The last, external control variable is 'Export barriers'. Leonidou (2004) investigated which barriers hinder export for SMEs. We use seven of these potential export barriers (as seen in Ramaswami and Yang, 1990 and in Wilkinson and Brouthers, 2006) and added one to the list that is relevant for the creative sector.

'Poor knowledge of potential markets', 'lack of ability or time to follow-up trade leads', 'no mechanism to generate trade leads', 'strong foreign competition', 'lack of staff', 'strong exchange rate of the euro' and 'trade barriers' are the variables used by Wilkinson and Brouthers (2006). 'Lack of protection in creative and intellectual property rights' is added to our list (Flanders Investment & Trade Los Angeles, 2009). The eight barriers are summed up to constitute the variable 'export barriers'.

After examining for extreme observations, observations 16, 21 and 46 show abnormal values for model 1 with only host country EPPs. Three dummy variables are added to the different models to exclude bias of the results.

Three models have been analyzed. The first only incorporates the host country EPPs, the second one only the home country EPPs and the last one both EPPs. For each model we divided the respondents into two subgroups of firms that are purely creative and those that are not. Purely creative firms have their own designer or design department; the others don't.

6.4   RESULTS AND IMPLICATIONS

Appendix 6.1 gives the average, standard deviation, variance and minimum and maximum value for every variable. This will help us with the interpretation of the regression models. A short description of every variable is added here.

Correlation matrices can be found in Appendixes 3, 4 and 5 for every model. In every correlation matrix the same variables show significant correlations. Between 'Reserves top management' and 'Marketing reserves' there is a strong correlation; the value is just above 0.5, which can indicate multicollinearity. But the low Variance Inflation Factors (VIF) contradict this, with scores for all variables lower than two. The generally applied rule is that the VIF value must be lower than five to exclude multicollinearity (Studenmund, 2006). We also notice a – logically – strong correlation between 'Export performance satisfaction' and 'Export intensity' ($r = 0.518$), but no VIF value higher than two.

Table 6.1 shows all three models and their subgroups. First of all, we find that export intensity shows a very significant, positive relation with export performance satisfaction. This result is perfectly in line with our expectations. Also growth in foreign turnover has a positive and significant impact. These two results need no further explanation.

On the side of the internal resources, we see different results when we distinguish between the 'purely creative firms', having their own designer or design department, and those that do not. For the purely creative firms, marketing reserves seem to be positively related to export performance satisfaction while for the other group, it is the extra production capacity which is positively related to export performance satisfaction. These results are in line with Alvarez (2004); Leonidou (2004); Leonidou et al. (2002); Wilkinson and Brouthers (2006). The results suggest that extra marketing effort is particularly effective to promote and stimulate exports in the creative firms and the design industry. This is a first important conclusion for creative SMEs: if they want to promote or stimulate their products or services on foreign markets, they should invest considerably in marketing effort.

On the side of the external resources, we find that among the EPPs organized in the international export market only the individual 'Product sample booths' at international fairs seem to have a consistent significant positive effect ($p < 0.05$) on export performance satisfaction in all models. For 'Export days in the host country', model 3 alone shows a significant positive effect. Only the sector-oriented EPPs focusing on a specific sector and organized in the host (export) country seem to have a positive, significant effect on export performance satisfaction.

Table 6.1 Linear multiple regressions

Variables	Model 1	Purely creative	Not creative	Model 2	Purely creative	Not creative	Model 3	Purely creative	Not creative
Export performance	1.740***	0.482	0.709	1.726***	1.297**	1.303*	1.910***	1.267*	1.689
Marketing reserves	0.489**	0.510	0.036	0.363	0.816*	0.131	0.240	0.735(*)	0.133
Reserves top management	−0.067	0.188	0.461	−0.042	−0.228	0.361	0.028	0.010	0.140
Reserves production capacity	−0.200	−0.276	0.725*	0.171	−0.335	1.033**	0.182	−0.545	1.280*
Growth in foreign turnover	0.002*	0.002*	0.005	0.002*	0.002(*)	0.018	0.002*	0.002(*)	0.018
Export intensity	0.371***	0.426***	0.428***	0.308***	0.423***	0.249**	0.258***	0.432**	0.179
Export barriers	−0.023	0.139*	−0.091	0.004	0.038	−0.136*	−0.032	0.003	−0.140
Contact days				0.013	0.177	0.019	0.000	0.217	0.009
Export days in home country				−0.023	0.135	−0.253	−0.013	0.115	−0.180

	(1)	(2)	(3)	(4)	(5)	(6)	(7)	(8)	(9)
Inviting foreign buyers				0.000	0.000	0.007	-0.006**	-0.004	-0.012
Seminars				0.017	-0.205	0.154	0.019	-0.194	0.121
Export days in host country	0.008	0.011	0.008				0.020**	0.074	0.035
Catalogue stands	-0.007	-0.015	-0.026				-0.004	-0.008	0.019
PSB	0.025**	0.010	0.052**				0.039**	0.032	0.028
Group stands	0.006	-0.001	0.033				0.010	0.001	0.056
P&B	-0.002	0.001	0.000				0.001	-0.004	0.004
Dummy16	2.182***								
Dummy21	-2.325***	2.627***							
Dummy46			2.429***						
N	65	34	31	65	34	31	65	34	31
R^2	0.582	0.656	0.730	0.361	0.500	0.554	0.470	0.568	0.654
Adj R^2	0.476	0.459	0.549	0.243	0.283	0.330	0.307	0.208	0.308
F	5.466***	3.333***	4.047***	3.049***	2.302**	2.480**	2.894***	1.578	1.892

Note: *** p, 0.01, ** p, 0.05, * p, 0.1, (*)p, 0.2.

Source: Authors' calculations.

Other EPPs, like catalogue booths or trade missions and export days in
the home country, do not show significant effects on export performance
satisfaction. EPPs organized in the home country and aiming at identifying agents and distributors with both subgroups: 'Export days in home
country' and 'Inviting foreign buyers' are insignificant or even negatively
related to export performance satisfaction.

We supposed that identifying agents and distributors would improve
export performance satisfaction (Hypotheses 1 and 2). The results only
show a significant positive unstandardized coefficient (0.020 with $p < 0.05$)
for 'Export days in the host country' in model 3. Onkelinx and Sleuwaegen
(2009) also concluded this need: personal contact with distributors in the
host country would facilitate the first contact. Moreover Wilkinson and
Brouthers (2006) also found a positive relationship. On the other hand,
'inviting foreign buyers to the home country' has the opposite effect, a
negative one ($p < 0.05$). The invitation of foreign buyers to your home
country does not seem to be very useful to export performances of creative
SMEs. A reason for this difference can be because 'Export days in host
country' are more sector specific, while 'the invitation of foreign buyers in
the home country' is mostly organized on a regional (not sectorial) basis
by FIT. Effective export promotion should be focused on selective sectors
and be just as flexible as the international market itself. Export promo-
tions with the focus on all or too many sectors seem not very effective
(Islam and Cook, 1999; Onkelinx and Sleuwaegen, 2008).

The next three hypotheses discuss three different actions on trade
shows. The first one, 'Catalogue booths' is negative but insignificant.
This is in line with Hypothesis 3. The second, 'Product sample booths', is
positive and significantly correlated ($p < 0.05$) with export performances
for model 1 and 3 and for the non-creative SMEs in model 1. Hypothesis
4 is confirmed and thus in line with Wilkinson and Brouthers (2006).
Third, 'Group stands', is positive but not significant and as a consequence
Hypothesis 5 is not supported. This difference may be due to the fact that
our respondents made more use of PSBs than of group stands, which leads
to insignificant results for group stands.

The difference in use probably is due to the fact that group stands are
more expensive than PSBs and while using a PSB, firms can still clearly
be distinguished from the other Flemish participants. This cuts back costs
and therefore is more frequently used and more effective. The costs are
very high for most creative SMEs; more financial support is needed when
participating in group stands.

Hypothesis 6 is reinforced by our results, 'Trade missions, prospection
and business trips' are not significantly correlated with export performance satisfaction. These findings confirm previous work on export promo-

tion (Alvarez, 2004; Moini, 1998; Spence 2003; Wilkinson and Brouthers, 2000).

Hypothesis 7 expects a negative influence of seminars, export days in the home country and contact days on the export performance satisfaction, as found in the study of Wilkinson and Brouthers (2000). We found no significant impact of any of the three above-mentioned export promotion programs on the dependent variable. Wilkinson and Brouthers (2000) argued that objective market information is negatively associated with export success. Previous studies from Simpson and Kujawa (1974) and Walters (1983) sum up some reasons to explain why objective market information activities don't have an influence on export success: (1) Because these firms aren't getting the right information; (2) companies have difficulties evaluating the available information; (3) they are not equipped or not willing to use the information delivered by these instruments; and (4) they are not interested in these types of activities and prefer other instruments.

These results are in line with those of Wilkinson and Brouthers (2006) who found that, even after controlling for internal firm resources, the use of trade shows and programs identifying agents and distributors contributes negatively to SME satisfaction with export performance. In their study of 2000, they also found that international trade missions and objective market information programs are negatively associated with direct exports. For the creative sector, we can conclude that only EPPs organized in the host countries, and oriented towards a particular industry or sector, seem to be effective. This observation is of great importance in practice, since it indicates that it is important for governmental organizations to focus on sector- or industry-specific actions in the host country. EPPs in the home country (of origin) and/or oriented towards larger markets, covering various industries, seem to lose a large part of their effects.

6.5   CONCLUSIONS

The purpose of this study was to evaluate the effects of export promotion instruments on export performance satisfaction of SMEs in the creative sector. The nine export promotion instruments are Export days in the host country, Catalogue booths, Product sample booths, Group stands, Prospection and business trips, Seminars, Inviting foreign buyers, Export days in the home country and Contact days. Based on the literature, we expect a significant influence on the export performance satisfaction of firms from Export days in the host country, Product sample booths, Group stands and Inviting foreign buyers.

With an online questionnaire we collected data for a linear multiple regression analysis. The population consisted of companies in the creative sector in Flanders which had already come in contact with FIT. With 80 respondents we had a relatively low response rate of 5 per cent. After further analysis, only 65 responses could be used for our research. The collected data consisted of a dependent variable export performance satisfaction, export promotion programs, internal resources and control variables.

The internal resources, 'marketing reserves' and two control variables: 'growth in foreign turnover' and 'export intensity' have a significant influence on export performance satisfaction. The internal resource, 'firms' reserves in production' is only significant for the not purely creative sector; 'marketing reserves' are clearly significant for the 'purely creative firms'. These results suggest that extra marketing effort is particularly effective to promote and stimulate exports in the creative firms and the design industry.

Concerning the export promotion instruments, we only get a consistent significant positive effect for 'Product sample booths'. These typically sector-oriented export promotion activities that send a representative of the firm to international fairs seem to be the most effective. For 'Export days in the host country', only model 3 shows a significant positive effect. All other EPPs show insignificant or even negative effects on export promotion satisfaction.

Important restrictions for this research are the low response rate, the subjective parameter for 'export performance satisfaction' and the static approach, not taking into account the dynamic process of internationalization.

The results lead to the following management and policy recommendations. First of all, we mention the importance of the internal resources, mainly 'marketing reserves' and 'firms' reserve in production capacity'. They represent a success factor for internationalizing SMEs. Hence it is important that managers of creative SMEs invest in marketing and that export promotion organizations support them in this topic.

Secondly, only 'Product sample booths' have a positive and significant influence on export performance satisfaction. When the available public budget is allocated, export promotion organizations should keep these results in mind. Also for firms it is very relevant to know what the most effective instruments are to focus on. Nevertheless, some vigilance is appropriate, since 'PSBs' aren't always significant for the subgroups of purely creative and not purely creative SMEs. Further investigation of the reason for this difference is recommended before taking profound decisions.

Thirdly the use of 'Trade missions, prospection and business trips' and of 'Inviting foreign buyers' is not immediately useful, since they are negatively and/or insignificantly related to the export performance satisfaction of SMEs in the creative sector. These programs are often not sector specific and therefore less useful than 'Product sample booths' which are, in contrast, often sector specific.

Due to the limitation in current research there is definitely enough room for further investigation, especially in the growing creative sector.

NOTE

1. FIT is a Flemish governmental organization for international trade. Their purpose is to improve international trade of Flemish firms (specifically of SMEs) and at the same time attract foreign investments to Flanders.

REFERENCES

Alvarez, R.E. (2004), 'Sources of export success in small and medium-sized enterprises: the impact of public programs', *International Business Review*, **13**, 383–400.

Anderson, O. and L.S. Kheam (1998), 'Resource-based theory and international growth strategies: an exploratory study', *International Business Review*, **7**, 163–84.

Beeman, D.R., H. Hosebrock and O. Tran (2007), 'Do structured international trade missions improve corporate performance?', *Economic Development Journal*, **6**(3), 41–8.

Bloodgood, J., H. Sapienza and J. Almeida (1996), 'The Internationalization of new high-potential US ventures: antecedents and outcomes', *Entrepreneurship Theory and Practice*, **20**, 61–76.

Cavusgil, S.T., and J. Naor (1987), 'Firm management characteristics as discriminators of export marketing activity', *Journal of Business Research*, **15**(3), 221–35.

Cavusgil, S.T., G. Knight and J.R. Riesenberger (2008), *International Business: Strategy, Management and the New Realities*, upper saddle River: Pearson Education.

Crick, D., S. Chaudry and S. Batstone (2001), 'An investigation into the overseas expansion of small Asian-owned UK firms', *Small Business Economics*, **16**, 75–94.

Dhanaraj, C. and P.W. Beamish (2003), 'A resource-based approach to the study of export performance', *Journal of Small Business Management*, **41**(3), 242–61.

DiPietro, W.P. and E. Anoruo (2006), 'Creativity, innovation and export performance', *Journal of Policy Modeling*, **28**, 133–9.

Etemad, H. (2004), 'Internationalization of SMEs: a grounded theoretical framework and overview', *Canadian Journal of Administrative Science*, **21**(1), 1–21.

FIT (2009), 'Statistieken', Flanders Investment & Trade, available at: http://www.flanderstrade.be/site/wwwnl.nsf/statistiekenhome?openform.

Flanders Investment & Trade Los Angeles (2009), 'Vlaamse Designproducten: Een

Amerikaans Marktperspectief', Los Angeles: Flanders Investment & Trade Los Angeles.

Flanders Investment & Trade (2010), 'De wereld inpakken is verrassend eenvoudig. Actieprogramma 2010', Brussels: Flanders Investment & Trade.

Gemünden, H.G. (1991), 'Success factors of export marketing: a meta-analytic critique of the empirical studies', in S.J. Paliwoda et al. (eds), *New Perspectives on International Marketing*, London: Routledge, pp. 33–62.

Gençtürk, E.F. and M.Y. Kotabe (2001), 'The effect of export assistance program usage on export performance: a contingency explanation', *Journal of International Marketing*, **9**(2), 51–72.

Geringer, J.M. and L. Herbert (1991), 'Measuring performance of international joint ventures', *Journal of International Business Studies*, **22**(2), 249–64.

Hollaender, I., M. Cools and Y. Nauwelaerts (2010), 'Supply–demand gap between small exporting creative firms and professional service providers', Working Paper, RENT conference, University of Maastricht, EIASM.

Islam, M. and P. Cook (1999), 'New challenges for trade promotion: export strategies for small firms', *International Trade Forum*, **1**, 9–12.

Julien, P-A. and C. Ramangalahy (2003), 'Competitive strategy and performance of exporting SMEs: an empirical investigation of the impact of their export information search and competencies', *Entrepreneurship Theory and Practice*, **27**(3), Spring, 227–45.

Kuivaleinen, O., S. Sundqvist, K. Puurmaleinen and J.W. Cadogan (2004), 'The effect of environmental turbulence and leader characteristics on international performance: are knowledge-based firms different?', *Canadian Journal of Administrative Sciences*, **21**(1), 35–50.

Lederman, D., M. Olarreaga and L. Payton (2010), 'Export promotion agencies: do they work?', *Journal of Development Economics*, **91**, 257–65.

Leonidou, L.C. (2004), 'An analysis of the barriers hindering small business export development', *Journal of Small Business Management*, **42**(3), 279–302.

Leonidou, L.C., C.S. Katsikeas and S. Samiee (2002), 'Marketing strategy determinants of export performance: a meta-analysis', *Journal of Business Research*, **55**, 51–67.

Maenhout, T., I. De Voldere, J. Onkelinx and L. Sleuwaegen (2006), 'Creatieve industrie in Vlaanderen', Flanders DC Research report, Leuven.

Moini, A.H. (1998), 'Small firms exporting: how effective are government export programs?', *Journal of Small Business Management*, **36**(1), 1–15.

Nauwelaerts, Y. and T. Franck (2007), 'Kritische succesfactoren van startende en jonge bedrijven in de design sectoren', *Tijdschrift voor Economie en Management*, **52**(1), 65–94.

Onkelinx, J. and L. Sleuwaegen (2008), 'Internationalization of SMEs', Flanders DC Research report, Leuven.

Onkelinx, J. and L. Sleuwaegen (2009), 'Determinants of successful internationalization of SMEs in Flanders', Research report Flanders District of Creativity, Leuven.

Power, D. and J. Jansson (2008), 'Cyclical clusters in global circuits: overlapping spaces in furniture trade fairs', *Economic Geography*, **84**(4), 423–48.

Ramaswami, S.N. and Y. Yang (1990), 'Perceived barriers to exporting and export assistance requirements', in S.T. Cavusgil and M.R. Czinkota (eds), *International Perspectives on Trade Promotion and Assistance*, Westport, CT: Quorum Books.

Robertson, C. and S.K. Chetty (2000), 'A contingency-based approach to understanding export performance', *International Business Review*, 9, 211–35.

Robson, P.J.A. and R.J. Bennett (2000), 'SME growth: the relationship with business advice and external collaboration', *Small Business Economics*, 15, 193–208.

Rugman, A.M. and J. D'Cruz (2000), *Multinationals as Flagship Firms: A New Theory of Regional Business Networks*, Oxford: Oxford University Press.

Rutten, P., W. Manshanden, J. Muskens and O. Koops (2004), 'De creatieve industrie in Amsterdam en de regio', TNO rapport, Delft.

Seringhaus, F.H.R. and P.J. Rosson (1998), 'Management and performance of international trade fair exhibitors: government stands vs independent stands', *International Marketing Review*, 15(5), 398–412.

Seringhaus, F.H.R. and P.J. Rosson (2000), 'Exhibitors at international trade fairs: the influence of export support', LTA 4/00, 505–16.

Simpson, C. and D. Kujawa (1974), 'The export decision process: an empirical inquiry', *Journal of International Business*, 5(1), 107–17.

Spence, M.M. (2003), 'Evaluating export promotion programmes: UK overseas trade missions and export performance', *Small Business Economics*, 20, 83–103.

Statbel (2009), 'Distribution of the total consumption/expenses in 2007 for Flanders', available at: http://statbel.fgov.be/nl/statistieken/cijfers/arbeid_leven/inkomens/spreiding/index.jsp.

Studenmund, A.H. (2006), *Using Econometrics: a Practical Guide*, Boston, MA: Pearson Addison Wesley.

Walters, P.G.P. (1983), 'Export information sources, a study of their usage and utility', *International Marketing Review*, 1(2), 34–43.

Wilkinson, T. and L.E. Brouthers (2000), 'An evaluation of state sponsored promotion programs', *Journal of Business Research*, 47, 229–36.

Wilkinson, T. and L.E. Brouthers (2006), 'Trade promotion and SME export performance', *International Business Review*, 15, 233–52.

Wolff, J.A. and T.L. Pett (2000), 'Internationalization of small firms: an examination of export competitive patterns, firm size, and export performance', *Journal of Small Business Management*, 38(2), April, 34–47.

APPENDIX 1 SUMMARY OF THE VARIABLES

Variables	Export performance	Marketing reserves	Reserve top management	Reserve production capacity	Growth in foreign turnover	Export intensity	Export barriers	Seminars
Mean	3.33846	0.65	0.76	0.77	24.59	4.02	4.6970	1.38
SD	0.87397	0.480	0.432	0.425	78.057	1.307	2.18364	5.101
Variance	0.764	0.231	0.186	0.180	6092.953	1.707	4.768	26.024
Minimum	1	0	0	0	-10	1	0	0
Maximum	5	1	1	1	600	5	8	40

Variables	Contact days	Inviting foreign buyers	Export days in the home country	Export days in host country	Catalogue stands	PSB	Group stands	Prospection and business trips
Mean	1.06	10.76	0.65	2.83	1.20	4.73	71	20.12
SD	6.224	44.508	2.663	12.847	4.652	7.257	0.365	36.866
Variance	38.735	1980.925	7.092	165.033	21.638	52.663	0.593	1359.124
Minimum	0	0	0	0	0	0	0	0
Maximum	50	300	20	100	32	25	5	200

Source: Authors' calculations based on survey.

APPENDIX 2 DEFINITIONS OF THE VARIABLES

Export performance satisfaction – dependent variable	Estimation of the foreign sales growth, the number of foreign markets, the market share abroad, and the overall export performances
Marketing reserves – internal resource	The firm has enough personnel for marketing when internationalizing
Reserves top management – internal resource	The firm has enough available time of the top management
Firms' reserves in production capacity – internal resource	The firm has enough production capacity
Growth in foreign turnover – control variable	Average yearly growth percentage in export over the last 5 years
Export intensity – control variable	Five phazes of export intensity:
	1. Accidental export: little interest in exports. Focus on the home market. Export is rather accidental
	2. Exploratory export: Investigates the possibilities of exporting but exports are less than 5% of the total turnover. Finances, management and production capacity aren't willingly made available for export activities
	3. Experimental export: Exports are on an experimental basis and between 5% and 20% of the total turnover, with a focus on neighbor countries or countries with the same culture
	4. Active export: Exports are between 20% and 40% of the total turnover and find place on a regular basis
	5. Dedicated export: Exports are more than 40% of the total turnover. A dedicated exporter seeks export opportunities around the world, mostly in very distant countries with a totally different culture
Export barriers – control variable	Number of export barriers the firm has to deal with
Export days in the host country	Number of times the firm has participated in export days in the host country in the last 5 years

Catalogue stand	Number of times the firm has participated in catalogue stands in the last 5 years
Product Sample Booth (PSB)	Number of times the firm has participated in PSBs in the last 5 years
Group stand	Number of times the firm has participated in group stands in the last 5 years
Prospection and business trip	Number of times the firm has participated in prospection and business trips in the last 5 years
Seminars	Number of times the firm has participated in seminars in the last 5 years
Export days home country	Number of times the firm has participated in export days in the home country in the last 5 years
Contact days	Number of times the firm has participated in contact days in the last 5 years
Inviting foreign buyers	Number of times the firm has participated in inviting foreign buyers in the last 5 years

Source: Authors' calculations.

APPENDIX 3   CORRELATION MATRIX MODEL 1: ONLY HOST COUNTRY EPPs

Variables	1	2	3	4	5	6	7	8	9	10	11	12
1. Export performance	1.000											
2. Marketing reserves	0.208*	1.000										
3. Reserve top management	0.192	0.548**	1.000									
4. Reserve production capacity	0.285*	0.206*	0.280*	1.000								
5. Growth in foreign turnover	0.276*	0.071	0.009	0.082	1.000							
6. Export intensity	0.518**	0.025	0.165	0.365**	0.123	1.000						
7. Export barriers	0.039	0.063	0.059	0.066	-0.061	0.022*	1.000					
8. Export days in host country	0.193	0.063	0.084	0.017	-0.041	0.091	0.218	1.000				
9. Catalogue stands	0.067	0.187	0.149	0.080	-0.044	0.140	0.165	-0.023	1.000			
10. PSB	0.357	0.202	0.098	0.086	0.007	0.203	0.164	0.183	0.036	1.000		
11. Group stands	0.035	-0.059	0.130	-0.049	-0.073	0.095	0.141	0.149	-0.073	-0.055	1.000	
12. P&B	0.171	0.083	0.253*	-0.138	-0.103*	0.261	-0.157	0.143	-0.012	0.123	0.094	1.000
13. Dummy16	0.089	-0.169	-0.219*	0.068	-0.007*	-0.288	-0.038	-0.028	-0.033	-0.083	-0.038	0.022
14. Dummy21	-0.344*	0.093	-0.219*	-0.228*	-0.039	-0.096	-0.096	-0.028	-0.033	-0.048	-0.038	-0.069

Note: * $p < 0.05$; ** $p < 0.01$.

Source: Authors' calculations.

APPENDIX 4   CORRELATION MATRIX MODEL 2: ONLY HOME COUNTRY EPPs

Variables	1	2	3	4	5	6	7	8	9	10	11
1. Export performance	1.000										
2. Marketing reserves	0.208*	1.000									
3. Reserve top management	0.192	0.548**	1.000								
4. Reserve production capacity	0.285*	0.206*	0.280*	1.000							
5. Growth in foreign turnover	0.276*	0.071	0.009	0.082	1.000						
6. Export intensity	0.518**	0.025	0.165	0.365**	0.123	1.000					
7. Export barriers	0.039	0.063	0.059	0.066	-0.061	0.022	1.000				
8. Seminars	0.075	-0.157	-0.186	0.093	-0.052	0.137	0.182	1.000			
9. Export days in home country	0.063	-0.227*	-0.247*	0.194	-0.025	0.151	0.151	0.951**	1.000		
10. Inviting foreign buyers	0.083	0.139	0.115	0.058	-0.046	0.137	0.100	0.051	-0.040	1.000	
11. Contact days	0.018	-0.229*	0.053	-0.210*	-0.040	-0.021	0.141	0.061	0.100	0.100	1.000

Note: **p < 0.01, *p < 0.05.

Source: Authors' calculations.

APPENDIX 5 CORRELATION MATRIX MODEL 3: HOME AND HOST COUNTRY EPPs

Variables	1	2	3	4	5	6	7	8	9	10	11	12	13	14	15	16
1. Export performance	1.000															
2. Marketing reserves	0.208*	1.000														
3. Reserves top management	0.192	0.548**	1.000													
4. Reserves production capacity	0.285*	0.206*	0.280*	1.000												
5. Growth in foreign turnover	0.276*	0.071	0.009	0.082	1.000											
6. Export intensity	0.518**	0.025	0.165	0.365**	0.123	1.000										
7. Export barriers	0.039	0.063	0.059	0.066	-0.061	0.022	1.000									
8. Seminars	0.075	-0.157	-0.186	0.093	-0.052	0.137	0.182	1.000								
9. Export days in home country	0.063	-0.227*	-0.247*	0.194	-0.025	0.151	0.151	0.951**	1.000							

153

Variables	1	2	3	4	5	6	7	8	9	10	11	12	13	14	15	16
10. Inviting foreign buyers	0.083	0.139	0.115	0.058	-0.046	0.137	0.100	0.051	-0.040	1.000						
11. Contact days	0.018	-0.229*	0.053	-0.210*	-0.040	-0.021	0.141	0.061	0.100	0.100	1.000					
12. Export days in host country	0.193	0.063	0.084	0.017	-0.041	0.091	0.218*	0.005	-0.039	0.612*	0.251*	1.000				
13. Catalogue stands	0.067	0.187	0.149	0.080	-0.044	0.140	0.165	-0.003	-0.008	-0.060	-0.044	-0.023	1.000			
14. PSB	0.357**	0.202	0.098	0.086	0.007	0.203	0.164	0.008	-0.060	0.416*	0.071	0.183	0.036	1.000		
15. Group stands	0.035	-0.0.59	0.130	-0.049	-0.073	0.095	0.141	-0.030	-0.064	0.072	0.470**	0.149	-0.073	-0.055	1.000	
16. P&B	0.171	0.083	0.253*	-0.138	-0.103	0.261*	-0.157	-0.017	-0.053	0.150	0.073	0.143	-0.012	0.123	0.094	1.000

Note: **p < 0.01, *p < 0.05.

Source: Authors' calculations.

154

7. Do firms benefit from investing in basic scientific research? An empirical investigation for pharmaceutical firms

Stijn Kelchtermans, Bart Leten and René Belderbos

7.1 INTRODUCTION

Nelson (1959) has argued that a private enterprise economy fails to provide adequate incentives for firms to invest in basic (scientific) research, due to the uncertain nature of basic research and appropriability problems of the outcome of basic research, that is, knowledge. Despite these difficulties, there may be rational reasons for profit-seeking private firms to conduct basic research with their own research money (Rosenberg, 1990). Firms that perform basic research may benefit, for example, from 'first-mover advantages'. First-mover advantages refer to a wide set of advantages that firms can obtain from being the first to possess new knowledge resulting from basic research, such as the acquisition of valuable assets (whose value becomes apparent from the new knowledge) or the creation of new products and production processes which, in case of effective patent protection, may (at least temporarily) block competing firms. In addition, firms can improve the efficiency of their technology activities by doing basic research. Scientific knowledge, resulting from basic research activities, helps firms to gain a better understanding of the technological landscape in which they search for new inventions, informs them about the most profitable directions for applied research, and helps them to better interpret findings of applied research (Rosenberg, 1990; Fleming and Sorenson, 2004). Internal basic research capabilities also allow firms to better monitor, interpret and absorb scientific knowledge that is conducted externally to firms (Cohen and Levinthal, 1990; Gambardella, 1992).

Only a limited number of prior empirical studies have examined the

impact of in-house basic (scientific) research on the technological performance of firms.[1] The results of these studies are mixed. Using data on the
14 largest US-based drug manufacturers, Gambardella (1992) found that
firms with stronger in-house scientific research skills produced a greater
number of inventions. For a sample of 20 pharmaceutical firms, Cockburn
and Henderson (1998) found positive effects of in-house scientific research
when it was undertaken in collaboration with university scientists. Lim
(2004) found no effect of internal basic scientific research on the technological performance of pharmaceutical firms, while a negative effect was
found for semiconductor firms. Using a sample of pharmaceutical and
biotechnology firms, Fabrizio (2009) found that firms conducting more
scientific research produce higher-value inventions.

Our study extends and improves on this body of prior empirical work
in two important respects. First, we use a more accurate indicator of
firms' involvement in basic research than prior studies. Prior studies have
predominantly used the number of corporate scientific articles as proxy
for their engagement in basic research.[2] However, scientific articles are an
imperfect measure of basic research because a large share of scientific articles in the pharmaceutical industry reports on results of applied research
activities such as clinical trials (Hicks et al., 1994). Second, we examine
the nature of the basic research–firm performance relationship more in
detail than prior studies by using a more flexible functional form to model
the impact of basic research on firms' technological performance. More
specifically, we relax the assumption that in-house basic research has
a linear effect on performance, and use a dummy variable approach to
examine the magnitude of the effect of basic research for different levels
of involvement in basic research. Our analysis draws on a unique panel
dataset (1995–2002) on the R&D, patent and publication activities of 33
large, R&D-intensive US, European and Japanese pharmaceutical firms.
In-house involvement in basic research is measured by firm publications in
Web of Science journals that publish basic research findings.

7.2   BASIC RESEARCH AND TECHNOLOGICAL PERFORMANCE: EXISTING RESEARCH

Basic research has received many definitions (Rosenberg, 1990). We
adopted the definition of the National Science Foundation (NSF) where
basic research is defined as the systematic study directed towards greater
knowledge or understanding of the fundamental aspects of phenomena
and observable facts without specific immediate commercial applications
in mind, although research may be in fields of present or potential com-

mercial interest of those performing the research activities (NSF, 2009). Applied to the pharmaceutical industry, basic research includes attempts to reveal the mechanisms and processes of diseases, but does not include applied research activities such as compound screening, clinical trials and dosage testing (Lim, 2004).

There is broad agreement among economists that basic research is a major source of economic growth and welfare (Mansfield, 1980; Griliches, 1986; Adams, 1990).[3] Although exact estimates of the societal returns to investments in basic research differ among empirical studies, they all show a positive correlation between investments in basic research and productivity growth, after controlling for conventional inputs such as labor and investments in physical capital. Basic research activities generate knowledge that becomes available for society to draw upon in technological activities (Klevorick et al., 1995). Numerous important technical inventions were the direct result of advances in scientific knowledge resulting from basic research. A famous example is the development of the transistor at the Bell Telephone Laboratories in 1948 as a result of basic research activities of company scientists on the workings of semiconductors (Nelson, 1962). Other examples of radical inventions that were motivated by advances in the state of the art of science include nylon, radar and hybrid corn (Nelson, 1962).

Empirical studies have shown that firms actively use scientific knowledge resulting from basic research activities in their applied technology activities (Klevorick et al., 1995). Mansfield (1995 and 1998) surveyed samples of US firms across different industries, and found that, during the period 1975–85, 11 per cent of firms' new products and 9 per cent of new processes could not have been developed (or with substantial delay) in the absence of basic research conducted by universities. These numbers are higher for the period 1986–94 (respectively 15 per cent and 11 per cent), suggesting that basic research findings have become more important for industrial technology activities over time. Another indication of the growing reliance of industrial technology activities on basic scientific knowledge can be found in the analysis of citations of scientific literature in patent documents. For instance, Narin et al. (1997) reported a threefold increase in the number of citations of scientific literature in industrial patents in the United States during the early and mid-1990s.

Basic research is an important source of knowledge for industrial innovation in many industries, but particularly in the pharmaceutical industry (McMillan et al., 2000). Patents in drugs and medicine classes cite significantly more scientific articles than patents in other classes (Narin et al., 1997; Narin and Olivastro, 1992). The strong reliance of pharmaceutical firms on basic research also becomes apparent from the case histories of the discovery of 21 important drugs described by Cockburn and Henderson (1998). Fundamental insights resulting from basic scientific research played an important role in the discovery of 16 of these drugs.

While there is a strong agreement on the importance of basic research for industrial innovation activities, there is a debate among economists whether it is rational for firms to be involved themselves in basic research. Nelson (1959) argues that firms are reluctant to invest in basic research due to high degrees of uncertainty, long timeframes to bear fruit, and appropriability problems of the outcome of basic research, that is, knowledge. Knowledge is (at least partly) believed to be a public good and therefore freely available to other firms, including firms that did not contribute to the production of this knowledge (Arrow, 1962).[4] Despite these difficulties, there are rational reasons for firms to conduct in-house basic research. First, basic research and scientific knowledge resulting from this research impacts on firms' search processes for new inventions. Invention is, to a large extent, a process of (re)combination of existing and novel components (Schumpeter, 1934; Hargadon and Sutton, 1997; Fleming, 2001). The search for a new invention is an uncertain and complex process, in a multi-dimensional landscape of possible new combinations, which is constrained by bounded rationality, firms' routines and prior technological activities (Nelson and Winter, 1982; Leten et al., 2010). Scientific knowledge provides firms with an understanding of the technological landscape in which they search for new inventions (Rosenberg, 1990).[5] Scientific knowledge allows firms to anticipate the results of research experiments without performing them, and helps them to prioritize research avenues and to avoid costly and time-consuming research trials that lead to low-value outcomes (Fabrizio, 2009). Scientific knowledge also helps firms to evaluate the outcomes of applied research and to perceive its implications (Rosenberg, 1990). Second, in-house basic research helps firms to develop the absorptive capacity to monitor, appraise and utilize findings emanating from basic research that is conducted outside the firms (Gambardella, 1992). Increasing costs and complexity of invention processes have increased the importance for firms to be 'connected' to the outside world and tap into external knowledge sources, which may be done by investing in-house in basic research (Chesbrough, 2003).

In reality, most firms do not conduct basic research (Rosenberg, 1990). Basic industrial research is concentrated in two different respects. First, the majority is conducted in science-based industries, such as pharmaceuticals, electrical machinery and aerospace (Mansfield, 1980). Second, within these sectors a handful of firms perform most of the basic research activities. These firms are typically large firms with diverse product and technology portfolios who are confident that they will be able to put both anticipated and unexpected findings from basic research into commercial use (Nelson, 1959). The link between basic research and invention activities is particularly strong in the pharmaceutical industry (Lim, 2004). Most pharmaceutical firms follow a rational drug design approach in drug discovery. In this approach, firms first conduct basic research to learn (that is create knowledge) about the biochemical mechanisms that cause a certain disease, after which they search for compounds that inhibit the mechanisms (Pisano, 1997). While most firms in the pharmaceutical industry conduct basic research, case studies of US pharmaceutical firms have shown that firms have put a different emphasis on in-house basic research in their technology activities (Gambardella, 1992). This observation formed the starting point from which to study in detail the impact of in-house basic research on firms' technological performance.

7.3   DATA AND EMPIRICAL MODEL

We constructed a panel dataset on the patent and publication activities of 33 top R&D spending pharmaceutical firms. The sample firms are selected as top R&D spenders from the '2004 EU Industrial R&D Investment Scoreboard'. This scoreboard lists the top 500 corporate investors in R&D whose parent is located in the EU, and the top 500 companies whose parent is located outside the EU (mainly US and Japan), based on corporate R&D expenditures in 2003. The sample firms have their headquarters in the United States, Europe and Japan and are observed over a period of eight years (1995–2002). The R&D investments of the sample firms totaled US$40.2 billion in 2002. In terms of the mean R&D budget across years, the smallest budget amounts to US$175 million (Sepracor) and the largest R&D budget reaches almost US$6 billion (Pfizer).

Our measure of the technological performance of the firms is based on patent data. There are numerous advantages of the use of patent indicators (Pavitt, 1985; Basberg, 1987; Griliches, 1990): patents contain detailed information on the technological content, owners and prior art of patented inventions; patent data is objective in the sense that it has been processed and validated by patent examiners; and patent data is easily available from patent offices and covers long time series. Like any indicator, patent indicators are also subject to a number of drawbacks: not all inventions are patented and those that are patented vary in their technical and economical value (Trajtenberg, 1990; Gambardella et al., 2008). The first problem can be addressed by limiting patent analyses to industries with high patent propensities and studying firm-level patent time series.[6] The 'value' problem can be taken care of by weighting patent counts by the number of forward patent citations received by patents (Trajtenberg, 1990; Harhoff et al., 1999; Hall et al., 2005; Czarnitzki et al., 2010). Both approaches are followed in this chapter.

Since company names in patent databases are not unified and patents may be applied for under names of subsidiaries or divisions of a parent firm, we collected patent data at the consolidated parent firm level. Therefore, we searched, for each parent firm, for patents under the name of the parent firm as well as all their majority-owned subsidiaries. For this purpose, we used yearly lists of companies' subsidiaries included in corporate annual reports, yearly 10-K reports filed with the SEC in the US, and, for Japanese firms, information on foreign subsidiaries published by Toyo Keizai in the yearly 'Directories of Japanese Overseas Investments'. The consolidation was conducted on a yearly basis to take into account (frequent) changes in the group structure of sample firms over time. Acquisitions are considered part of a parent firm from the year the acquisition transaction has been completed.

Patent data are taken from the European Patent Office (EPO). The technological performance of the sample firms (dependent variable) is measured as the number of EPO patent applications of a parent firm in a year, weighted by the number of forward patent citations received by those patents over a fixed time window of four years. The number of forward patent citations is calculated on a fixed time window because the number of forward citations to any patent depends on the length of the citation window (Hall et al., 2005; Trajtenberg, 1990). Forward patent citations are calculated on the EPO patent citation database described in Webb et al. (2005).

7.4   BASIC RESEARCH

We used information on scientific publications authored by the sample firms and published in peer reviewed international journals to assess firms' involvement in basic research. Publication data are extracted from yearly updates of the Science Citation Index database of ISI/Thomson Scientific; documents of the type article, letter, note and review have been selected. Publication data is collected at the consolidated parent firm level, following a similar approach to the one followed for the collection of patent data. This approach consists of identifying all publications on which the parent firms, or their subsidiaries, are listed as publishing institutes. The consolidation exercise is conducted annually. In line with studies of Hicks et al. (1994) and Cockburn and Henderson (1998) we find that pharmaceutical firms publish extensively; the sample firms published on average 263 publications per year in the SCI database over the period 1995–2002. We collected bibliographic information (journal name, volume, pages and so on) for all the publications in which the 33 sample firms are listed as one of the authors' institutions.

Publications are classified as 'basic research' based on the journal in which they are published and the journal classification scheme by CHI Research Inc. (Narin et al., 1976; Narin and Hamilton, 1996), which classifies each of the SCI journals in one of four research levels, in a spectrum ranging from very applied, targeted research to basic research. Journals that are classified in levels 3 and 4 are considered as reporting mainly on findings of basic research. About 74.5 per cent of SCI publications of the sample firms are published in basic research journals. The remaining 25.5 per cent of SCI publications report on applied research activities of the sample firms (for example clinical trials) and are not used in the construction of the internal basic research variables.

The basic research variable is constructed on the basis of a four-year moving time window. The basic research expertise of a firm in year t is measured as the sum of firm publications that are published in basic research journals in the past four years (t-4 to t-1) by subsidiaries that were part of the firm in year t. The variable is divided by the size of the firm's R&D expenditures in year t-1 to make it independent of the scale of firms' R&D activities, in line with prior empirical work.

7.5   CONTROL VARIABLES

Our empirical models control for various firm-level factors that are likely to impact directly on firms' technological performance, and which may be correlated with firms' involvement in basic research, and therefore bias the empirical results on basic research if not controlled for in the regression models. First, we control for differences in the scale of the firms' R&D expenditures, taking a one-year time lag between R&D expenditures and firm patents. The data on firms' R&D expenditures is collected from corporate annual financial reports (Worldscope and Compustat databases) and is measured in millions of US dollars. Second, we control for differences in the prior patent productivity of firms, measured as the one-year lagged ratio of the number of firm patents to R&D expenditures. Third, we include an indicator for the level of technology diversification in a firm's patent portfolio such that both scale and scope of R&D activities of firms are controlled for in the regression models

(Arora et al., 2009, Henderson and Cockburn, 1996; Nesta and Saviotti, 2005; Leten et al., 2007). Technology diversification is measured as the 'spread' of patents in a firm's four-year patent portfolio over technology classes. Technology class information on patents is derived from the International Patent Classification (IPC) classes assigned to patents. We distinguished between 120 different 3-digit IPC classes. The technology diversification variable is the inverse of the so-called Herfindahl index: it takes higher values when the level of technology diversification increases. Both linear and quadratic terms of technology diversification are included in the regression model to test for the existence of an inverted U-shape relationship between technology diversification and firm technological performance (for example Henderson and Cockburn, 1996; Leten et al., 2007). Finally, the empirical models include time dummies (1995 as base category) to account for time-specific factors affecting the technological performance (forward citation-weighted patent numbers) of the sample firms.

7.6   METHODS

The dependent variable (citation-weighted patent count) is a count variable with only non-negative integer values. In this case, non-linear count data models are preferred to standard linear regression models as they explicitly take into account the non-negativity and discreteness of the dependent variable. Negative Binomial count data models, which control for over-dispersion in the dependent variable, are used (Cameron and Trivedi, 1998). We have used fixed effects panel data estimators in all regression models to control for unobserved (time-invariant) firm characteristics, such as R&D management capabilities that could affect technological performance. Besides including fixed effects, our empirical specification has other features that alleviate concerns of potential endogeneity and biases stemming from unobserved factors. First, the temporal ordering of the variables in the model – where past publication activity explains current performance – avoids reverse causality where higher technological performance and the ensuing higher availability of R&D resources may lead to more in-house scientific research. Second, we include several key time-varying firm characteristics as control variables (R&D expenses, patent intensity, and technology diversification) that are likely to pick up time variant firm traits such as developments in corporate R&D resources and capabilities.

Table 7.1   Descriptive statistics

N = 247	Mean	St. Dev.	Min	Max
Citation Weighted Patent Count	136.37	154.13	1.00	651.00
R&D Expenses (million $)	864.95	946.29	21.71	5176.00
Patent Intensity (patents per million $ R&D)	0.17	0.17	0.02	1.04
Technology Diversification (inverse Herfindahl index of IPC-classes in 4-year patent portfolio)	3.36	0.94	1.70	5.69
Basic Scientific Research	1.09	0.77	0.00	5.42

Table 7.2   Correlation coefficients

N = 247	1	2	3	4	5	6
1 Citation Weighted Patent Count	1.00					
2 Log (R&D Expenses)	0.62	1.00				
3 Patent Intensity	0.11	−0.45	1.00			
4 Technology Diversification	0.10	−0.08	0.47	1.00		
5 Technology Diversification^2	0.08	−0.10	0.48	0.99	1.00	
6 Basic Scientific Research	−0.17	−0.36	0.37	0.36	0.36	1.00

7.7   SUMMARY STATISTICS

Summary statistics of the dependent and explanatory variables can be found in Table 7.1. Note that there is substantial variation between the sample firms in the basic research variable, with the maximum several times larger than the minimum and mean values.

Table 7.2 reports the coefficients of correlation between the variables of interest. As to be expected, the correlation between technology diversification and its squared term is considerable; none of the other reported correlations is excessively high.

7.8   EMPIRICAL RESULTS

The empirical results of the fixed effects Negative Binomial regression models of the relationship between basic research and the technological performance of firms are reported in Table 7.2. Model 1 includes only the

Table 7.3 Fixed-effect Negative Binomial regression of the effect of basic scientific research on firms' technological performance

	Model 1	Model 2	Model 3
Log (R&D expenses)	0.21**	0.28***	0.28**
	(0.10)	(0.11)	(0.12)
Patent intensity	0.93**	0.65	0.64
	(0.37)	(0.42)	(0.41)
Technology Diversification	0.63*	0.60*	0.55*
	(0.33)	(0.33)	(0.33)
Technology Diversification^2	−0.06	−0.06	−0.06
	(0.04)	(0.04)	(0.04)
Basic scientific research		0.15*	
		(0.08)	
10th perc. ≤ scientific research			0.42**
< 20th perc.[a]			(0.17)
20th perc. ≤ scientific research			0.52***
< 30th perc.			(0.17)
30th perc. ≤ scientific research			0.43**
< 40th perc.			(0.18)
40th perc. ≤ scientific research			0.54***
< 50th perc.			(0.18)
50th perc. ≤ scientific research			0.68***
< 60th perc.			(0.19)
60th perc. ≤ scientific research			0.70***
< 70th perc.			(0.20)
70th perc. ≤ scientific research			0.68***
< 80th perc.			(0.21)
80th perc. ≤ scientific research			0.79***
< 90th perc.			(0.23)
90th perc. ≤ scientific research			0.86***
			(0.24)
Intercept	−2.22	−3.26**	−3.37*
	(1.48)	(1.63)	(1.78)
Time dummies	*included*	*included*	*included*
Number of observations	247	247	247
Number of firms	33	33	33
Wald Chi^2	96.38***	104.08***	118.49***
Log Likelihood	−981.33	−979.61	−972.42

Notes:
a. The base category is scientific research < 10th perc.
Significance of coefficients is indicated by *(0.1), **(0.05) and ***(0.01).
Standard errors are reported in parentheses. All models include firm-level fixed effects.

control variables and acts as a point of comparison for the other models. The R&D expenditures and patent intensity variables have the expected positive signs and are both statistically significant. Technology diversification has a positive, and significant, linear term, and a negative, but insignificant, quadratic term, indicative of a positive linear effect of diversification on firm performance.

Model 2 adds the basic research variable to the set of controls. This allows for checking whether basic research has a linear effect on technological performance. The basic research variable is positive and significant, showing that firms can increase their technological performance by performing more basic research. Note that the coefficient has the interpretation of a semi-elasticity, which informs us about the (average) magnitude of the effect of basic research on technological performance. In particular, an increase of 1 unit for the basic research variable (measured by the number of basic research publications per million US dollars in R&D) increases technological performance by 15 per cent.

In model 3, we examine the basic research–technological performance relationship more in detail by modeling the impact of basic research on firm performance via a more flexible functional form. We relax the assumption that basic research has a linear effect,[7] and use a dummy variable approach to examine the magnitude of the effect of basic research for different levels of involvement in basic research. More specifically, we replace the basic research variable by 10 dummy variables, each dummy corresponding to a particular 'decile' of values of the basic research variable for the sample firms. Table 7.4 shows the lower and upper bound values of each of the 10 dummy variables.[8] The first dummy takes the value 1 for observations with values for basic research lower than 0.4 (10th percentile of sample values). This variable functions as the base category and is not included in the estimations; the effect is incorporated in the estimation for the intercept. The second dummy takes the value 1 for observations that have basic research values between 0.4 and 0.5, corresponding to values between percentiles 10 and 20 of the sample, and so on.

A log-likelihood ratio test ($Chi^2 = 14.39$; p-value = 0.07) shows that the explanatory power of model 3 is significantly higher than model 2, implying that the impact of basic research on technological performance can be modeled more accurately via the dummy specification in model 3. The coefficients of the dummy variables for basic research are all positive and significant. This indicates that the technological performance of firms with the lowest levels of in-house basic research (that is firms with a basic research intensity not higher than the 10th percentile, the base category) is significantly lower than the performance of the other firms. There are two more interesting things to note from the coefficients of the dummy

Table 7.4   Descriptive statistics for firms' basic scientific research

Statistic	Value	Category[a]	Number of firms[b]
0th perc.	0.0	basic scientific research <10th perc.	6
10th perc.	0.4	10th perc. ≤ basic scientific research < 20th perc.	9
20th perc.	0.5	20th perc. ≤ basic scientific research < 30th perc.	14
30th perc.	0.7	30th perc. ≤ basic scientific research < 40th perc.	12
40th perc.	0.8	40th perc. ≤ basic scientific research < 50th perc.	14
50th perc.	0.9	50th perc. ≤ basic scientific research < 60th perc.	12
60th perc.	1.1	60th perc. ≤ basic scientific research < 70th perc.	13
70th perc.	1.3	70th perc. ≤ basic scientific research < 80th perc.	15
80th perc.	1.6	80th perc. ≤ basic scientific research < 90th perc.	10
90th perc.	2.1	90th perc. ≤ basic scientific research	7
Mean	1.1	All categories	33

Notes:
a.   Basic scientific research is measured in the same way as it is included in the empirical model.
b.   I.e. the number of firms that belong to the category in at least one year.

variables. First, the magnitude of the coefficients increases when going from low to high levels of basic research. We have performed pair-wise Wald tests to test whether differences in the size of coefficients are statistically significant. These tests indicate that the coefficient for the top dummy category (percentile 90 to 100) is significantly different, not only from the base category, but also from several other dummy categories, up to the median value of basic research (percentile 40 to 50). Second, the 'marginal change' from one to another dummy category (change in coefficients of subsequent dummies) is by far the largest between the base category (percentile 0 to 10) and the second category (percentile 10 to 20), measured by the coefficient size of dummy 1 (0.42). The average marginal change between dummies 1 and 9 is only 0.05. Both models do agree that technological performance is a monotonically increasing function of basic research intensity.

Figure 7.1 visualizes our research findings. It depicts mean predicted citation-weighted patents (on the vertical axis) for different values of basic research (on the horizontal axis) and two models (2 and 3). While the graphs for both models indicate a positive effect of basic research on technological performance, it is clear that the dummy specification allows for a better estimation of the relationship under study. Most noticeable, the graph of model 3 shows that the largest relative gains of basic research are

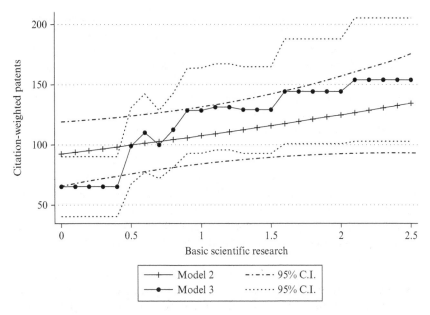

Figure 7.1   Predicted technological performance as a function of basic scientific research

found when firms move from low (including no investments) to moderate levels of basic research.

7.9 CONCLUSIONS

This study examined the effects of basic research on the technological performance of pharmaceutical firms. Our study extends prior empirical work on this topic in two important respects. First, we use a more accurate indicator of firms' involvement in basic research by constructing this indicator on the subset of firm publications that appeared in journals that report basic scientific research findings. Second, we examine the nature of the basic research–technological performance relationship more in detail by using a more flexible functional form to estimate the impact of basic research on performance. We relax the assumption that basic research has a linear effect, and use a dummy variable approach to examine the effect of basic research for different levels of involvement in basic research.

Our analysis draws on a unique panel dataset (1995–2002) on the R&D,

patent and publication activities of 33 large US, European and Japanese pharmaceutical firms. Fixed-effects panel data analyses show that pharmaceutical firms can increase their technological performance by conducting more basic research and that the magnitude of this effect is substantial. Technological performance is a monotonically increasing function of basic research intensity (measured by the number of basic research publications per million US dollars invested in R&D), with the largest marginal gains present at lower levels of basic research (including cases of no investments in basic research). This finding suggest that the benefits of basic research, such as the creation of absorptive capacity to recognize and utilize the fruits of external basic science and improved search heuristics for applied research, may not require relatively large investments in basic research to materialize. After the large initial gains from getting involved in basic research, technological performance is further enhanced if involvement in basic research intensifies, but the marginal effects of greater involvement are smaller.

Our analysis has a number of limitations, which suggest interesting avenues for future research. First, we focused our analysis on large firms in the pharmaceutical industry, and one should be careful when generalizing our findings to firms in other sectors. The industry we analyzed is exceptional with respect to the relevance of basic scientific research for technology activities (McMillan et al., 2000; Rosenberg, 1990) and appropriability conditions due to a high efficacy of patenting (Lim, 2004). However, we conjecture that our results may hold for other industries where basic research plays an important role in technology development, such as semiconductors and electronics (Pavitt, 1984; Klevorick et al., 1995). Second, further research should investigate in more detail the conditions for successfully translating basic research into technological performance. Under which circumstances does involvement in basic scientific research have the most pronounced effect? For example, collaboration with public research organizations and universities may attenuate the finding that firms that do less basic research benefit less in terms of technological performance since such collaborations may allow for more substantial knowledge flows compared with basic research performed in-house by the firm independently. In general, a more complete analysis would not only include the basic activities performed inside the firm but would also take into account to what extent firms draw on externally conducted basic research in universities and public research institutes in their innovation processes. While recent research has examined some performance consequences of drawing on external basic research (measured by references to scientific literature in firms' patent applications, for example Fabrizio, 2009), the roles of internal and external sources of basic scientific knowledge have not been analyzed jointly nor is it understood to what extent they may complement each other.

NOTES

1. Mansfield (1980) and Griliches (1986) examined the impact of in-house basic research on the economic performance of firms, and found a positive effect of basic research on total factor productivity.
2. The study of Lim (2004) is a notable exception. While he measures basic research via publications in basic research journals, his analysis of the relationship between basic research and firms' technological performance does not control for differences in firms' R&D inputs, which may partly explain heterogeneity in empirical results.
3. An elaborate overview of the empirical literature that studied the economic benefits from basic scientific research can be found in the overview article of Salter and Martin (2001).
4. Based on the idea that a private enterprise economy does not provide sufficient incentives for firms to invest in basic science, and to avoid a loss in social welfare from under-investing in basic science, governments in most developed countries invest in basic science at universities and public research institutes (Pavitt, 1991).
5. Fleming and Sorenson (2004) label this as the 'map' function of scientific knowledge.
6. The majority of inventions in the pharmaceutical industry are patented (Arundel and Kabla, 1998; Campbell, 2005) and firm-specific patent application policies are likely to be relatively stable over time.
7. More specifically, we change the specification of the linear predictor $X'_{it}\beta$. Note that for both the linear and the dummy specification, the *marginal effect* on the dependent variable is non-linear due to the exponential function in the negative binomial model: $E(Y_{it}) = e^{X'_{it}\beta}$. We compare the predictions of the conditional mean of the dependent variable for both models in Figure 7.1.
8. The table also lists, for each of the 10 categories, the number of sample firms that have a minimum of one observation (firm/year level) in that category. Most categories contain observations for 10 to 15 firms. Since our sample consists of 33 firms, these numbers indicate that many firms 'change' categories over time, which is important as we employ fixed-effects (that is, within-firm) estimators in our regressions.

REFERENCES

Adams, J.D. (1990), 'Fundamental stocks of knowledge and productivity growth', *Journal of Political Economy*, **98**, 673–702.

Arora, A., A. Gambardella, L. Magazinni and F. Pammili (2009), 'A breath of fresh air? Firm type, scale, scope and selection effects in drug development', *Management Science*, **55**(10), 1638–53.

Arundel, A. and I. Kabla (1998), 'What percentage of innovations are patented? Empirical estimates from European firms', *Research Policy*, **27**, 127–41.

Arrow, K. (1962), 'Economic welfare and the allocation of resources for invention', in R. Nelson (ed.), *The Rate and Direction of Inventive Activity*, Princeton, NJ: Princeton University Press.

Basberg, B. (1987), 'Patents and the measurement of technological change: a survey of the literature', *Research Policy*, **16**, 131–41.

Cameron, A. and P. Trivedi (1998), *Regression Analysis of Count Data*, Cambridge: Cambridge University Press.

Campbell, J.J. (2005), *Understanding Pharma. A Primer on How Pharmaceutical Companies Really Work*, Raleigh, NC: Pharmaceutical Institute, Inc.

Chesbrough, H. (2003), *Open Innovation: the New Imperative for Creating and Profiting from Technology*, Boston, MA: Harvard Business School Press.

Cockburn, I. and R. Henderson (1998), 'Absorptive capacity, coauthoring behavior, and the organization of research in drug discovery', *The Journal of Industrial Economics*, **46**(2), 157–82.

Cohen, W. and D. Levinthal (1990), 'Absorptive capacity: a new perspective on learning and innovation', *Administrative Science Quarterly*, **35**, 128–52.

Czarnitzki, D., K. Hussinger and B. Leten (2010), 'Market value and heterogeneity of patent citations', paper presented at the Pacific Rim Innovation Conference, Melbourne, January.

Fabrizio, K.R. (2009), 'Absorptive capacity and the search for innovation', *Research Policy*, **38**(2), 255–67.

Fleming, L. (2001), 'Recombinant uncertainty in technological search', *Management Science*, **47**, 117–32.

Fleming, L. and O. Sorenson (2004), 'Science as a map in technological search', *Strategic Management Journal*, **25**, 909–28.

Gambardella, A. (1992), 'Competitive advantages from in-house scientific research: the US pharmaceutical industry in the 1980s', *Research Policy*, **21**, 391–407.

Gambardella, A., D. Harhoff and B. Verspagen (2008), 'The value of European patents', *European Management Review*, **5**(2), 69–84.

Griliches, Z. (1986), 'Productivity, R&D and basic research at the firm level in the 1970s', *The American Economic Review*, **76**(1), 141–54.

Griliches, Z. (1990), 'Patent statistics as economic indicators – a survey', *Journal of Economic Literature*, **28**(4), 1661–707.

Hall, B., A. Jaffe and M. Trajtenberg (2005), 'Market value and patent citations', *Rand Journal of Economics*, **36**(1), 16–38.

Harhoff, D., F. Narin, F. Scherer and K. Vopel (1999), 'Citation frequency and the value of patented inventions', *Review of Economics and Statistics*, **81**(3), 511–15.

Hargadon, A. and R. Sutton (1997), 'Technology brokering and innovation in a product development firm', *Administrative Science Quarterly*, **42**, 716–49.

Henderson, R. and I. Cockburn (1996), 'Scale, scope and spillovers: the determinants of research productivity in drug discovery', *Rand Journal of Economics*, **27**(1), 32–59.

Hicks, D., T. Ishizuka, P. Keen and S. Sweet (1994), 'Japanese corporations, scientific research and globalization', *Research Policy*, **23**, 375–84.

Klevorick, A.K., R. Levin, R. Nelson and S. Winter (1995), 'On the sources and significance of inter-industry differences in technological opportunities', *Research Policy*, **24**, 185–205.

Leten, B., R. Belderbos and B. Van Looy (2007), 'Technological diversification, coherence and performance of firms', *The Journal of Product Innovation Management*, **24**(6), 567–79.

Leten, et al. (2010), 'Entry and performance in new technology domains: relatedness, opportunities and competition', MSI Working Paper, KU Leuven, Belgium.

Lim, K. (2004), 'The relationship between research and innovation in the semi-conductor and pharmaceutical industries (1981–1997)', *Research Policy*, **33**, 287–321.

McMillan, G.S., F. Narin and D.L. Deeds (2000), 'An analysis of the critical role of public science in innovation: the case of biotechnology', *Research Policy*, **29**, 1–8.

Mansfield, E. (1980), 'Basic research and productivity increase in manufacturing', *The American Economic Review*, **70**(5), 863–73.

Mansfield, E. (1995), 'Academic research underlying industrial innovations: sources, characteristics and findings', *The Review of Economics and Statistics*, **77**, 55–65.

Mansfield, E. (1998), 'Academic research and industrial innovation: an update of empirical findings', *Research Policy*, **26**, 773–76.

Narin, F., G. Pinski and H.H. Gee (1976), 'Structure of the biomedical literature', *Journal of the American Society for Information Science*, **27**, 25–45.

Narin, F. and K. Hamilton (1996), 'Bibliometric performance measures', *Scientometrics*, **36**, 293–310.

Narin, F. and D. Olivastro (1992), 'Status report – linkage between technology and science', *Research Policy*, **21**(3), 237–49.

Narin, F., K. Hamilton and D. Olivastro (1997), 'The increasing linkage between US technology and public science', *Research Policy*, **26**, 317–30.

National Science Foundation (NSF) (2009), 'Business R&D innovation survey'.

Nelson, R. (1959), 'The simple economics of basic scientific research', *The Journal of Political Economy*, **67**(3), 297–306.

Nelson, R. (1962), 'The link between science and invention: the case of the transistor', in R. Nelson (ed.), *The Rate and Direction of Inventive Activity*, Princeton, NJ: Princeton University Press.

Nelson, R. and S. Winter (1982), *An Evolutionary Theory of Economic Change*, Cambridge, MA and London: Harvard University Press.

Nesta, L. and P. Saviotti (2005), 'Coherence of the knowledge base and the firms' innovative performance: evidence from the US pharmaceutical industry', *The Journal of Industrial Economics*, **53**(1), 123–42.

Pavitt, K. (1984), 'Sectoral patterns of technical change – Towards a taxonomy and theory', *Research Policy*, **13**(6), 343–73.

Pavitt, K. (1985), 'Patent statistics as indicators of innovative activity: possibilities and problems', *Scientometrics*, **7**(1), 77–99.

Pavitt, K. (1991), 'What makes basic research economically useful?', *Research Policy*, **20**, 109–19.

Pisano, G. (1997), *The Development Factory*, Boston, MA: Harvard Business School Press.

Rosenberg, N. (1990), 'Why do firms do basic research (with their own money)?', *Research Policy*, **19**(2), 165–74.

Salter, A. and B. Martin (2001), 'The economic benefits of publicly funded research: a critical review', *Research Policy*, **30**, 509–32.

Schumpeter, J.A. (1934), *Business Cycles*, New York: McGraw-Hill Book Company.

Trajtenberg, M. (1990), 'A penny for your quotes: patent citation and the value of innovation', *Rand Journal of Economics*, **21**, 172–87.

Webb, C., H. Dernis, D. Harhoff and K. Hoisl (2005), 'Analyzing European and international patent citations: a set of EPO patent database building blocks', OECD Science, Technology and Industry Working Papers, 2005/9, OECD Publishing.

8. FDI motives and host country productivity effects of US MNEs

John Cantwell and Roger Smeets

8.1 INTRODUCTION

The cumulative ambiguity in empirical results regarding the productivity-enhancing effects of inward Foreign Direct Investment (FDI) or *spillovers* has led scholars to start investigating such effects in more detail (Smeets, 2008). Some studies try to disentangle the knowledge diffusion channels through which such effects allegedly take place (Javorcik, 2004; Görg and Strobl, 2005), while others have considered the moderating role of factors such as the absorptive capacity of local firms (Girma, 2005; Girma and Görg, 2007) or the geography of inter-firm patterns of location (Barrios et al., 2006; Nicolini and Resmini, 2007).

A more recent stream of literature has approached the issue by acknowledging the fact that multinationals (MNEs) and their foreign subsidiaries are not homogeneous, and as such may generate different (productivity) effects on host-country firms (Feinberg and Keane, 2005). In this vein, some authors have investigated the influence of differences in MNE ownership structures (Javorcik and Spatareanu, 2008), parent nationality (Buckley et al., 2007a and 2007b) and market orientation (Girma et al., 2008; Smeets and Wei, 2010).

One form of MNE heterogeneity that has to date received much less attention in the FDI spillover literature is that of heterogeneity in investment motives, and in particular the distinction between *technology seeking (TS) FDI* vis-à-vis *technology exploiting (TE) FDI*.[1] Various scholars have examined, *inter alia*, the characteristics of companies involved in these two types of FDI (Kuemmerle, 1999; Le Bas and Sierra, 2002; Cantwell and Mudambi, 2005; Berry, 2006) and the regional characteristics that attract these different FDI types (Cantwell and Piscitello, 2005; 2007). These studies find persistent differences between the two types of FDI, which suggests that their effects on their host-country environment may also differ.

Contrary to some recent contributions by Girma (2005) and Driffield and Love (2007), our main claim in this chapter is that TS FDI will generate positive productivity effects in the host country, and that the existence of these effects will be at least as or even more likely as those of TE FDI. We support this claim by three arguments which can be discerned in the literature. These arguments relate to the R&D intensity of TS FDI, the characteristics of firms that engage in either FDI type, and the general nature of knowledge diffusion.

We then empirically test the relationship between TS and TE FDI on the one hand, and productivity effects on the other, using a new industry-level dataset of the foreign activities of US MNEs in 15 OECD countries over the period 1987–2003. Our results are supportive of the expectation that TS FDI is highly conducive to positive productivity effects in the host country, and moreover, that these effects arise more generally than those from TE FDI.

The rest of the chapter is structured as follows: in the subsequent section we will review the literature on FDI motives, and spell out the three arguments that support our claim regarding the positive productivity effects of TS FDI. Section 3 presents the data and the empirical methodology that we employ in this chapter, and section 4 reports and discusses the empirical results. Section 5 concludes.

8.2 THEORY

8.2.1 FDI Motives and Productivity Effects

The traditional literature of the MNE either implicitly or explicitly refers to the TE motive of Foreign Direct Investment (Hymer, 1960; Dunning, 1977). That is, in order to overcome its *liability of foreignness*, a MNE and its subsidiary have to possess some firm-specific competitive advantage in order to be able to compete with local (foreign) firms. This firm-specific advantage (Rugman, 1981) or nationality of ownership advantage (Dunning, 1958) has often been associated with a technological competence or asset (Markusen, 2002) that is capable of being transferred and thus exploited in other suitably advantaged locations.

Yet in more recent years, a complementary motive for FDI has been increasingly recognized, in which a MNE is argued to benefit from the international scope of its activities by seeking or sourcing technology-based assets from its foreign-located counterparts. The articulation within the firm of this MNE motive or strategy may be the initially unplanned outcome of the evolution over time of selected subsidiaries (Birkinshaw and Hood, 1998) that, as they have matured, have become increasingly capable of local initiatives, entrepreneurship and new business network creation (Birkinshaw, 1997; Forsgren et al., 2005). This locally competence creating type of FDI has sometimes been termed TS or asset-augmenting FDI (Dunning and Narula, 1995; Kuemmerle, 1999; Le Bas and Sierra, 2002).

Inspired by the recent trend to examine more closely the interaction between MNE heterogeneity of motives and host-country locational characteristics, Girma (2005) and Driffield and Love (2007) study the extent to which these differing FDI motives generate different productivity effects in the UK. In both these studies, the distinction between TE and seeking FDI is based, *inter alia*, on relative R&D intensities (RDIs) between the home and the host country.[2] It is argued that since FDI with a TS motive is aimed at seeking or sourcing technology in the host country in fields in which the MNE is lacking, it can reasonably be expected that the RDI of the home country industry of the MNE is lower than that of the host country industry, assuming that MNEs are at least on average representative of the areas from which they originate. Hence, if the ratio of home country RDI over host country RDI is less than 1, FDI is defined to be of a TS type. If it is greater than 1, it is termed TE FDI.

Since TS FDI (by definition or assumption) originates in terms of its country of ownership from less R&D-intensive industries when compared to the equivalent industries in the host locations in which it is sited, it is hypothesized that TS FDI will not induce any knowledge diffusion to local actors in the host country. The reverse holds for TE FDI, which is thus expected to induce positive knowledge diffusion, given the relative home country technological advantage. Both Girma (2005) and Driffield and Love (2007) find broad support for these hypothesized effects.[3]

In the remainder of this section we will question the basic premise behind this argument, that is that TS FDI is characterized as that which runs between industries with home–host RDI ratios smaller than 1. In fact, we will argue that considering differences in relative RDIs is not a suitable method to distinguish between TS and TE FDI motives. Our line of reasoning follows three alternative strands of thinking on this issue: the (expected) R&D intensity of TS FDI; the general firm characteristics of TS firms; and the reciprocal nature of knowledge diffusion. We then formulate two hypotheses regarding the productivity effects of TE and TS FDI.

8.2.2 Subsidiary Mandates and R&D Responsibilities

A recent and increasing body of microeconomic literature has investigated the relationship between subsidiary mandates (which may include either or both TE or seeking roles) and the corresponding R&D assignments or responsibilities that are likely to be received by the subsidiaries in question. Although such studies do not directly address the question of the productivity effects generated by MNE subsidiaries, they do shed some light on the extent and nature of R&D responsibilities of TS affiliates.

Feinberg and Gupta (2004) investigate the determinants of R&D assignments by MNEs to their foreign subsidiaries, distinguishing between external (to the firm) and internal determinants of this decision. Among other factors, they argue and show that the extent to which the external host country environment provides knowledge spillover opportunities is positively related to the extent of R&D responsibilities assigned to subsidiaries in the host country. The argument here is that increased R&D at the subsidiary level allows the subsidiary to better absorb the external knowledge (Cohen and Levinthal, 1989; Minbaeva et al., 2003). It also implies that subsidiaries with a TS mandate are more effective at acting on this mandate if they receive significant R&D responsibilities from the parent.

Cantwell and Mudambi (2005) investigate the relationship between the R&D responsibilities assigned to foreign subsidiaries, and the output mandates that such subsidiaries have received from their parents. In their sample of UK subsidiaries of non-UK MNEs, one thing that clearly stands out is the substantially larger RDI of subsidiaries with a competence creating mandate (CC), versus those with a competence exploiting (CE) mandate.[4] It should be noted that in their study a CC mandate refers to local subsidiary responsibilities for product development and international strategy development within their MNE group, and so it is measured independently of the R&D activities of a subsidiary.[5] Moreover, their empirical tests also demonstrate that in addition to the observed quantitative difference in RDI between subsidiary types, there is also a qualitative difference in the motives for and hence in the nature of R&D undertaken. In particular, R&D assignments to CE subsidiaries are more sensitive to local demand conditions, whereas those of CC subsidiaries respond more to the level of regional development, resources, infrastructure and science base in the host location, a result which is further corroborated in Cantwell and Piscitello (2005; 2007).

Marin and Bell (2006) study the productivity effects of foreign subsidiaries located in Argentina in the period 1992–96. To examine these effects, they propose *inter alia* an 'active subsidiary model', in which knowledge spillovers to domestic firms arise only if subsidiaries are technologically active. Their empirical results provide strong support for this model, implying that knowledge spillovers from foreign subsidiaries mainly arise as a result of their own local competence-creating and TS activities.

Furthermore, a recent study by Phene and Almeida (2008) on foreign subsidiaries of US MNEs in the semiconductor industry adds to this result, as these authors demonstrate that subsidiaries with higher technology sourcing capabilities also engage in larger-scale innovative efforts. In addition, their study finds consistent evidence of the importance of knowledge obtained from host country firms in stimulating subsidiary innovation. This would actually suggest a positive feedback effect, whereby TS subsidiaries obtain more R&D responsibilities; as a result they are able to source more knowledge from host country firms, and in turn they become even more innovative.

What all these studies clearly demonstrate is that the RDI of foreign subsidiaries with a TS (or competence-creating) mandate is not at all obviously lower than that of the host country firms active in the sector in which the subsidiaries are operating. The study of Cantwell and Mudambi (2005) also demonstrates that in comparison with CE subsidiaries, CC subsidiaries have a clearly larger RDI. As a consequence, TS FDI is likely to generate positive productivity effects in its host-country environment. Additionally, given its greater RDI, such productivity effects are likely to be at least as large as, or even larger than those of TE FDI.

8.2.3 Firm Heterogeneity and TS FDI

A substantial amount of research has either implicitly or explicitly considered the nature or characteristics of the firms that engage in TS FDI. In particular, the question of whether high-productivity (leader) or low-productivity (laggard) firms engage in this type of FDI has featured prominently in this debate. Many of the earlier empirical industry-level studies have suggested that laggards are more likely to engage in TS FDI, as they stand to gain the most from it (Kogut and Chang, 1991; Hennart and Park, 1993; Neven and Siotis, 1996). This conclusion has also been formalized (Fosfuri and Motta, 1999; Siotis, 1999).

However, more recent microeconomic evidence suggests quite the contrary. Notably, in a study of Japanese investors in the United States, Berry (2006) convincingly demonstrates that leaders are more likely to engage in TS FDI, a result which is corroborated, *inter alia*, by Le Bas and Sierra (2002), Branstetter (2006) and Griffith et al. (2006). Berry (2006) explains this finding by arguing that unlike leaders, laggard firms have neither the absorptive capacity nor the intra-firm technology transfer skills necessary to benefit from TS FDI. Formalizing these arguments, Smeets and Bosker (2011) also demonstrate the likelihood of leaders engaging in TS FDI, and provide an empirical illustration of this.

The implication of these more recent and more detailed studies on firm heterogeneity and FDI motives is that leaders, and not laggards, are more likely to engage in TS FDI. Consequently, the implication is that in terms of spillover or diffusion potential, TS FDI can be expected to generate productivity spillover effects that are at least as large as those of TE FDI.

8.2.4   The Reciprocal Nature of Knowledge Diffusion

A third reason to expect that TS subsidiaries are as least as conducive to positive productivity effects as TE subsidiaries has to do with the alleged reciprocal nature of knowledge diffusion.

Already in 1989, Cantwell had argued that in order to benefit from knowledge feedbacks, MNEs' subsidiaries have to internalize foreign technology development, which implies that their own operations have to be firmly embedded in the host-country environment. This in turn will generate larger knowledge diffusion potential from the subsidiaries to the host-country firms. As such, two-way knowledge diffusion is essentially just part of the logic of MNE expansion (Cantwell, 1989).

Frost (2001) makes a similar argument which he also formulates from an embeddedness perspective. He argues that the norm of reciprocity requires sufficient contributory innovative capacity on behalf of firms which themselves wish to capture external knowledge. Specifically, he claims that 'subsidiaries with greater innovation scale may be more likely to access and utilize local sources of knowledge during the innovation process' (2001, p. 107). His empirical analysis of patent citations made by a sample of US-based subsidiaries of foreign MNEs during the period 1980–90 provides broad empirical support for this conjecture.

In a study of FDI in China, Wei et al. (2008) substantiate this finding. Utilizing a 3SLS model to simultaneously investigate the knowledge diffusion effect from FDI to the host economy and vice versa, they find very strong and robust evidence of mutual (i.e. two-way) knowledge diffusion effects. This result again implies that when successful in TS, subsidiaries are most likely to also diffuse some knowledge of their own. Similar findings are documented in Liu et al. (2006).

These findings provide a third argument as to why TS FDI may be at least as conducive to knowledge diffusion as TE FDI: it appears that in order for a subsidiary to benefit from knowledge spillovers generated by domestic firms – and as such perform its TS task – it also needs to contribute to its local environment in terms of knowledge diffusion itself.

8.2.5   Wrapping Up

Summarizing, based on previous literature we have developed three arguments to support our claim of positive productivity effects of TS FDI: the RDI of this type of FDI has been demonstrated to be substantial; recent microeconomic evidence indicates that high-productivity leader firms are more likely to engage in this type of FDI; and the demonstrated reciprocal nature of knowledge diffusion implies that TS FDI is only successful when it also contributes to the productivity of its local environment.

From a methodological point of view, most of the microeconomic studies discussed above do not base the distinction between TS and TE FDI on relative R&D intensities. For example Cantwell and Mudambi (2005) derive the competence-creating motive of subsidiaries both from their outward orientation and the extent of new product development, independent of the R&D efforts of the subsidiary. Even though such an approach might be more complicated at higher levels of aggregation, this suggests that distinguishing between TS and TE FDI should preferably go beyond the use of relative R&D intensities.

Also, we would like to note explicitly that we do not argue here that TE FDI does not generate productivity effects in the host country: since this type of FDI by definition exploits a competitive (technology) asset of the MNE, there is at least a potential for knowledge diffusion. Moreover, given that it will also be integrated in the local economy in terms of supplier and customer networks, there are also sufficient diffusion mechanisms present for this type of FDI (see Beugelsdijk et al., 2008). However, based on the foregoing we expect TS FDI to be at least as likely to generate productivity effects as is TE FDI.

Thus, we end up with the following two hypotheses that we will investigate empirically in the remainder of this chapter:

Hypothesis 1: TE FDI will have positive host country productivity effects.

Hypothesis 2: TS FDI will have positive host country productivity effects that are at least as likely as those of TE FDI.

8.3   DATA AND METHODOLOGY

8.3.1   Measuring FDI Motives

In the empirical part of this chapter we will illustrate our arguments using industry-level data of subsidiary activities of US MNEs in 15 OECD countries and eight industries over the period 1987–2003.[6] We use industry-level data from the Bureau of Economic Analysis (BEA) in order to measure the activities of foreign affiliates of US MNEs. The BEA provides data regarding the operations of foreign subsidiaries on, *inter alia,* the amount of their annual sales, their net fixed capital stocks, the number of persons employed, and the technology license receipts of subsidiaries.

As mentioned in the previous section, the distinction between TS and TE FDI should preferably go beyond the use of relative R&D intensities. Here we exploit the fact that, in our view, there are two important aspects to a TS strategy: first, the subsidiary receiving the TS mandate should be sufficiently integrated into the MNE's internal network in order to be able to transfer the acquired technology across the firm as a whole (Berry, 2006; Monteiro et al., 2008). Second, new (to the firm) knowledge or technology actually has to be acquired or generated by the foreign subsidiary in the host country.

In order to capture the first aspect on subsidiary intra-MNE integration, we exploit the fact that our dataset decomposes total foreign affiliate sales into local sales (i.e. destined for the host country), sales back to the US parent, and sales to third countries (other than the host or home country). Using this decomposition, we compute the following ratios:

$$\text{local FDI}_{ijt} = \frac{\text{local sales}_{ijt}}{\text{total sales}_{ijt}} \times FDI_{ijt}$$

$$\text{parent FDI}_{ijt} = \frac{\text{exports to US parent}_{ijt}}{\text{total sales}_{ijt}} \times FDI_{ijt}$$

$$\text{export FDI}_{ijt} = \frac{\text{exports to third countries}_{ijt}}{\text{total sales}_{ijt}} \times FDI_{ijt} \qquad (8.1)$$

where i, j and t index industry, country and time respectively. *FDI* is a measure of MNE presence. We will use fixed capital stocks as our main measure of MNE presence, but we will also test the sensitivity of our results using employment levels.

Following the reasoning above, we expect *parent FDI* to capture the first aspect of a TS strategy, as it measures the strength of subsidiary–parent linkages. Of course, the extent to which the focal subsidiary is integrated with other (third country) subsidiaries is also part of intra-MNE integration. However, the industry-level data do not allow us to decompose *export FDI* into intra-firm versus arm's length exports, so we cannot accurately measure these linkages. Still, we include *export FDI* in the analyses in order to gauge its productivity effects and consider the (dis)similarities to *parent FDI* and *local FDI*.

The second aspect of a TS strategy relates to the fact that subsidiaries that (successfully) pursue a TS strategy can be expected to contribute to the knowledge and technology stock of the firm as a whole. Utilizing

Table 8.1   FDI investment motives

	Positive technology license receipts	Zero technology license receipts
Parent FDI	TS FDI	Efficiency-seeking FDI
Local FDI	Competence-creating FDI	TE FDI

data on technology license receipts of foreign affiliates, we are able to capture this second aspect. These license receipts are paid to subsidiaries by third parties (among which the US parent) so that they can license technology acquired or generated by the subsidiary. Hence, it accurately captures the extent to which such subsidiaries have been able to acquire or generate new knowledge or technology. Specifically, if such receipts are positive, we take this as evidence that a subsidiary has engaged in some degree of TS activities. Together, these two aspects allow us to classify FDI subsidiary motives in a two-by-two matrix as shown in Table 8.1. In the upper-left corner, where sales are dominantly back to the US parent and technology license receipts are positive, the investment motive is one of TS. In the opposite bottom-right corner, sales are mainly local and no new technology is acquired. This corresponds to the traditional TE motive for FDI. The remaining two options are of less interest to our purposes, but we tentatively label them to enhance interpretation of the empirical results. In the upper-left corner, subsidiaries are firmly integrated into the intra-MNE network but do not acquire host-country technology. This resembles another traditional motive for FDI, which is efficiency or resource-seeking FDI (see Beugelsdijk et al., 2008). Finally, in the bottom-left corner, subsidiaries are locally (host-country) oriented but still acquire or generate new technology. We tentatively label this as resembling a competence-creating strategy, as this is usually associated with more autonomous subsidiaries (Cantwell and Mudambi, 2005).

8.3.2   Empirical Model

The model we wish to estimate takes the following form (with lower case letters denoting logs):

$$\omega_{ijt} = \beta_0 + \beta_1 \mathbf{FDI}_{ij,t-1} + \beta_2 \mathbf{X}_{ijt} + \eta_i + v_j + \upsilon_t + \varepsilon_{ijt} \qquad (8.2)$$

where i, j and t index country, industry and time respectively, ω is total factor productivity (TFP), **FDI** is a vector with the different types of FDI in (8.1) in period $t-1$ to take into account the lag between MNE activity and productivity effects, **X** is a vector of control variables, η, v and υ are fixed effects, and ε is an idiosyncratic error term. The parameters of interest are contained in the vector β_1 and measure the effect of the different types of FDI on industry productivity. We use two control variables in the vector X: (the log of) industry-level exports, measured in millions of US dollars and also taken from the STAN database (*Exports*), and (the log of) industry-level R&D stocks, computed from data on R&D expenditures (from the OECD ANBERD database – *R&D*) using the perpetual inventory method and imposing a generic annual depreciation rate of 15 per cent (Hall and Mairesse, 1995). Since industry-level exports also contain the exports of the US MNEs in our sample that we use in constructing the different FDI types, we net out those exports from the industry aggregate.

TFP (ω) estimates are derived as the residuals from log-linear Cobb-Douglas production functions that we estimate for each industry separately:

$$y_{ijt} = \gamma_{0j} + \gamma_{1j}l_{ijt} + \gamma_{2j}k_{ijt} + \omega_{ijt} \qquad (8.3)$$

where i, j and t index country, industry and time respectively, y is value-added, l is labor and k is capital. The data for y and k are obtained from the OECD STAN database, and the data on l from the Groningen Growth and Development Center (GGDC). Value-added and capital stocks are measured in millions of US dollars, and the latter are computed from data on capital expenditures using the perpetual inventory method and imposing a generic annual depreciation rate of 5 per cent (Hall and Mairesse, 1995). Employment is measured in thousands of total hours worked. We estimate (8.3) with Generalized Least Squares (GLS).[7] All variables have been deflated using industry-level GDP deflators. When appropriate, variables measured in foreign currencies have been transformed into US dollars using 1995 PPP exchange rates.

We follow Girma and Görg (2007) and assume that (the log of) *TFP* follows an AR(1) process with fixed effects (which are already included in model (8.2)):

$$\omega_{ijt} = \rho\omega_{ij,t-1} + \eta_i + v_j + \upsilon_t + \varepsilon_{ijt} \qquad (8.4)$$

so that combining this process with the model in equation (8.5) yields the following empirical model:

$$\omega_{ijt} = \beta_0 + \rho\omega_{ij,t-1} + \beta_1 FDI_{ij,t-1} + \beta_2 X_{ijt} + \eta_i + v_j + \upsilon_t + \varepsilon_{ijt} \quad (8.5)$$

This is the model that we will estimate.

As mentioned above, our sample covers 15 OECD host countries and

Table 8.2   Descriptive statistics and pairwise correlations

	1	2	3	4	5	6	7
1. TFP[a]	1.00						
2. Lagged TFP[a]	0.93	1.00					
3. R&D[a]	0.13	0.12	1.00				
4. Exports[a]	−0.01	−0.02	−0.62	1.00			
5. Local FDI[b]	−0.11	−0.08	−0.31	0.12	1.00		
6. Parent FDI[b]	0.23	−0.20	0.05	−0.09	0.00	1.00	
7. Export FDI[b]	0.10	0.06	−0.28	0.25	−0.43	−0.23	1.00
Mean	0.12	0.09	−8.15	9.26	3.58	0.54	2.18
s.d.	0.37	0.37	1.55	1.45	1.77	0.90	1.53

Notes:
a. Variables measured in logs.
b. One-period lagged values

Eight manufacturing industries over the period 1987–2003. However, the panel is very unbalanced due to missing observations for many countries. Moreover, data on technology license payments were only available from 1994 onward, so that those parts of the analyses using this variable use a limited sample. All variables have been deflated using industry-level GDP deflators.[8] When appropriate, variables measured in foreign currencies (in the case of OECD data) have been transformed into US dollars using PPP exchange rates. Table 8.2 presents some summary statistics and correlations for the variables in our model.

8.3.3   Estimation Strategy

In the empirical FDI knowledge diffusion literature, the potential endogeneity of FDI is a well-known problem: if foreign investors set up their subsidiaries in more productive countries, sectors or regions, any inferred productivity effects from FDI in model (8.5) will be spurious. Using lagged FDI variables could to some extent address this problem; however, this solution is less suited in situation where the series are persistent over time. Reverting to instrumental variable (IV) regression analysis would provide an alternative way out of this situation (Beugelsdijk et al., 2008), but such an approach is not straightforward in the present context: even though the gravity literature provides a number of potentially exogenous instruments for FDI (see Frankel and Romer, 1999), these mainly function at the country level rather than the industry level that we explore in this chapter.

Additionally, the lagged dependent variable $\omega_{ij,t-1}$ captures dynamic adjustments of sectoral productivity. To the extent that productivity depends on its past realizations (for example due to learning effects or business cycles), its inclusion is important to control for 'sluggish' adjustment of the productivity and to obtain unbiased coefficient estimates of the other explanatory variables (Baum, 2006). However, it again induces endogeneity since $\omega_{ij,t-1}$ is by definition correlated with the error term.

Under these circumstances, it is appropriate to revert to Generalized Method of Moments (GMM) estimation (Baum, 2006; Roodman, 2009). One specific estimator in this context is difference-GMM by Arrelano and Bond (1991) which transforms the model in (8.5) into first differences:

$$\Delta y_{ijt} = \hat{\rho}\Delta y_{ijt-1} + \hat{\beta}_1\Delta \mathbf{FDI}_{ijt-1} + \hat{\beta}_2\Delta \mathbf{X}_{ijt} + \Delta \upsilon_t + \Delta \varepsilon_{ijt} \qquad (8.6)$$

This removes the fixed effects in the error term, but it does not solve the endogeneity problem since $\omega_{ij,t-1}$ in $\Delta\omega_{ij,t-1}$ is now correlated with ε_{ijt-1} in $\Delta\varepsilon_{ijt}$. However, under the assumptions that the error term is not serially correlated and that explanatory variables are not correlated with *future* realizations of the error term, deeper lags of the explanatory variables are orthogonal to the error term, and hence may serve as proper instruments (see Carkovic and Levine, 2005). Thus the following moment conditions are used:

$$E(\omega_{i,t-s} \cdot (\varepsilon_{it} - \varepsilon_{i,t-1})) = 0 \ \text{s.t.} \ s \geq 2; t = 3,\ldots,T \qquad (8.7)$$

$$E(FDI_{i,t-s} \cdot (\varepsilon_{it} - \varepsilon_{i,t-1})) = 0 \ \text{s.t.} \ s \geq 2; t = 3,\ldots,T$$

To the extent that these explanatory variables are persistent over time or close to a random walk, lagged levels contain little information about future changes, and as such they will make for weak instruments (Carkovic and Levine, 2005; Roodman, 2009).

Blundell and Bond (1998) solve this problem by extending the outlined approach to also include the levels equation in model (8.5), and using lagged differences – that is, $\Delta\omega_{ij,t-1}$ and $\Delta FDI_{ij,t-s}$ – to instrument the endogenous variables y and *FDI*. These instruments are uncorrelated with the fixed effects in the error term, that is:

$$E((\omega_{ij,t-s} - \omega_{ij,t-s-1}) \cdot (\eta_i + v_j + \varepsilon_{ijt})) = 0 \ \text{s.t.} \ s \geq 1. \qquad (8.8)$$

$$E((FDI_{ij,t-s} - FDI_{ij,t-s-1}) \cdot (\eta_i + v_j + \varepsilon_{ijt})) = 0 \ \text{s.t.} \ s \geq 1.$$

For estimation purposes, the Blundell–Bond estimator builds a system of both models in (8.5) and (8.6) but treats them as a single equation. As such, this estimator is called the system-GMM estimator, and it is adopted here as it exploits more information in the data than the difference-GMM estimator alone.

Given the relatively limited amount of observations in our sample ($N = 559$ in the largest sample), we are forced to restrict the number of lags used in instrumentation to avoid over-fitting of the model (Roodman, 2009). Following Driffield and Love (2007), we first impose a maximum lag structure of four years.[9] However, further inspection indicates that the error term in model (8.6) is autocorrelated up to AR(4), which renders the first four lags of the instruments for the endogenous variables in model (8.6) invalid. Hence, in the analyses below, we use lags 5–8 to instrument the endogenous variables.

Moreover, we employ the one-step estimator: as shown by Madariaga and Poncet (2007), although the two-step estimator is more efficient, it is only appropriate in relatively large samples, otherwise it heavily biases the coefficient estimates. Finally, we utilize the small sample correction proposed by Roodman (2009), include time dummies in order to minimize the occurrence of contemporaneous (cross-section) correlation, and report robust standard errors.

8.4   EMPIRICAL RESULTS

8.4.1   Results

Table 8.3 presents the system-GGM estimation results of the system of the models in (8.5) and (8.6), with subsidiary activities split into *local FDI*, *parent FDI* and *export FDI* as defined in (8.1). The first three columns use fixed capital stocks as the measure of MNE presence in (8.1), whereas columns 4–6 use employment levels.

Column 1 of Table 8.3 presents the total sample results. The coefficient of lagged *TFP* is positive and significant, indicating positive feedback effects of productivity. *R&D stocks* are also positive and significant, as expected. *Exports* are positive but insignificant.

All three FDI types show up with a positive and significant coefficient. It is noteworthy that *local FDI* has a somewhat smaller estimated coefficient relative to *parent FDI* and *export FDI*. However, since we have not yet distinguished between activities with positive versus zero technology license receipts, these are essentially average effects that do not allow us to differentiate between the different FDI motives of Table 8.1.

We split up the sample according to the level of technology license receipts in columns 2 and 3. Column 2 shows the results for those activities with positive technology license receipts. Following Table 8.1, *parent*

Innovation and creativity

Table 8.3   Productivity effects of different FDI types

	Fixed capital stocks			Employment levels		
	(1) Total Sample	(2) Tech License Pay > 0	(3) Tech License Pay = 0	(4) Total Sample	(5) Tech License Pay > 0	(6) Tech License Pay = 0
Lag TFP[a]	0.918**	0.936**	0.910**	0.928**	0.961**	0.923**
	(0.025)	(0.029)	(0.025)	(0.031)	(0.025)	(0.027)
R&D Stock[a]	0.035**	0.010	0.019*	0.033**	0.005	0.018†
	(0.009)	(0.010)	(0.008)	(0.011)	(0.008)	(0.009)
Exports[a]	0.012	0.002	−0.000	0.022*	−0.004	−0.011
	(0.011)	(0.010)	(0.010)	(0.009)	(0.012)	(0.014)
Local FDI[b]	0.021*	0.008	0.013	0.010	−0.015	0.008
	(0.008)	(0.009)	(0.009)	(0.014)	(0.012)	(0.016)
Parent FDI[b]	0.028**	0.037**	0.088**	0.037**	0.033*	0.146†
	(0.007)	(0.008)	(0.033)	(0.013)	(0.015)	(0.081)
Export FDI[b]	0.032**	0.017	0.018*	0.036†	0.007	0.023
	(0.010)	(0.011)	(0.009)	(0.019)	(0.018)	(0.019)
Constant	0.256*	0.189†	0.332*	0.195*	0.200*	0.444**
	(0.114)	(0.104)	(0.128)	(0.092)	(0.096)	(0.134)
Time Dummies	Yes	Yes	Yes	Yes	Yes	Yes
F-stat	149.1**	376.3**	181.4**	107.2**	350.7**	340.5**
Hansen-test	49.9	19.9	24.1	47.6	26.7	17.9
AR(1)	−5.08**	−4.27**	−2.32**	−5.01**	−4.54**	−3.15**
AR(5)	−1.04	−2.16	0.41	−0.88	−2.25	−0.63
N	559	177	112	559	177	112

Notes:
Dependent variable is (Log) Total Factor Productivity (TFP). System GMM-estimates –
One step robust estimator, lags $>=5$ used for endogenous variables.
** 1% sig.; * 5% sig.; † 10% sig.
a.   Variables measured in logs.
b.   One-period lagged values.

FDI corresponds to TS FDI in column 2, whereas *local FDI* resembles CC FDI. As is clear from the table, only *parent FDI* shows up positive and significantly, implying that TS FDI generates positive productivity effects, contrary to CC FDI. *Export FDI* is also insignificant in this subsample.

Column 3 shows the results for the activities that did not receive any technology license receipts in the period of study. The results are partly similar to those in column 2. That is, *local FDI* is still insignificant while *parent FDI* is highly significant. What is more, *export FDI* is now also positive and significant. Following the classification in Table 8.1, this can be taken to imply that TE FDI has no discernible productivity effects, whereas efficiency-seeking FDI does. The interpretation that we should attach to the results of *export FDI* is unclear, due to the reasons mentioned above. On the one hand, to the extent that this variable captures inter-subsidiary linkages, it could be another proxy for efficiency-seeking FDI and thus reinforce the results of *parent FDI*. On the other hand, to the extent that it captures arm's length sales, it could be a proxy for TE FDI and thus provide evidence in favor of positive productivity effects of this FDI motive.[10]

Columns 4–6 in Table 8.3 repeat these regressions, now using foreign employment levels as the measure of MNE presence. The results of columns 1–3 are by and large replicated. *Parent FDI* consistently shows up with a positive and significant sign, indicating that both TS FDI (column 5) and efficiency-seeking FDI (column 6) generate positive productivity effects. *Local FDI* on the other hand is nowhere significant, implying that neither CC FDI (column 5) nor TE FDI (column 6) generate positive productivity effects. *Export FDI* also is no longer significant except for the total sample results in column 4.

Finally, the test statistics at the bottom of the table all demonstrate the existence of first-order autocorrelation – which is due to the inclusion of a lagged dependent variable – but from lag 5 onwards, the correlation in the error term disappears. This implies that our 5–8 period lagged instruments are indeed exogenous, which is confirmed by the Sargan–Hansen statistic, which is not significant.

8.4.2 Discussion

First and foremost, our results confirm our second hypothesis, which states that TS FDI generates positive productivity effects that are at least as likely to occur as those of TE FDI. Regardless of the measure of MNE presence that we use, *parent FDI* is significantly positive in the subsample with positive technology license receipts. Recalling the classification in Table 8.1, this combination of intra-MNE integration – captured by *parent FDI* – and technology acquisition or generation – captured by the positive technology license receipts – exactly captures the TS motive for FDI. Moreover, its effect always outweighs those of TE FDI (i.e. *local FDI* in columns 3 and 5) so that indeed its positive productivity effects are more likely to occur than those of TE FDI.

Our first hypothesis is not confirmed: when we use fixed capital stocks as the proxy for MNE presence we find no significant effects of *local FDI* in any of the subsamples. Again referring to Table 8.1, this indicates that neither CC FDI nor TE FDI yield positive productivity effects. This result arises regardless of whether we use fixed capital stocks or employment levels as the proxy for MNE presence.

Although we might disqualify our first hypothesis based on these results, we already indicated that the significant positive effects of *export FDI* in column 3 of Table 8.3 could also (partly) capture a TE motive. Yet for this type of FDI, the results are sensitive to changing the proxy for MNE presence between the first and last three columns of Table 8.3. Nonetheless, there might be a substantive explanation for these different results. In their meta-study of empirical FDI knowledge spillover studies, Görg and Strobl (2001) find that the measure of MNE presence used has an important effect on whether or not productivity effects are found. Wei and Liu (2006) and Wei et al. (2008) combine this finding with a theoretical argument: They relate different measures of MNE presence to different knowledge diffusion mechanisms. Specifically, measuring MNE presence through capital stocks (as in columns 1–3 in Table 8.3) will be a good proxy for diffusion through demonstration effects, whereas measuring it in terms of employment (as in columns 4–6 in Table 8.3) will generally be a proxy for diffusion through labor turnover. By extension, our results might be taken to indicate that TS FDI and efficiency FDI generate productivity effects through both these mechanisms, whereas *export FDI* only does so through demonstration effects. Still, we are reluctant to give the final verdict here regarding the interpretation of the results of *export FDI*, but instead take these as a stepping stone for future research.

8.5 CONCLUSION

In this chapter we have proposed that, contrary to recent empirical evidence, FDI motivated by a technology-seeking (TS) strategy is at least as likely to induce positive productivity effects in the host country as technology-exploiting (TE) FDI. We support this proposition by three arguments: first, a number of recent empirical microeconomic studies have demonstrated that the R&D and innovation intensity of MNE subsidiaries with a TS mandate is substantial, and even likely to outperform that of TE subsidiaries. Second, there is increasing theoretical and empirical evidence that productivity leaders rather than laggards engage in TS FDI, implying high knowledge spillover potential. Third, it has been demonstrated that productivity spillovers are most likely to be mutual, flowing not only from the MNE to domestic firms but also the other way around. This implies that to seek technology successfully, subsidiaries also have to be prepared to diffuse some of their own.

Based on these three arguments we hypothesize positive productivity effects of TS FDI, also arguing that they are more likely to occur than those of TE FDI. We test these propositions, using data on US MNEs' foreign activities in 15 OECD countries and eight industries over the period 1987–2003. In order to single out TS FDI (and TE FDI), we consider two important elements of such an investment motive: first, a subsidiary should be sufficiently integrated into the intra-MNE network. Second, the subsidiary should actually and successfully engage in knowledge or technology acquisition.

Overall, our empirical results provide quite consistent support for our hypothesis on TS FDI. Regardless of the MNE presence proxy used (fixed capital stocks or employment levels), we find consistent positive and significant productivity effects of TS FDI. Regarding TE FDI, we find no support for our hypothesis. Regardless of which MNE presence proxy we use, we find no significantly positive effects of TE FDI.

Our results have a number of implications for future theoretical and empirical work. This study demonstrates the importance of heterogeneity in FDI motives for the observed productivity effects. Even though earlier theoretical and conceptual work has invested substantial effort in characterizing the differences between TS and TE FDI as well as the differences in their determinants, this literature has not yet brought together these different insights in order to spell out clearly their consequences for the host country, for example in terms of productivity effects, and derive clear testable hypotheses for this. From a theoretical point of view, the game-theoretic literature on R&D decentralization decisions (Sanna-Randaccio and Veugelers, 2007) and FDI motives (Fosfuri and Motta, 1999; Siotis, 1999) provides useful building blocks to consider these issues in more formal detail.

Empirically, a clear limitation of the present study is its reliance on (rather aggregate) industry-level data, and the implication that we need proxies for FDI with TE and seeking motives, rather than more factual indicators (see Cantwell and Mudambi, 2005). We believe that there is a strong need for more empirical work using firm-level data and clearly distinguishing between investment motives. Given that many previous studies have already investigated many other aspects of these types of FDI at the firm level, as indicated above, this should be a manageable avenue of future research.

Another limitation is the fact that our sample of host countries is limited to OECD countries only. This is caused by the fact that detailed industry-level information on the dependent and explanatory (control) variables in our model are hard to come by for developing countries. However, it might be expected that the types of FDI differ substantially for developed versus developing countries. Including developing countries in the sample could substantially add to the variation in the FDI types and as such to the identification of the parameters in our model.

Finally, another factor that might be driving part of our results is the fact that for many observations, we do not have data on technology license receipts, which seriously reduces the sample sizes of the two subsamples in Table 8.3 above. Future research might try to come up with different ways of measuring the success of actual knowledge or technology acquisition which allows for a more general and broader analysis in a larger sample.

NOTES

1. Two recent exceptions are Girma (2005) and Driffield and Love (2007).
2. RDI is measured as R&D expenditures as a percentage of value-added (at the industry level).
3. The study by Driffield and Love (2007) also makes an additional distinction based on whether or not there is an efficiency-seeking motive for the FDI involved. Essentially, this efficiency-seeking motive is expected to depress any positive diffusion effects of FDI because of the negative competition effects (based on lower host-country labor costs) it generates.
4. Specifically, in their Table 4(b) (p. 1120) they show an RDI (measured as a subsidiary's R&D over sales ratio) of 5.1 per cent versus 2.9 per cent of competence-creating versus competence-exploiting subsidiaries respectively.
5. Strictly speaking, CC and TS FDI are not exactly identical. CC subsidiaries are usually considered to operate more independently than TS subsidiaries. Also see Table 8.1.
6. The Appendix contains a full list of countries and industries included in the analysis.
7. There is a large amount of microeconometric literature on the potential biases when estimating production functions like (8.3) without taking into account the possible correlation between inputs and productivity (Olley and Pakes, 1996; Levinsohn and Petrin, 2003). However, as noted by Bitzer et al. (2008), such problems do not arise at the industry level because output or value-added can be argued to be stochastic at this level of aggregation. In this case, OLS or GLS of (8.3) leads to consistent estimates.
8. Although Kafouros and Buckley (2008) argue and demonstrate that the use of common deflators is not appropriate when dealing with R&D expenditures, we are not aware of more specific deflators for these countries and sectors on the scale used in our sample. As such, we use GDP deflators for R&D as well.
9. Additionally, because our panel exhibits some gaps, instead of transforming the data using first differences we follow Roodman (2009) and use orthogonal deviations. This entails substracting the time-averaged value of all foregoing realizations of a variable instead of just its previous (one-period) observation (see Roodman, 2009: p. 20). This also implies that the AR tests reported in Table 8.3 are run on differenced residuals.
10. More generally, this variable might capture so-called export platform FDI (see Ekholm et al., 2007; Smeets and Wei, 2010) which can be argued to be an alternative manifestation of a TE strategy.

REFERENCES

Arellano, M. and S. Bond (1991), 'Some tests of specification for panel data: Monte Carlo evidence and an application to employment equations', *Review of Economics and Statistics*, **14**, 328–52.

Barrios, S., L. Bertinelli and E. Strobl (2006), 'Co-agglomeration and spillovers', *Regional Science and Urban Economics,* **36**(4), 467–81.

Baum, C.F. (2006), *An Introduction to Modern Econometrics Using Stata*, College Station, TX: Stata Press.

Berry, H. (2006), 'Leaders, laggards, and the pursuit of foreign knowledge', *Strategic Management Journal,* **27**(2), 151–68.

Beugelsdijk, S., R. Smeets and R. Zwinkels (2008), 'The impact of horizontal and vertical FDI on host country's economic growth', *International Business Review,* **17**, 452–72.

Birkinshaw, J.M. (1997), 'Entrepreneurship in multinational corporations: the characteristics of subsidiary initiatives', *Strategic Management Journal,* **18**(3), 209–27.

Birkinshaw, J.M. and N. Hood (1998), 'Multinational subsidiary evolution: capability and charter change in foreign-owned subsidiary companies', *Academy of Management Review,* **23**(4), 773–95.

Bitzer, J., I. Geishecker and H. Görg (2008), 'Productivity spillovers through vertical linkages: evidence from 17 OECD countries', *Economics Letters,* **99**(2), 328–31.

Blundell, R. and S. Bond (1998), 'Initial conditions and moment restrictions in dynamic panel data models', *Journal of Econometrics,* **87**, 110–43.

Branstetter, L. (2006), 'Is Foreign Direct Investment a channel of knowledge spillovers? Evidence from Japan's FDI in the United States', *Journal of International Economics,* **68**(2), 325–44.

Buckley, P.J., J. Clegg and C. Wang (2007a), 'Is the relationship between inward FDI and spillover effects linear? An empirical examination of the case of China', *Journal of International Business Studies,* **38**, 447–59.

Buckley, P.J., J. Clegg and C. Wang (2007b), 'The impact of foreign ownership, local ownership and industry characteristics on spillover benefits from Foreign Direct Investment in China', *International Business Review,* **16**(2), 142–58.

Cantwell, J.A. (1989), *Technological Innovation and Multinational Corporations*, Oxford: Basil Blackwell.

Cantwell, J.A. and R. Mudambi (2005), 'MNE competence creating subsidiary mandates', *Strategic Management Journal,* **26**(12), 1109–28.

Cantwell, J.A. and L. Piscitello (2005), 'Recent local of foreign-owned research and development activities by large multinational corporations in the European regions: the role of spillovers and externalities', *Regional Studies,* **39**(1), 1–16.

Cantwell, J. and L. Piscitello (2007), 'Attraction and deterrence in the location of foreign-owned R&D activities: the role of positive and negative spillovers', *International Journal of Technological Learning, Innovation and Development,* **1**(1), 83–111.

Carcovic, M. and R. Levine (2005), 'Does Foreign Direct Investment accelerate economic growth?', in T.H. Moran, E.M. Graham and M. Blomström (eds), *Does Foreign Direct Investment Promote Development?*, Washington, DC: Institute for International Economics, pp. 195–220.

Cohen, W. and D.A. Levinthal (1989), 'Innovation and learning: the two faces of R&D', *Economic Journal,* **99**(397), 569–96.

Driffield, N. and J.H. Love (2007), 'Linking FDI motivation and host economy productivity effects: conceptual and empirical analysis', *Journal of International Business Studies,* **38**, 460–73.

Dunning, J.H. (1958), *American Investment in British Manufacturing Industry*, London: George Allen and Unwin.

Dunning, J.H. (1977), 'Trade, location of economy activity and MNE: a search for an eclectic approach', in B. Ohlin, P.O. Hesselborn and P.S. Wijkman (eds), *The International Allocation of Economic Activity*, Basingstoke: Macmillan, pp. 395–418.

Dunning, J.H. and R. Narula (1995), 'The R&D activities of foreign firms in the United States', *International Studies of Management and Organization*, 25(1–2), 39–73.

Ekholm, K., R. Forslid and J.R. Markusen (2007), 'Export platform foreign direct investment', *Journal of the European Economic Association*, 5(4), 776–95.

Feinberg, S.E. and A.K. Gupta (2004), 'Knowledge spillovers and the assignment of R&D responsibilities for foreign subsidiaries', *Strategic Management Journal*, 25(8–9), 823–45.

Feinberg, S. and M. Keane (2005), 'The intra-firm trade of US MNCs: findings and implications for models and policies towards trade and investment', in T.H. Moran, E.M. Graham and M. Blomström (eds), *Does Foreign Direct Investment Promote Development?*, Washington, DC: Institute for International Economics, pp. 245–71.

Forsgren, M., U. Holm and J. Johanson (2005), *Managing the Embedded Multinational: A Business Network View*, Cheltenham, UK and Northampton, MA, USA: Edward Elgar Publishing.

Fosfuri, A. and M. Motta (1999), 'Multinationals without advantages', *Scandinavian Journal of Economics*, 101(4), 617–30.

Frankel, J.A. and D. Romer (1999), 'Does trade cause growth?', *The American Economic Review*, 89(3), 379–99.

Frost, T.S. (2001), 'The geographic sources of foreign subsidiaries' innovations', *Strategic Management Journal*, 22, 101–23.

Girma, S. (2005), 'Absorptive capacity and productivity spillovers from FDI: a threshold regression analysis', *Oxford Bulletin of Economics and Statistics*, 67(3), 281–306.

Girma, S. and H. Görg (2007), 'The role of efficiency gap for spillovers from FDI: evidence from the UK electronics and engineering sectors', *Open Economies Review*, 18(2), 215–32.

Girma, S., H. Görg and M. Pisu (2008), 'Exporting, linkages and productivity effects from Foreign Direct Investment', *Canadian Journal of Economics*, 41(1), 320–40.

Görg, H. and D. Greenaway (2004), 'Much ado about nothing? Do domestic firms really benefit from Foreign Direct Investment?', *World Bank Research Observer*, 19(2), 171–97.

Görg, H. and E. Strobl (2001), 'Multinational companies and productivity spillovers: a meta-analysis', *The Economic Journal*, 111(475), F723–F739.

Görg, H. and E. Strobl (2005), 'Spillovers from foreign firms through worker mobility: an empirical investigation', *Scandinavian Journal of Economics*, 107(4), 693–709.

Griffith, R., R. Harrison and J. Van Reenen (2006), 'How special is the special relationship? Using the impact of US R&D spillovers on UK firms as a test of technology sourcing', *American Economic Review*, 96(5), 1859–75.

Hall, B. and J. Mairesse (1995), 'Exploring the relationship between R&D and productivity in French manufacturing firms', *Journal of Econometrics*, **65**(1), 263–93.

Hennart, J.F. and Y.R. Park (1993), 'Greenfield vs. acquisition: the strategy of Japanese investors in the United States', *Management Science,* **39**(9), 1054–70.

Hymer, S.H. (1960), 'The international operations of national firms: a study of direct foreign investment', Ph.D. dissertation, Massachusetts Institute of Technology, Cambridge, MA.

Javorcik, B.S. (2004), 'Does foreign direct investment increase the productivity of domestic firms? In search of spillovers through backward linkages', *American Economic Review,* **94**(3), 605–27.

Javorcik, B.S. and M. Spatareanu (2008), 'To share or not to share: does local participation matter for spillovers from Foreign Direct Investment?', *Journal of Development Economics*, **85**(1–2), 194–217.

Kafourous, M.I. and P.J. Buckley (2008), 'Under what conditions do firms benefit from the research efforts of other organizations?', *Research Policy*, **37**(2), 225–39.

Kogut, B. and S.J. Chang (1991), 'Technological capabilities and Japanese foreign direct investment in the United States', *Review of Economics and Statistics,* **73**(3), 401–13.

Kuemmerle, W. (1999), 'Foreign direct investment in industrial research in the pharmaceutical and electronics industries: results from a survey of multinational firms', *Research Policy,* **28**(2–3), 179–93.

Le Bas, C. and C. Sierra (2002), 'Location versus home country advantages in R&D activities: some further results on multinationals' location strategies', *Research Policy,* **31**(4), 589–609.

Levinsohn, J. and A. Petrin (2003), 'Estimation production function using inputs to control for unobservables', *Review of Economic Studies*, **70**(2), 317–42.

Liu, X., C. Wang and Y. Wei (2006), 'Trade orientation and mutual productivity spillovers between foreign and local firms in China', *Journal of Asia Business Studies*, **1**(1), 46–53.

Madariaga, N. and S. Poncet (2007), 'FDI in Chinese cities: spillovers and impact on growth', *The World Economy*, **30**(5), 837–62.

Marin, A. and M. Bell (2006), 'Technology spillovers from foreign direct investment (FDI): the active role of MNE subsidiaries in Argentina in the 1990s', *Journal of Development Studies*, **42**(4), 678–97.

Markusen, J.R. (2002), Multinational Firms and the Theory of International Trade, Cambridge, MA: MIT Press.

Minbaeva, D., T. Pedersen, I. Björkman, C.F. Fey and H.J. Park (2003), 'MNE knowledge transfer, subsidiary absorptive capacity, and HRM', *Journal of International Business Studies,* **34**(6), 586–99.

Monteiro, F., N. Arvidsson and J. Birkinshaw (2008), 'Knowledge flows within multinational corporations: explaining subsidiary isolation and its performance implications', *Organization Science*, **19**(1), 90–107.

Neven, D. and G. Siotis (1996), 'Technology sourcing and FDI in the EC: an empirical evaluation', *International Journal of Industrial Organization,* **14**(5), 543–60.

Nicolini, M. and L. Resmini (2007), 'Productivity spillovers and multinational enterprises: in search of a spatial dimension', DYNREG Working Paper 10, Economic and Social Research Institute, Dublin.

Phene, A. and P. Almeida (2008), 'Innovation in multinational subsidiaries:

the role of knowledge assimilation and subsidiary capabilities', *Journal of International Business Studies*, **39**(5), 901–19.

Roodman, D. (2009), 'How to do xtabond2: an introduction to difference and system GMM in Stata', *The Stata Journal*, **9**(1), 86–136.

Rugman, A. (1981), *Inside the Multinational*, Basingstoke: Palgrave-Macmillan.

Sanna-Randaccio, F. and R. Veugelers (2007), 'Multinational knowledge spillovers with decentralised R&D: a game-theoretic approach', *Journal of International Business Studies,* **38**(1), 47–63.

Siotis, G. (1999), 'Foreign direct investment strategies and firms' capabilities', *Journal of Economics & Management Strategy,* **8**(2), 251–70.

Smeets, R. (2008), 'Collecting the pieces of the FDI knowledge spillovers puzzle', *World Bank Research Observer*, **23**, 107–38.

Smeets, R. and E.M. Bosker (2011), 'Leaders, laggards, and technology seeking strategies', *Journal of Economic Behavior & Organization*, **80**, 481–97.

Smeets, R. and Y. Wei (2010), 'Productivity effects of US MNEs: the roles of market orientation and regional integration', *Regional Studies*, **44**, 949–63.

Wei, Y. and X. Liu (2006), 'Productivity spillovers from R&D, exports and FDI in China's manufacturing sector', *Journal of International Business Studies*, **37**(4), 544–57.

Wei, Y., X. Liu and C. Wang (2008), 'Mutual productivity spillovers between foreign and local firms in China', *Cambridge Journal of Economics*, forthcoming.

APPENDIX

Sample Countries and Sectors

Countries	Sectors
Australia	Computers and electronic products
Belgium	Chemicals
Canada	Machinery
Denmark	Electrical equipment, appliances and components
Finland	Transportation equipment
France	Food and kindred products
Germany	Primary and fabricated metals
Ireland	Utilities
Italy	
Netherlands	
Norway	
Poland	
Spain	
Sweden	
United Kingdom	

9. Reverse technology diffusion: on the diffusion of technological capabilities from competence-creating subsidiaries to headquarters of the MNE

Katarina Blomkvist

9.1 INTRODUCTION

According to recent research in the field of international business, developing and diffusing technology throughout the MNE network constitutes one of its most important policies and sources of competitive advantage (Bartlett and Ghoshal, 1989; Gupta and Govindarajan, 1991; Nohria and Ghoshal, 1997; Argote and Ingram, 2000; Piscitello, 2004; Mudambi, 2002; Mudambi et al., 2007). The general story often depicts the MNE as an increasingly interconnected and superior creature for leveraging technology domestically as well as internationally, where autonomous innovative activity by foreign subsidiaries serves an important source for the technological development of the MNE as a whole (Pearce, 1989; Håkanson and Nobel, 1993; Nobel and Birkinshaw, 1998).

Over time foreign subsidiaries have become responsible for an increasing share of research and development in the MNE (Cantwell, 1989; Dunning, 1994; Cantwell, 1995; Zander, 1997, 1999; Frost, 2001; Cantwell and Mudambi, 2005). In the earlier phases of MNE development, foreign subsidiaries are looked upon as extensions of the parent firm using technology supplied from home and attending to adaptation work and servicing local customers in foreign locations (Dunning, 1980). However, some foreign subsidiaries came to access external resources in the local environment, and became involved in local and independent technological development (Birkinshaw and Hood, 1998; Forsgren, 1989; Forsgren et al., 1992; Pearce, 1999). Accordingly, certain foreign subsidiaries have turned into important sources of technological capabilities that are significant for the entire multinational group (Cantwell, 1995;

Papanastassiou and Pearce, 1997; Zander, 1999; Cantwell and Mudambi, 2005).

The ability of the MNE to leverage knowledge from geographically dispersed foreign subsidiaries is perceived as a must for firm success (Bartlett and Ghoshal, 1989; Kogut and Zander, 1992; Hedlund, 1994), and global diffusion of capabilities is viewed by several scholars as the main *raison d'être* of MNEs (Kogut and Zander, 1992, 1993; Doz et al., 2001; Andersson et al., 2007). Consequently, the importance of reverse diffusion has increased as it allows the MNE to draw upon the knowledge and capabilities residing in its network and to take advantage of the scope economies of learning within the entire multinational group (Ghoshal and Bartlett, 1988; Yamin, 1999).

Earlier studies on reverse diffusion within MNEs have emphasized the questions why and how reverse transfer can benefit headquarters (Piscitello and Rabbiosi, 2007), highlighting determinants and obstacles of such flows (Szulanski, 1996; Gupta and Govindarajan, 2000). Previous research has also addressed organizational mechanisms used by MNEs in order to enhance reverse transfer (Foss and Pedersen, 2002; Björkman et al., 2004), and differences between greenfield and acquired subsidiaries regarding reverse transfer of technology and knowledge (Björkman et al., 2004; Bresman et al., 1999; Gupta and Govindarajan, 2000; Håkanson and Nobel, 2001). But while there is growing recognition of the strategic role of foreign subsidiaries as sources of new technological capabilities (Birkinshaw and Hood, 1998; Zander, 1999; Cantwell and Mudambi, 2005), and of the increased importance of reverse diffusion of knowledge and capabilities within the MNE (Kogut and Zander, 1993; Gupta and Govindarajan, 2000; Mudambi and Navarra, 2004; Piscitello and Rabbiosi, 2007; Yang et al., 2008), the speed of reverse diffusion of technological capabilities has not received direct theoretical or empirical attention.

The aim of this chapter is to examine longitudinal patterns in the speed of reverse diffusion of technological capabilities. In particular, it is argued that, over time, the speed of diffusion of technological capabilities from foreign subsidiaries to headquarters has increased but also that the establishment of a subsidiary, either through a greenfield investment or through the acquisition of an existing unit in the host country, has important implications for the speed of reverse diffusion of technological capabilities. Addressing the issue is also important from a managerial point of view, especially in light of the increasing importance attributed to the leveraging of knowledge and technology throughout the MNE network in order for MNEs to achieve and maintain competitive advantage and performance (Gupta and Govindarajan, 1991; Mudambi, 2002; Mudambi et al., 2007; Piscitello, 2004; Ambos et al., 2006).

To test for this a dataset containing the complete patenting activity in foreign locations by 21 Swedish multinationals over the 1893–1990 period was used. The findings show a statistically significant increase in the speed of diffusion from competence-creating subsidiaries to headquarters, suggesting an increase in the likelihood of diffusion of just below 3 per cent for each year in the 1893–1990 period and 10 per cent in the 1960–90 period. The results support work that suggests enhanced intra-MNE diffusion and sharing of technologies within the MNE (Gupta and Govindarajan, 1991; Mudambi, 2002; Mudambi et al., 2007; Piscitello, 2004) and increased importance of foreign subsidiaries as sources of significant technological capabilities (Birkinshaw and Hood, 1998; Zander, 1999; Frost et al., 2002). The results reveal no statistical difference in the pace of reverse diffusion depending on whether the origin was greenfield or acquired foreign subsidiaries. Yet, the results indicate that the speed of reverse diffusion of technological capabilities is faster by acquired competence-creating subsidiaries.

The disposition of the chapter is as follows. The next section reviews the literature on the evolution of foreign subsidiaries and development of reverse diffusion within MNEs and presents the hypotheses concerning the speed of reverse technology diffusion. In the subsequent section, the sample, method and data collection are discussed, after which the results from the empirical analyses are presented. The final section contains a concluding discussion, including managerial implications and issues for future research.

9.2   THE DEVELOPMENT OF COMPETENCE-CREATING SUBSIDIARIES

In the early phases of development of today's well-established MNEs they were dependent on home-based advantages and technologies developed at home (Hymer, 1960; Dunning, 1980; Caves, 1982), and the initial reason for making foreign direct investments (FDI) was to exploit ownership advantages (Dunning and Narula, 1995) in foreign locations. Hence, headquarters served as the main provider of technology, and technological capabilities were diffused from headquarters to its subsidiaries in foreign locations. Thus, the underlying driving force behind diffusion of technological capabilities was to explore home-based advantages.

The internationalization of MNEs has included gradually increased commitments to foreign markets and increasingly sophisticated operations in these locations. Over time, sales and manufacturing operations in foreign locations have become more important and advanced, leading to a specialization in production (Stopford and Dunning, 1983; Dunning, 1983, 1992), and the shifting of R&D activities to foreign locations. Subsidiaries were no longer responsible for only one market or region; rather, they acquired more important roles within the MNE, such as centers of excellence (Holm and Pedersen, 2000; Frost et al., 2002), subsidiaries with world product mandates (Birkinshaw and Morrison, 1995), or global innovators (Gupta and Govindarajan, 1991), creating several centers of decision-making and lateral communication flows within the MNE (Dunning, 1992). In line with these developments, some foreign subsidiaries have developed from passively receiving centrally developed capabilities to performing R&D activities and generating technology advancements important for the entire multinational group (Dunning, 1994; Cantwell, 1995; Nobel and Birkinshaw, 1998; Zander, 1997, 1999).

Hence, over time foreign subsidiaries have come to contribute actively and significantly to the emergence and diffusion of new technological capabilities in the MNE (Hedlund, 1986; Ghoshal and Bartlett, 1988; Bartlett and Ghoshal, 1989; Sölvell and Zander, 1998; Holm and Pedersen, 2000; Andersson et al., 2002). Ultimately, some foreign subsidiaries may have developed into competence-creating subsidiaries (Cantwell and Mudambi, 2005) which actively contribute to the technological and strategic renewal of the MNE.

There has also been a change in managerial attitudes toward more geocentric managerial attitudes, facilitating the emergence and exchange of technology and capabilities throughout the multinational network (Perlmutter, 1969). This is in sharp contrast to the ethnocentric attitudes, typically prevailing in the early internationalization and development phases of the MNE. The effects on organizational design were seen in high volumes of unidirectional communication and information flows from headquarters to subsidiaries, often in the form of orders and advice. The general attitude of headquarters managers would be to 'manufacture the complex products in our country and keep the secrets among our trusted home-country nationals' (Perlmutter, 1969, p.11). Thus, the geocentric approach reflects more collaborative and balanced two-way communication between headquarters and subsidiaries, and as a consequence the potential emergence of new significant technological capabilities in foreign subsidiaries as well as the subsequent diffusion of these capabilities and practices to headquarters.

9.2.1 Capability Diffusion from Subsidiaries to Headquarters

In line with the development of competence-creating subsidiaries serving as sources of technological capabilities that are significant for the entire multinational group, reverse diffusion of capabilities from foreign subsidiaries to headquarters has become increasingly important (Ghoshal, 1987; Yamin, 1999; Mudambi, 2002; Yang et al., 2008). The ability of headquarters to build upon and use knowledge developed in foreign subsidiaries allows it to exploit local capabilities, enlarge the overall MNE technological portfolio and act as an intermediary regarding capability exchange within the multinational group (Yang et al., 2008). Thus, reverse diffusion serves as a mechanism through which MNEs can realize the scope of economies of learning inherent throughout its geographically dispersed network (Ghoshal and Bartlett, 1988).

From a subsidiary perspective it is important to serve and be recognized as a provider of strategically important capabilities (Holm and Pedersen, 2000). It is argued that subsidiaries evolve over time concerning their technological advancements and responsibilities, and that this evolution can occur in both directions (Birkinshaw and Hood, 1998; Birkinshaw and Fry, 1998; Foss and Pedersen, 2002), and while certain subsidiaries gain mandates, others see their roles within the organization reduced or even eliminated. Thus, in line with the increased competitive situation among subsidiaries of MNEs, serving as a source of strategically important capabilities is a must in order for a subsidiary to sustain a specific position or mandate within the MNE (Forsgren and Pedersen, 2000; Gupta and Govindarajan, 2000; Mudambi and Navarra, 2004), and further development of a subsidiary's own capabilities at the expense of diffusion to other actors in the multinational network has proved to negatively influence its position within the MNE (Forsgren et al., 2000).

Compared with conventional flows of technology from headquarters to abroad, reverse transfer is more complex (Yang et al., 2008) because a subsidiary may need to convince headquarters that its capabilities are important and will contribute positively to the operations of headquarters or other actors in the MNE as headquarters is only interested in capabilities that are beneficial from their perspective (Gupta and Govindarajan, 2000; McDonald et al., 2005). Moreover, due to the principal–agent relationship of headquarters and subsidiaries, headquarters' dedication to learn from its subsidiaries is less compared with the obligation of subsidiaries to learn from the parent firm (Kogut and Zander, 1993; Gupta and Govindarajan, 2000). Hence, reverse diffusion can be viewed as a complex process, where the foreign subsidiary may need to persuade headquarters that its capabilities will be beneficial and answer the needs of headquarters (Yang et al., 2008).

9.2.2   Speed of Reverse Diffusion of Technological Capabilities

It is likely that technological capabilities not only diffuse more extensively but also that they diffuse more rapidly within the modern MNE. In terms of the international exploitation of innovations and new technologies, it has been argued that enhanced international competition and short-ened product life cycles have contributed to increasingly rapid transfer of technology within the multinational network. Mansfield and Romeo (1980) found that the mean age of 65 US technologies transferred to overseas subsidiaries in developed countries was six years but also that transfer speed had increased somewhat between the 1960s and 1970s.[1] Moreover, because of the interdependence of foreign R&D operations in the more modern MNE, reverse diffusion is increasingly important for headquarters in being able to coordinate a global strategy (Ambos et al., 2006). Hence, the expectation in the current chapter is that, over time, the speed of reverse diffusion of new technological capabilities is likely to have increased within MNEs; that is, new technological capabilities that emerge in the more modern MNE would experience more rapid diffusion from competence-creating subsidiaries to headquarters (Hedlund, 1986; Bartlett and Ghoshal, 1989).

Hypothesis 1: Over time, there has been an increase in the speed at which technological capabilities emerging in competence-creating subsidiaries are diffused to headquarters.

In the last decades, acquisitions have generally been the preferred mode of international expansion (Hood and Young, 1979; Dunning, 1988; Holm and Pedersen, 2000). The shift in entry mode from greenfield investments to acquisitions has been found to have a considerable effect on the overall share and profile of foreign technological activity in the MNE (Zander, 1999; Puranam et al., 2006). Acquired subsidiaries are more likely to act in asset-seeking ways, thus developing more substantial technological capabilities and having a greater strategic impact than greenfield estab-lishments (Cantwell and Mudambi, 2005). Two main reasons for acqui-sitions are fast penetration of foreign markets and rapid access to new knowledge assets, leading to an enlargement of the MNE's technological base (Prahalad and Hamel, 1990; Hitt et al., 1996) and an increase in the potential recombination of technological capabilities within the MNE (Hedlund, 1986; Hedlund and Ridderstråle, 1995).

It is suggested that certain factors ease the process of reverse diffu-sion within MNEs. Normative integration between headquarters and subsidiaries facilitates the diffusion of innovations, and it is claimed that subsidiaries sharing the overall strategy, goals and values of the MNE generate higher degrees of reverse diffusion (Bartlett and Ghoshal, 1989). Accordingly, diffusion of capabilities from foreign subsidiaries to headquarters will be higher when there are beliefs and values shared by headquarters and subsidiary (Ghoshal et al., 2004). Moreover, knowledge relevance and absorptive capacity between two units are believed to positively influence reverse diffusion of capabilities (Yang et al., 2008; Cohen and Levinthal, 1990). According to Schulz (2003) knowledge relevance can be defined as 'the degree to which external knowledge has the potential to connect to local knowledge'. Drawing upon relevance theory, the more the sending unit's knowledge has implications for the receiving unit, the more relevant and easier it will be for the receiving unit to obtain these implications. For a given degree of willingness to send and receive knowledge, the more the knowledge is connected and relevant, the more effective the transfer will be (Yang et al., 2008); hence, the more knowledge overlaps between subsidiary and headquarters, the more likely it is that headquarters will take an interest in and understand the subsidiary's knowledge. Consequently, these circumstances suggest that the speed of diffusion of technological capabilities is faster from greenfield competence-creating subsidiaries than from acquired competence-creating subsidiaries because, in terms of technological base, greenfield subsidiaries can be expected to be generally more integrated with and similar to headquarters than acquisitions (Yamin, 1999).

On the other hand, acquisitions that are perceived as strategically important from a headquarters' perspective have a positive influence on reverse diffusion of knowledge (Yang et al., 2008). Headquarters often have a special interest in acquired subsidiaries and their technological capabilities, especially if they are considered to be strategically important, as they are relatively more likely to contribute with significantly new technological capabilities important for the entire MNE (Zander, 1999; Björkman et al., 2004; Gupta and Govindarajan, 2000) than greenfield subsidiaries, and are often acquired because of their technological assets and future growth potential (Doz and Prahalad, 1991; Hitt et al., 1996). Hence, this suggests that the diffusion of technological capabilities to headquarters may be faster from acquired subsidiaries than from foreign greenfield subsidiaries.

Previous studies of reverse diffusion of knowledge among greenfield and acquired subsidiaries have found mixed results (Björkman et al., 2004; Bresman et al., 1999; Gupta and Govindarajan, 2000; Håkanson and Nobel, 2001). According to Gupta and Govindarajan (2000), there is no difference in technology flows from greenfield and acquired subsidiaries to headquarters. However, other findings indicate that reverse knowledge transfer is more extensive for greenfield subsidiaries than for acquired subsidiaries (Yamin, 1999), and mixed results have been found when controlling for the role of the subsidiary (Mudambi et al., 2007). Thus, two competing hypotheses concern the pace at which technological capabilities diffuse from greenfield and acquired competence-creating subsidiaries to headquarters:

Hypothesis 2a: The speed of reverse diffusion of technological capabilities will be higher from greenfield subsidiaries than from acquired advanced foreign subsidiaries.

Hypothesis 2b: The speed of reverse diffusion of technological capabilities will be higher from acquired subsidiaries than from greenfield advanced foreign subsidiaries.

9.3 RESEARCH DESIGN

9.3.1 Sample

To test for and explore patterns of diffusion of new technological capabilities, the chapter draws on the US patenting activity by 21 Swedish multinationals over the 1893–1990 period. Out of these subsidiaries, 108 were located in Europe (most importantly Germany, 15; Switzerland, 14; United Kingdom, 12; Denmark, 11; and Finland, 10), 18 in the United States, and 31 in other countries (most importantly Canada, 9; Australia, 5; Japan, 3; and Mexico, 3). The sample firms represent a quite broad spectrum of industries, including pulp and paper, motor vehicles, pharmaceuticals, and telecommunications equipment (Appendix A). According to earlier studies, these firms represent a significant number of inventions and also R&D expenditure in Swedish industry (Wallmark and McQueen, 1986; Håkanson and Nobel, 1993); however, they are not necessarily representative of firms in other countries. On the other hand, all the sample firms have long exposure to international markets and international business, and should therefore serve as a useful testing ground for identifying patterns of diffusion of technological capabilities.

In order to define the sample firms and subsidiaries in a way that allows for longitudinal comparisons, a historical examination of each individual firm identified possible name changes as well as potential changes in ownership through mergers and acquisitions. The data includes the patenting activity by all majority owned subsidiaries for the periods during which they belonged to the parent companies. These subsidiaries were identified by systematically going through the history of each individual sample firm, using the publications *Svenska Aktiebolag: Handbok för Affärsvärlden, Koncernregistret: KCR*, and *Who Owns Whom: Continental Europe*. Complementary publications such as publications on company histories, were also used in the consolidation process (for a sample of the consolidated firms, see Appendix B).

The empirical analysis covers both competence-creating subsidiaries that were originally established as greenfield subsidiaries, and subsidiaries that were added as the result of foreign acquisitions. It should be re-emphasized that the data only include competence-creating subsidiaries, that is, subsidiaries which have once proven their capacity to contribute significantly to the technological and strategic development of the multinational group. Proof of this capacity is that the subsidiaries have been awarded at least one US patent, which by definition requires that inventions be novel, non-obvious, and constitute useful additions to the existing stock of knowledge. (Additional methodological notes and comments are to be found in Appendix C.)

9.3.2 Data and Data Collection

The study uses patents as a marker or indicator of the emergence and diffusion of technological capabilities. Patents are a frequently used technology indicator, in the international business literature and elsewhere (for example Jaffe, 1986; Archibugi and Pianta, 1992; Almeida and Phene, 2004; Feinberg and Gupta, 2004), and possess the specific advantage of providing consistent and comparable information over extended periods of time. Patenting also correlates highly with alternative measures of technological activity and innovative performance, such as research and development expenditure and new product introductions. In a study comprising a large number of companies in four high-tech industries, Hagedoorn and Cloodt (2003, pp. 1375, 1365) found 'no major systematic disparity amongst R&D inputs, patent counts, patent citations and new product announcements', concluding that 'future research might also consider using any of these indicators to measure the innovative performance of companies in high-tech industries'.

The present study relies on the firms' patenting in the United States. The completion of a US patent application requires that the nationality of the inventor be recorded (rather than the nationality of the research unit). Under the assumption that the nationality of the inventor in most cases coincides with the geographical location of invention, it is possible to find out where the research and development underlying the invention was carried out. On every patent application the name, nationality and address is stated for the inventor.[2] Thus, for every US patent registered under the name of any of the sample firms and their subsidiaries, it is known whether the patent *originated* in, for example, Germany, the United Kingdom, the United States or any other country.[3] This is an important advantage because company-specific patenting policies (for example involving the registration of patents under the name of the parent company rather than that of the inventing subsidiary) could otherwise conceal the correct geographical distribution of technological activity and invention.

One advantage of using US patenting data is that the general attractiveness of the large US market encourages patenting of inventions that are believed to be of relatively high quality and commercial value. It has been found that Swedish firms' patenting in the United States does not differ significantly from patenting in other large markets such as Germany or France (Archibugi and Pianta, 1992). One potential drawback of using US patenting data is that it tends to inflate the patenting activity by US subsidiaries (because they have a relatively higher propensity to patent in what is their home market).

Although information from patents must be treated with some caution (Schmookler, 1950; Pavitt, 1988), no substantial biases are anticipated in the present study. Most of the sample firms are active in medium to high-tech industries, where patenting is considered an important competitive device. Patenting propensity varies across the sample firms, causing variation in the number of patents associated with each firm, but this does not in itself affect patterns in the diffusion of new technological capabilities.

9.3.3 Variables

Main variables
The first main variable of interest is the *emergence of technological capabilities*. The emergence of technological capabilities occurs when any subsidiary of the MNE is awarded a patent in a technology in which the multinational group has not been previously active. Entry into new technologies and associated technological capabilities is measured at the level of about 400 classes of technology as defined by the US Patent Office.[4] At this level of aggregation, it is possible to distinguish between relatively narrowly defined technological capabilities, such as paper making and fiber preparation and pulse or digital communications. For the purposes of this chapter, the classification should strike a good balance between more aggregate groups (the use of which would result in fewer identified entries into new technological capabilities) and finer levels of disaggregation.

The emergence of technological capabilities is set to the year in which the subsidiary received its first patent in a technology that is new to the entire multinational group. It needs to be added that, whereas patenting in a new technology is seen as an indicator of the emergence of new technological capabilities in the multinational group, the formation of capabilities is not a discrete event but a gradual process which typically precedes the first patenting by a number of years. More recently, the granting of a US patent has delayed the application by about two years and the emergence of technological capabilities is likely to have preceded the application by an additional, unknown number of years. Yet, *ceteris paribus*, the information gained from the patenting records should still provide relatively consistent information about changes in the patterns of emergence of technological capabilities and the ensuing diffusion process. It is further notable that there is only information about the event that first signals the formation of technological capabilities in the multinational group, and except for the first recorded occurrence(s) of the diffusion of these capabilities, the firms' depth of involvement in each individual technology will not be explained further.[5]

The second main variable of interest is *reverse diffusion of technological capabilities*. In this chapter, diffusion is concerned with the process by which a specific technological capability first emerges in a foreign subsidiary and later on in headquarters. It is measured by US patent data, that is reverse diffusion takes place when, after a greenfield or acquired subsidiary has been awarded a patent in a technology that is new to the entire MNE, patenting activity in the same technology is also recorded at headquarters.[6] Although the empirical investigation reveals patterns in reverse diffusion of technological capabilities, it is necessary to add that the main mechanisms behind diffusion remain unknown. Diffusion may have been brought about in several different and possibly overlapping ways (Wilkins, 1974), including the transfer of technology, knowledge exchange as part of inter-subsidiary collaboration or internationally coordinated research and development projects. In some cases, the diffusion of technological capabilities may also be the result of independent work on the same technologies by both a subsidiary and headquarters.

While the main source of reverse diffusion in the current study remains unknown, the principal driver is probably not that of traditional transfer to exploit the technological capabilities in the local market, as the Swedish market in all probability is of insignificant size and commercial importance. Rather, drawing upon previous work, reverse transfer may represent a selection process through which some subsidiaries' innovations are elevated to a higher level within the MNE (Yamin, 1999) and serve as the mechanism through which headquarters can realize the economies of learning inherent in its geographically dispersed network of foreign subsidiaries (Ghoshal and Bartlett, 1988). Thus, the driver behind reverse diffusion is more likely to be headquarters' enhanced innovative capacity (Piscitello and Rabbiosi, 2007), access to local knowledge, and the coordination of a global strategy (Ambos et al., 2006).

The third main variable of interest is *type of subsidiary; greenfield or acquired advanced foreign subsidiary*. The aim of this variable is to capture potential differences in the ability or desirability to diffuse technological capabilities from greenfield and acquired competence-creating subsidiaries to headquarters. It was measured through a dummy variable coded 0 and 1.

Control variables

Ideally, the data should have incorporated a variety of control variables capturing the external and internal environment of a subsidiary, and the organizational structure, that is the degree of centralization and different control mechanisms for intra-MNE diffusion, such as incentives and evaluation programs for knowledge development and exchange, previous subsidiary diffusion and subsidiary size. But the length of the time period under study in combination with the unavailability of data at the subsidiary level precludes the use of a comprehensive set of controls. However, a number of location, industry and market variables were included as controls.

The industrial context is likely to have an influence on the diffusion of capabilities within the MNE. Manufacturing industries have turned out to have patterns of knowledge flows different from those in service-based industries (Grosse, 1996; Lahti and Beyerlein, 2000); thus, three industry dummy variables (coded 0 and 1) were introduced to control for industry-dependent effects on diffusion patterns. These dummy variables are expected to reflect different propensities to centralize R&D activities (Papanastassiou and Pearce, 1998) and exchange knowledge with headquarters (Randoy and Li, 1998). The first dummy variable captured firms in the automotive industry (two firms), the second, firms in processing industries, such as pulp and paper and steel (four firms), and the third, firms involved in pharmaceuticals and chemicals (four firms). This left a mixed group of sample firms mainly active in mechanical engineering industries and often having a highly diversified product portfolio.

The potential effects of national culture on the diffusion process were controlled for by the use of culture clusters (Ronen and Schenkar, 1985). The aim of these variables was to capture cultural dissimilarities between the foreign country of a subsidiary and headquarters (which is Sweden in the present sample), that could influence both the ability and desirability of competence-creating subsidiaries to diffuse technological capabilities. More specifically, the sample subsidiaries were divided into five different cultural clusters. The first dummy variable captured subsidiaries in the Anglo-Saxon cluster (147 subsidiaries), the second subsidiaries in the Germanic cluster (63 subsidiaries), the third subsidiaries in the Nordic cluster (14 subsidiaries), and the fourth, subsidiaries in the rest of Europe (18 subsidiaries). This left a mixed group of subsidiaries located outside Europe (six subsidiaries).

Furthermore, size of the local market was included as a general proxy for the generosity of the local technological and business environment. The size is measured in annual GDP expressed in the log of millions of US dollars (constant 1990 terms), using data obtained from the Groningen Growth and Development Centre and the Conference Board, Total Economy Database (2006). It is expected that larger markets offer broader technological potential and may therefore be more important and followed more closely, leading to an earlier detection of new significant technological capabilities at headquarters, fostering a faster reverse diffusion process of technological capabilities.

9.3.4 Statistical Method

Variations of event history analysis (Allison, 1995) were used to analyze diffusion patterns and to test the hypotheses. In order to investigate the expected general increase in the pace of reverse diffusion, a Cox regression was employed, using the year of the first emergence of technological capabilities as the independent variable or covariate (higher numbers mean that the respective technological capabilities emerged toward the end of the 1893–1990 period) and the event of diffusion of the capabilities to headquarters as the dependent variable. A positive parameter estimate thereby signals that an increase in the year of emergence increases the hazard or pace of diffusion. The goodness of fit of the specific model is tested by the score statistic, that is the chi-square, which compares the specified model with an empty equivalent. The degrees of freedom represent the actual number of parameters specified in the model (Allison, 1995).

To investigate potential differences in the pace of diffusion for technological capabilities originally emerging either in greenfield or acquired competence-creating subsidiaries, non-parametric maximum likelihood Kaplan–Meier estimates were employed. The life-table method of Kaplan–Meier estimates survivor functions following event times having probability distributions. More specifically, the survivor function is the probability that an event time is greater than t, where t can take any non-negative number. In the case of no censoring, that is all observations experience an event, the survivor function is simply the proportion of observations with event times greater than t. The method makes it possible to test the null hypothesis that survivor functions for two or more groups are identical, which, in the present case, means testing for differences in the diffusion of technological capabilities originating at greenfield competence-creating subsidiaries versus capabilities emerging in acquired foreign subsidiaries. The Kaplan–Meier estimates are used in addition to the Cox regression analysis in order to graphically display the reverse diffusion process from greenfield and acquired competence-creating subsidiaries to headquarters.

9.4 FINDINGS

Over the entire period 1893–1990, 248 new technological capabilities emerged in the sample of foreign advanced subsidiaries (in each case marked by the first patent in a specific class of technology as defined by the US Patent Office). Out of these 248 technological capabilities, 133 were diffused within the MNE during the window of observation and 75 of these diffused to headquarters, 68 from greenfield subsidiaries and seven from acquired subsidiaries. The overall median estimated time for diffusion to headquarters from foreign advanced subsidiaries was 14 years (mean 14.1) between 1893 and 1990; however, shortening the window of observation indicates a substantial increase in the pace of reverse diffusion. Thus, the overall median estimated time for diffusion to headquarters from foreign advanced subsidiaries was seven years (mean 6.8) between 1960 and 1990, which suggests a substantial increase in the pace of reverse diffusion over time. The correlation matrix in Table 9.1 reveals generally modest correlations between the covariates. The variance inflation factor (VIF) was estimated to check for potential multicollinearity issues. With no VIF scores over three (Hair et al., 1998), the risk of significant misinterpretations of the results due to multicollinearity appears limited.

Table 9.1   Pearson correlation matrix

Covariates	1	2	3	4	5	6
1. Emergence	1.00					
2. Type of subsidiary	0.42**	1.00				
3. Processing industry	0.09	0.19**	1.00			
4. Pharmaceuticals/chemicals	0.01	−0.17**	−0.06	1.00		
5. Automobile industry	0.07	0.05	−0.04	−0.53	1.00	
6. GDP	0.28**	0.03**	0.14	−0.19	−0.18**	1.00

Note: ** Correlation is significant at the 0.01 level (two-tailed); * Correlation is significant at the 0.05 level (two-tailed).

Table 9.2   Cox regression: Determinants of pace of reverse diffusion 1983–90

Cox regression model	Estimate	s.e.	P	Hazard ratio
Covariates				
Year of emergence	0.028	0.008	0.001	1.029***
Acquisitions	0.692	0.638	0.278	1.997
GDP	0.480	0.439	0.274	1.617
Industry		Yes		
Culture clusters		Yes		
Model fit statistics				
Chi^2		36.021*** (10)		
Censoring information				
69.8% (173 observations)				

Notes: Estimates significant at the 0.05, 0.01 and 0.001 levels are indicated; with *, ** and *** respectively. All tests are two-tailed.

Speed of reverse diffusion: A Cox's regression analysis was employed to investigate the expected general increase in the speed of reverse diffusion in the period 1893–1990 (see Table 9.2). The results reveal a statistically significant increase in the speed of diffusion (p = 0.001). In other words, the later into the time period a new technological capability emerges, the faster it is diffused to headquarters. The finding confirms Hypothesis 1, arguing that the pace of diffusion of technological capabilities from competence-creating subsidiaries to headquarters increases over time. The parameter estimate suggests that the hazard of diffusion increases by just under 3 per cent each year. Additionally, a Cox's regression analysis was employed to investigate a shorter time period, 1960–90, and the results indicate a higher increase in the pace of reverse diffusion (p = 0.01) of 10 per cent, suggesting that over time there is a substantial increase in the pace of reverse diffusion (see Table 9.3).

The variable that captures the type of subsidiary shows no clear statistically significant difference regarding time to diffusion of technological capabilities between greenfield and acquired foreign subsidiaries. This is also in line with the results of the non-parametric maximum likelihood Kaplan–Meier estimates, which show no statistical difference (the likelihood ratio test does not reject the null hypothesis of no difference between the groups) regarding survival functions between the two strata as observed in median survival times (or the time to reverse diffusion of technological capabilities). However, although not statistically significant, differences in time to diffusion are found between greenfield and acquired

Table 9.3   Cox regression: Determinants of pace of reverse diffusion 1960–90

Cox regression model	Estimate	s.e.	P	Hazard ratio
Covariates				
Year of emergence	0.096	0.035	0.006	1.101**
Acquisitions	0.620	0.746	0.406	1.859
GDP	0.749	0.704	0.240	2.115
Industry		Yes		
Culture clusters		Yes		
Model fit statistics				
Chi^2		19.848**(10)		
Censoring information				
80.9 % (148 observations)				

Notes: Estimates significant at the 0.05, 0.01 and 0.001 levels are indicated with *, ** and *** respectively. All tests are two-tailed.

foreign subsidiaries. The median survival time for a technological capability that emerged in a greenfield advanced foreign subsidiary is 15 years (mean 15.1) versus 3.5 years (mean 3.7) for a capability initially emerging in an acquired advanced foreign subsidiary. This is graphically illustrated in Figure 9.1, where a wider survivor function (the black line) is observed for greenfield subsidiaries than for acquired subsidiaries (the grey line). Time to diffusion is the time between the emergence and the diffusion to headquarters of a technological capability in a foreign subsidiary. In other words, the results indicate that technological capabilities emerging in acquired competence-creating subsidiaries are diffused more quickly to headquarters (the shorter survival function) than technological capabilities emerging in greenfield competence-creating subsidiaries (the longer survival function).

Furthermore, the results indicate that reverse diffusion is faster from countries with high GDP, and in the automobile industry (a 62 per cent and 53 per cent increase in the likelihood of reverse diffusion respectively); however, these results were not significant. Significant results are found for the dummies controlling for culture clusters, where the figures specifically suggest that reverse diffusion is faster from locations outside Europe compared with locations in Germanic and Anglo-Saxon countries.

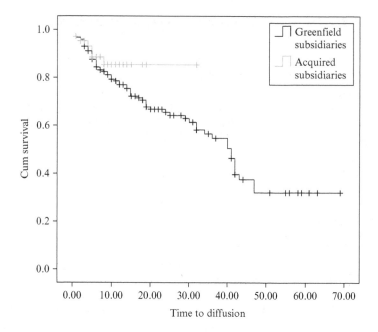

Figure 9.1   Kaplan–Meier survival functions of reverse diffusion of technological capabilities

9.5   DISCUSSION AND CONCLUSION

The main results suggest an increased speed of reverse diffusion. The diffusion from foreign advanced subsidiaries to headquarters has become faster over the investigated time period. The findings support those who have argued that the reason why MNEs exist and succeed is their ability to efficiently develop and leverage knowledge across borders (Gupta and Govindarajan, 1991; Kogut and Zander, 1993), and foreign subsidiaries' function as important sources of technological capabilities for headquarters and the entire multinational group (Cantwell, 1995; Pearce, 1999; Zander, 1999). Moreover, the results of an increased speed in reverse diffusion agree with previous research arguing that enhanced international competition and shortened product life cycles have contributed to increasingly rapid transfer of technology within the MNE (Mansfield and Romeo, 1980). The observed hazard rate suggests a substantial increase over time in the speed of diffusion of technological capabilities from competence-creating subsidiaries to headquarters.

The results demonstrate a clear difference between greenfield and acquired competence-creating subsidiaries regarding the diffusion speed to headquarters of technological capabilities emerging in these subsidiaries. Supporting previous research argues that acquisitions are often used in order to gain access to new technologies (Zander, 1999) and that headquarters therefore take a great interest in their technological assets and capabilities (Björkman et al., 2004). Several of the control variables showed results that were in line with those expectations; however, they were not significant. The diffusion speed from foreign subsidiaries to headquarters is higher from large and generous markets, such as the automotive or pharmaceutical industry.

Two particular limitations must be emphasized when analyzing the results and drawing conclusions. First, the sample used in this study is restricted to a limited and non-random sample. In essence, the firms represent a large and representative proportion of Swedish MNEs, but they may not be representative of MNEs in other countries. The results may be shared by other MNEs emerging in small home markets, but this remains an empirically open question. On the balancing side, the sample firms are corporations with long and extensive exposure to international markets and international business, which has led to the evolution of trends and patterns. Second, the data do not account for the reverse diffusion of technological capabilities emerging after 1990, but the length of the measured time period should have allowed for fundamental tendencies to surface and be detected. There is little evidence that the fundamental drivers behind reverse diffusion within the MNE should have changed significantly during the last fifteen years. If anything, the speed may be assumed to have quickened even more, and this would be in line with the observed trends in the current chapter.

9.6 SUMMARY

The objective of this chapter was to empirically investigate longitudinal patterns in the diffusion of technological capabilities from foreign advanced subsidiaries to headquarters, more specifically, to examine the speed of reverse diffusion and how it has changed over time. In doing so, this chapter adds to the current literature explaining knowledge and technology diffusion in the MNE, making a contribution by highlighting the speed of diffusion of technological capabilities from foreign subsidiaries to headquarters. Generally, the results suggest that the speed of reverse diffusion has increased during the window of observation; in other words, the later into the time period a new technological capability emerges, the faster it is diffused to headquarters. The pace of reverse diffusion has not received direct empirical attention before, and the empirical findings in this chapter support previous studies arguing that the diffusion of capabilities within the modern MNE takes place faster, something which previously was most often implicitly assumed.

This chapter raises important questions that future research in this area should consider addressing. First, research is needed on the influence of different control and incentive mechanisms on diffusion speed and patterns of technological capabilities by competence-creating subsidiaries in the MNE. It would also be interesting to look at the more specific role of headquarters regarding reverse diffusion of technological capabilities as well as the effect of reverse diffusion on headquarters and subsidiary innovativeness and overall performance. Second, this study is one of few attempts examining the difference in the diffusion speed of greenfield and acquired foreign subsidiaries, and in order to confirm the results additional studies drawing upon a broader sample are needed. Moreover, future studies should control for national origin and more specific subsidiary characteristics and attributes, such as how long the acquired subsidiaries have been a part of the MNE, and to what extent the capability is closely connected to the core technology of the MNE, which would increase our understanding of how the choice of entry mode influences diffusion patterns of technological capabilities in the MNE.

NOTES

1. Zander (1991) observed that among Swedish multinationals the average time to comprehensive transfer of manufacturing technology related to important innovations was about eight years.
2. A small proportion of all patents in the current dataset were associated with several individuals of different nationalities. In those cases, the recorded geographical location of technological activity and invention was that of the first inventor.
3. A small proportion of all patents in the current dataset were associated with several individuals of different nationalities. In those cases, the recorded geographical location of technological activity and invention was that of the first inventor.
4. The US Patent Office classification is primarily based on the nature and function of the inventions, not their primary adopters. The manual states that arts or instruments having like functions, producing like products, or achieving like effects, are classified together. The functions or effects that are chosen as a basis of classification must be proximate or essential, not remote or accidental. The categories of invention are product, process, apparatus, composition of matter, and certain varieties of plants. Accessories are generally classified with the instrument to which they are peculiar (Manual of Classification, Revision No. 1, June 1993, US Department of Commerce, Patent and Trademark Office).
5. Whereas an individual sample firm may have entered 75 new technologies and capabilities over the examined time period, 25 of which may have been recorded as diffused to other locations within the multinational group, in most cases there has been extensive

activity and patenting in each individual technology. In individual sample firms such as ASEA there has been a total of close on 2000 US patents over the entire period.
6. Headquarters is seen as synonymous with some unidentified units in the home country; in most cases these units are R&D units adjacent to headquarters.

REFERENCES

Allison, P.D. (1995), *Survival Analysis Using the SAS System: A Practical Guide*, Cary, NC: The SAS Institute.

Almeida, P. (1996), 'Knowledge sourcing by foreign multinationals: patent citation analysis in the US semi-conductor industry', *Strategic Management Journal*, **17**, 155–65.

Almeida, P. and A. Phene (2004), 'Subsidiaries and knowledge creation: the influence of the MNC and host country on innovation', *Strategic Management Journal*, **25**, 847–64.

Ambos, T.C., B. Ambos and B.B. Schlegelmilch (2006), 'Learning from the periphery: an empirical investigation of headquarters' benefits from reverse knowledge transfers', *International Business Review*, **15**(3), 294–312.

Andersson, U., M. Forsgren and U. Holm (2002), 'The strategic impact of external networks: subsidiary performance and competence development in the multinational corporation', *Strategic Management Journal*, **23**(11), 979–96.

Andersson, U., M. Forsgren and U. Holm (2007), 'Balancing subsidiary influence in the federative MNC: a business network view', *Journal of International Business*, **38**, 802–18.

Archibugi, D. and M. Pianta (1992), 'Specialization and size of technological activities in industrial countries: the analysis of patenting data', *Research Policy*, **21**(1), 2123–34.

Argote, L. and P. Ingram (2000), 'Knowledge transfer: a basis for competitive advantage in firms', *Organizational Behaviour and Human Decision Processes*, **82**(1), 150–69.

Bartlett, C.A. and S. Ghoshal (1989), *Managing Across Borders: the Transnational Solution*, Boston, MA: Harvard Business School Press.

Birkinshaw, J. and N. Fry (1998), 'Subsidiary initiatives to develop new markets', *Sloan Management Review*, **39**(3), 51–61.

Birkinshaw, J. and N. Hood (1998), 'Multinational subsidiary evolution: capability and charter change in foreign-owned subsidiary companies', *Academy of Management Review*, **23**(4), 773–95.

Birkinshaw, J. and A.J. Morrison (1995), 'Configurations of strategy and structure in subsidiaries of multinational corporations', *Journal of International Business Studies*, **26**(4), 729–53.

Björkman, I., W. Barner-Rasmusen and L. Li (2004), 'Managing knowledge transfer in MNCs: the impact of headquarters control mechanisms', *Journal of International Business Studies*, **35**, 443–55.

Bresman, H., J. Birkinshaw and R. Nobel (1999), 'Knowledge transfer in international acquisitions', *Journal of International Business Studies*, **30**, 439–62.

Cantwell, J.A. (1989), *Technological Innovation and Multinational Corporations*, Oxford: Basil Blackwell.

Cantwell, J.A. (1995), 'The globalisation of technology: what remains of the product cycle model', *Cambridge Journal of Economics*, **19**, 155–74.

Cantwell, J.A. and R. Mudambi (2005), 'MNE advanced foreign subsidiary mandate', *Strategic Management Journal*, **26**, 1109–28.

Caves, R.E. (1982), *Multinational Firms and Economic Analysis*, Cambridge, MA: Cambridge University Press.

Cohen, W. and D. Levinthal (1990), 'Absorptive capacity: a new perspective on learning and innovation', *Administrative Science Quarterly*, **35**, 128–52.

Doz, Y. and C. Prahalad (1991), 'Sustained product innovation in large, mature organizations: overcoming innovation-to-organization problems', *Academy of Management Journal*, **39**(5), 1120–53.

Doz, Y., J. Snatos and P. Williamsson (2001), *From Global to Metanational: How Companies Win in the Knowledge Economy*, Boston, MA: Harvard Business School Press.

Dunning, J.H. (1980), 'Toward an eclectic theory of international production: some empirical tests', *Journal of International Business Studies*, **11**(1), 9–31.

Dunning, J.H. (1983), 'Changes in the level and structure of international production – the last one hundred years', in M. Casson (eds), *The Growth of International Business*, London: George Allen and Unwin.

Dunning, J.H. (1988), *Explaining International Production*, London: Unwin Hyman.

Dunning, J.H. (1992), 'The competitive advantage of countries and the activities of transnational corporations', *Transnational Corporations*, **1**(1).

Dunning, J.H. (1994), 'Multinational enterprises and the globalization of innovatory capacity', *Research Policy*, **23**(1), 67–88.

Dunning, J.H. and R. Narula (1995), 'The R&D activities of foreign firms in the United States', *International Studies of Management and Organization*, **25**, 39–73.

Feinberg, S.E. and A.K. Gupta (2004), 'Knowledge spillovers and the assignment of R&D responsibilities to foreign subsidiaries', *Strategic Management Journal*, **25**, 823–45.

Forsgren, M. (1989), *Managing the Internationalization Process*, London: Routledge.

Forsgren, M. and T. Pedersen (2000), 'Subsidiary influence and corporate learning: centers of excellence in Danish foreign-owned firms', in U. Holm and T. Pederson (eds), *The Emergence and Impact of MNC Centers of Excellence*, London: Palgrave Macmillan.

Forsgren, M., U. Holm and J. Johanson (1992), 'Division headquarters go abroad – a step in the internationalization of the multinational corporation', *Journal of Management Studies*, **32**(4), 475–91.

Forsgren, M., J. Johansson and D. Sharma (2000), 'Development of MNC centers of excellence', in U. Holm and T. Pedersen (eds), *The Emergence and Impact of MNC Centers of Excellence*, London: Macmillan.

Foss, N.J. and T. Pederson (2002), 'Transferring knowledge in MNCs the role of sources of subsidiary knowledge and organizational context', *Journal of International Management*, **1**(8), 1–19.

Frost, T.S. (2001), 'The geographic sources of foreign subsidiaries' innovations', *Strategic Management Journal*, **2**(2), 101–23.

Frost, T.S., J.M. Birkinshaw and P.C. Ensign (2002), 'Centres of excellence in

Canada', in U. Holm and T. Pedersen (eds), *The Emergence and Impact of MNC Centers of Excellence: a Subsidiary Perspective*, Basingstoke: Macmillan.

GGDC, Groningen Growth and Development Centre and the Conference Board (2006), *Total Economy Database*, September 2006.

Ghoshal, S. (1987), 'Global strategy: an organizing framework', *Strategic Management Journal*, **8**(5), 425–40.

Ghoshal, S. and C.A. Bartlett (1988), 'Creation, adoption and diffusion of innovations by subsidiaries of multinational corporations', *Journal of International Business Studies*, **19**(3), 365–88.

Ghoshal, S., H. Korine and G. Szulanski (2004), 'Interunit communication in multinational corporations', *Management Science*, **40**, 96–110.

Grosse, R. (1996), 'International technology transfer in services', *Journal of International Business Studies*, **27**(4), 781–800.

Gupta, A.K. and V. Govindarajan (1991), 'Knowledge flows and the structure of control within multinational corporations', *Academy of Management Review*, **16**(4), 768–92.

Gupta, A.K. and V. Govindarajan (2000), 'Knowledge flows within the multinational corporation', *Strategic Management Journal*, **21**, 473–96.

Hagedoorn, J. and M. Cloodt (2003), 'Measuring innovation performance: is there an advantage in using multiple indicators?', *Research Policy*, **32**, 1365–79.

Hair, J.F., R.E. Anderson and W.C. Black (1998), *Multivariate Data Analysis*, 5th edn, Upper Saddle River, NJ: Prentice Hall.

Håkanson, L. and R. Nobel (1993), 'Foreign research and development in Swedish multinationals', *Research Policy*, **22**, 373–96.

Håkanson, L. and R. Nobel (2001), 'Organizational characteristics and reverse knowledge transfer', *Management International Review*, **41**(4), 395–420.

Hedlund, G. (1986), 'The hypermodern MNC – a heterarchy?', *Human Resource Management*, **25**(1), 9–35.

Hedlund, G. (1994), 'A model of knowledge management and the N-form corporation', *Strategic Management Journal*, **15**, 73–90.

Hedlund, G. and J. Ridderstråle (1995), 'International development projects: key to competitiveness, impossible, or mismanaged?', *International Studies of Management and Organization*, **25**(1–2), 121–57.

Hitt, M., R. Hoskisson, R. Johnson and D. Moesel (1996), 'The market for corporate control and firm innovation', *Academy of Management Journal*, **39**, 1084–119.

Holm, U. and T. Pedersen (eds) (2000), *The Emergence and Impact of MNC Centers of Excellence. A Subsidiary Perspective*, Basingstoke: Macmillan.

Hood, N. and S. Young (1979), *The Economics of Multinational Enterprise*, London: Longman.

Hymer, S. (1960), *The International Operations of National Firms: a Study of Direct Investments*, PhD dissertation, MIT.

Jaffe, A.B. (1986), 'Technological opportunity and spillovers of R&D: evidence from firms' patents, profits, and market value', *American Economic Review*, **76**, 984–1001.

Jaffe, A.B., M. Trajtenberg and R. Henderson (1993), 'Geographic localization of knowledge spillovers as evidence by patent citations', *Quarterly Journal of Economics*, **108**(3), 577–98.

Kogut, B. (1991), 'Country capabilities and the permeability of borders', *Strategic Management Journal*, **12**, 33–47.

Kogut, B. and U. Zander (1992), 'Knowledge of the firm, combinative capabilities, and the replication of knowledge', *Organization Science*, **3**, 383–97.

Kogut, B. and U. Zander (1993), 'Knowledge of the firm and the evolutionary theory of the multinational corporation', *Journal of International Business Studies*, **24**(4), 625–45.

Lahti, R.K.L. and M.M. Beyerlein (2000), 'Knowledge transfer and management consulting: a look at the firm', *Business Horizons*, **43**(1), 65–74.

Mansfield, E. and A. Romeo (1980), 'Technology transfer to overseas subsidiaries by US-based firms', *Quarterly Journal of Economics*, **95**, 737–50.

McDonald, F., H-J. Tüsselman, S. Voronkova and P. Dimitratos (2005), 'The strategic development of foreign-owned subsidiaries and direct employment in host locations in the United Kingdom', *Environment and Planning C*, **23**(6), 867–82.

Mudambi, R. (2002), 'Knowledge management in multinational firms', *Journal of International Management*, **8**(1), 1–9.

Mudambi, R. and P. Navarra (2004), 'Is knowledge power? Knowledge flows, subsidiary power and rent-seeking within MNCs', *Journal of International Business Studies*, **35**(5), 385–406.

Mudambi, R., L. Piscitello and L. Rabbiosi (2007), 'Mandates and mechanisms: reverse knowledge transfer in MNEs', paper presented at the conference 'Four decades of international business at Reading: looking to the future', 16–17 April, 2007, Reading, UK.

Nobel, R. and J. Birkinshaw (1998), 'Innovation in multinational corporations: control and communication patterns in international R&D operations', *Strategic Management Journal*, **19**, 479–96.

Nohria, N. and S. Ghoshal (1997), The Differentiated Network: Organizing Multinational Corporations for Value Creation, San Francisco: Jossey-Bass.

Papanastassiou, M. and R.D. Pearce (1997), 'Technology sourcing and the strategic roles of manufacturing subsidiaries in the UK: local competences and global competitiveness', *Management International Review*, **37**(1), 5–25.

Papanastassiou, M. and R.D. Pearce (1998), 'Individualism and interdependence in the technological development of MNEs: the strategic positioning of R&D in overseas subsidiaries', in J. Birkinshaw and N. Hood (eds), *Multinational Corporate Evolution and Subsidiary Development*, Basingstoke: Macmillan.

Pavitt, K. (1988), 'International patterns of technological accumulation', in N. Hood and J-E. Vahlne (eds), *Strategies in Global Competition*, London: Croom Helm.

Pearce, R.D. (1989), *The Internationalization of Research and Development by Multinational Enterprises*, Basingstoke: Macmillan.

Pearce, R.D. (1999), 'Decentralized R&D and strategic competitiveness: globalized approaches to generation and use of technology in multinational enterprises (MNEs)', *Research Policy*, **28**, 157–78.

Perlmutter, H.V. (1969), 'The tortuous evolution of the multinational corporation', *Columbia Journal of World Business*, January–February, pp. 9–18.

Phene, A. and P. Almeida (2008), 'Innovation in multinational subsidiaries: the role of knowledge assimilation and subsidiary capabilities', *Journal of International Business Studies*, **39**, 901–19.

Piscitello, L. (2004), 'Corporate diversification, coherence and economic performance', *Industrial and Corporate Change*, **13**(5), 757–87.

Piscitello, L. and L. Rabbiosi (2007), 'The impact of knowledge transfer on

MNEs' parent companies: evidence from the Italian case', in L. Piscitello and G. Santangelo (eds), *Do Multinationals Feed Local Development and Growth?*, Amsterdam: Elsevier, pp. 169–94.

Prahalad, C.K. and G. Hamel (1990), 'The core competence and the corporation', *Harvard Business Review*, May–June, pp. 71–91.

Puranam, P., H. Singh and M. Zollo (2006), 'Organizing for innovation: managing the coordination–autonomy dilemma in technology acquisitions', *Academy of Management Journal*, **49**(2), 263–80.

Randoy, T. and J. Li (1998), 'Global resource flows and MNE network integration', in J. Birkinshaw and N. Hood (eds), *Multinational Corporate Evolution and Subsidiary Development*, Basingstoke: Macmillan.

Ronen, S. and O. Shenkar (1985), 'Clustering countries on attitudinal dimensions: a review and synthesis', *Academy of Management Review*, **10**(3), 435–54.

Schmookler, M. (1950), 'The interpretation of patent statistics', *Journal of Patent Office Society*, **32**(2), 123–46.

Schulz, M. (2003), 'Pathways of relevance: exploring inflows of knowledge into subunits of multinational corporations', *Organization Science*, **14**(4), 4450–59.

Sölvell, Ö. and I. Zander (1998), 'International diffusion of knowledge: isolating mechanisms and the role of the MNE', in A.D. Chandler, P. Hagström and Ö. Sölvell (eds), *The Dynamic Firm – The Role of Technology, Strategy, Organization, and Regions*, New York: Oxford University Press.

Stopford, J.M. and J.H. Dunning (1983), *Multinationals – Company Performance and Global Trends*, Basingstoke: Macmillan.

Szulanski, G. (1996), 'Exploring internal stickiness: impediments to the transfer of best practice within the firm', *Strategic Management Journal*, **17**, 27–43.

Wallmark, T. and D. McQueen (1986), *100 Viktiga Innovationer under Tiden 1945–1980* [100 important innovations in the period 1945–1980], Lund: Studentlitteratur.

Wilkins, M. (1974), 'The role of private business in the international diffusion of technology', *Journal of Economic History*, **34**(1), 166–88.

Yamin, M. (1999), 'An evolutionary analysis of subsidiary innovation and "reverse" transfer in multinational companies', in F. Burton, M. Chapman and A. Cross (eds), *Multinational Enterprise, Transaction Costs and International Organization*, Macmillan AIB series, pp. 85–102.

Yang, Q., R. Mudambi and K.E. Meyer (2008), 'Conventional and reverse knowledge flows in multinational corporations', *Journal of Management*, **34**(5), 882–902.

Zander, I. (1997), 'Technological diversification in the multinational corporation – historical evolution and future prospects', *Research Policy*, **26**(2), 209–27.

Zander, I. (1991), 'Exploiting a technological edge: voluntary and involuntary dissemination of technology', published doctoral dissertation, Stockholm: Institute of International Business.

Zander, I. (1999), 'Whereto the multinational? The evolution of technological capabilities in the multinational network', *International Business Review*, **8**(3), 261–91.

APPENDIX A   THE SAMPLE OF CONSOLIDATED SWEDISH MULTINATIONAL FIRMS

Firm[a]	Principal field of industrial activity
AGA (1904)	Industrial gases
Alfa Laval (1878)	Separators, agricultural equipment
ASEA (1883)[b]	Power generation and distribution equipment
Astra (1913)	Pharmaceuticals
Atlas Copco (1873)	Pneumatic and hydraulic equipment
Electrolux (1910)	White goods, home appliances
Ericsson (1876)	Telecommunication equipment
ESAB (1904)	Welding equipment
Fagersta (1873)	Metals, rock drills
MoDo (1873)	Pulp and paper
Perstorp (1880)	Chemicals, conglomerate
Pharmacia (1911)	Pharmaceuticals
PLM (1919)	Packaging material
Saab-Scania (1891)	Automotive products, aircraft
Sandvik (1862)	Specialty steel and metals, hard materials
SCA (1925)	Pulp and paper
SKF (1905)	Ball- and roller bearings
Stora (1888)	Pulp and paper
Tetra Pak (1946)	Liquid packaging machinery
Trelleborg (1905)	Rubber products, conglomerate
Volvo (1915)	Automotive products, food

Notes:
a. Years in parentheses indicate the year of establishment.
b. ASEA merged with Swiss Brown Boveri et Cie. in 1987, and observations were truncated in 1988.

APPENDIX B   SAMPLE OF CONSOLIDATED SAMPLE FIRMS

Sandvik Aktiebolag	Sandco Limited
Sandviken Jernverk AB	Sandvik Coastal Inc.
AB Sandvik Coromant	Sandvik Conveyor GmbH
AB Sandvik Hard Materials	Sandvik Conveyor Inc.
AB Sandvik Rock Tools	Sandvik GmbH
Alston Tool + Gauge Company Ltd.	Sandvik Hard Materials Ltd.
Diagrit Grinding Company limited	Sandvik Inc.
Disston Inc.	Sandvik Kosta GmbH
Edsbyns Industri AB	Sandvik Rock Tools Inc.

Eurotungstene	Sandvik Special Metal Corporation
Fagersta Secoroc	Sandvik Steel of Colorado Inc. Mesne
Garnett-Bywater Limited	Sandvik Tobler S.A.
Greenleaf Corporation	Santrade Ltd.
Hack Saws Limited	Seco Tools AB
IMK Industriservice AB	Spooner Edmeston Engineering Ltd.
Madison Industries Inc.	Tobler S.A. Mecanique de P. F.-S.
Oberg C.O. + Co. AB	Tobler S.A.
Osprey Metals Limited	Uddeholm Strip Steel Aktiebolag
	Safety S.A.

APPENDIX C   METHODOLOGICAL NOTES

Patents as a proof of advanced technological capabilities using the number of US patents as proof of a subsidiary's capacity to contribute significantly to the technological and strategic development of the multinational group runs the risk of including in the sample those subsidiaries that only display serendipitous technological discoveries. It has not been possible to estimate the relative proportion of these subsidiaries in the current sample, and only a very small number of the identified subsidiaries were responsible for only one patent over the entire period.

A patent is an indicator of innovative performance, which narrows the focus to technological innovations, articulated knowledge, and the associated capabilities (Phene and Almeida, 2008), leaving out other types of innovations across different stages of the value chain. Patents only capture elements of capabilities that are mainly codified, leaving out an extensive amount of knowledge, especially in the context of strongly networked firms such as MNEs (Mudambi and Navarra, 2004). However, a patent can also be perceived as an explicit marker of the existence of a tacit capability underlying the patent; thus, in the current chapter patents are perceived as explicit knowledge of a process including a technological capability.

Finally, although patents as a measure of technology flows are well established in the literature (Jaffe et al., 1993; Almeida, 1996; Mudambi and Navarra, 2004), the empirical investigation only provides a picture of the patterns of technological capability diffusion in the MNE; it does not identify specific mechanisms of the diffusion process itself or the nature of the technological capability. Technological capability diffusion is based on the patenting activity of an advanced foreign subsidiary in a technological class that is new to the entire MNE, and the subsequent patenting activity, in the same technology class by headquarters (that is, if headquarters

apply for and receive a patent in that particular USPTO class). According
to Wilkins (1974), diffusion may have been brought about in several different and possibly overlapping ways, including the transfer of technology,
the international mobility of individuals between subsidiary and headquarters, knowledge exchange as part of inter-subsidiary collaboration or
internationally coordinated R&D projects. In some cases, the diffusion of
technological capabilities may also be the result of independent work on
the same technologies by both subsidiary and headquarters. This measure
is subject to noise, and reverse technological capability diffusion is not
completely captured by this variable. However, there is an extensive body
of literature using patent data to measure knowledge and capability flows
in the MNE, and it is argued that patent data have the advantage of being
objective and generally perceived as a good representative of knowledge
as a whole (Jaffe, 1986; Archibugi and Pianta, 1992; Almeida and Phene,
2004; Feinberg and Gupta, 2004; Mudambi and Navarra, 2004).

Identification of foreign subsidiaries the empirical analysis is based on
the assumption that, over time, the sample firms have maintained one subsidiary per country (an assumption supported by the historical accounts
and information on the international operations of the sample firms in
annual reports), although in some cases individual subsidiaries may have
included several legally separate entities. For many of the observations, it
is known that the parent firm has been awarded a US patent that had its
origin in a foreign country (assumedly because of corporate patenting policies), but the patenting records do not reveal the organizational identity of
the unit performing the actual research. In the analyses, it is assumed that
the research underlying a patent with, for example, UK inventors was also
carried out at the local UK subsidiary.

Period of investigation although the data cover the period 1893–1990,
the majority of entries into new technologies were recorded after 1950.
It should be expected that the reliability of data has improved over the
measured time period, especially as for most firms the United States may
have been perceived as relatively distant in the earlier parts of the twen-
tieth century (and hence not prioritized as a country in which patents were
sought). Accordingly, this serves as the main reason for dividing the analysis into two different time periods, 1893–1990 and 1960–90.

10. Innovation initiative within foreign subsidiaries in South Korea: determinants and outcomes

Axèle Giroud, Yoo Jung Ha and Mo Yamin

10.1 INTRODUCTION

Innovation is the process through which new products or processes are introduced within the firm; it represents the end of a process of knowledge sourcing and transformation, as well as the beginning of a process of exploitation which may result in an improvement in the performance of the innovating firm (Roper and Love, 2008). Within the context of the multinational corporation (MNC), localized subsidiary innovation (innovation initiative) refers to the extent to which subsidiaries develop and adopt new products, processes or administrative systems locally (Mu et al., 2007; Ghoshal and Bartlett, 1988).

The perspectives of organizational learning and knowledge (Cohen and Levinthal, 1990), and inter-firm networks (Forsgren, 2008) explain how subsidiaries have a local network of relationships that provides access to local knowledge. Authors have emphasized the importance of local resources for MNE innovation (Almeida, 1996; Pearce, 1999). In this chapter, both approaches are therefore considered. The literature first described how ownership-specific advantages were developed at the corporate HQ levels, and leveraged overseas through knowledge transfer. It is recognized now, however, that subsidiaries themselves can contribute significantly to the knowledge base of the MNC, creating ownership advantages through operations in dynamic host environments. Thus, foreign subsidiaries play a very important role by acquiring and creating valuable knowledge in their host country, in time, contributing back to the knowledge base of the entire MNEs (Zhao and Luo, 2005; Almeida and Phene, 2004; Birkinshaw and Hood, 2001; Cantwell and Piscitello, 1999).

There are few studies, however, on the specific case of South Korea, even though inward FDI has increased dramatically since the late 1990s (UNCTAD, 2008). One of the aims and contribution of this chapter is to fill this gap and investigate how subsidiaries located in South Korea learn from their operations in this environment and, in turn, contribute to the MNE.

Subsidiaries evolve through accumulation of resources and specialized capabilities (Frost, 2001; Birkinshaw and Hood, 1998), and their role within the multinational network evolves as a result of the headquarters' assignment, subsidiary choice and local environment determinism, these three mechanisms interacting to determine the subsidiary's role at any given point in time (Birkinshaw and Hood, 1998: 775). Therefore, it is acknowledged that the innovation initiative by foreign subsidiaries in South Korea will in part be determined by the dynamics of internal embeddedness, which is their level of interaction with other units of the MNE.

Following earlier work (Cassiman and Veugelers, 2002; Roper et al., 2008), we consider how foreign subsidiaries source knowledge (both internally within their MNE networks or externally within the host economy) to develop innovation initiative, transforming this knowledge into new products and processes, and finally exploiting this to achieve higher performance as business entities but also in terms of contributing, in turn, back to the MNE network. Roper et al. (2008) refer to the process as *innovation value chain*. Thus, another contribution of this chapter is to assess the benefits of innovation initiatives to both the subsidiary itself and the rest of the multinational network. The aim is to investigate the outcome of such innovation for output, performance, as well as reverse transfer to either the HQ or other units of the firm.

The chapter begins with a literature review to explore the background to the development and drivers of innovation initiative, together with the implication of such activities for the subsidiaries and the host economy as well as the multinational network. In the second part of the chapter, the methodology is discussed. Using data from the Korean Innovation Survey, a three-way least squares model is presented to provide answers to the hypotheses. The final section discusses the results and draws conclusions, with a focus on the dynamics of South Korea for building innovatory capacities amongst MNEs.

10.2   THEORETICAL CONSIDERATIONS

The literature first described how ownership-specific advantages were developed at the corporate HQ levels, and leveraged overseas through knowledge transfer. It is recognized now, however, that subsidiaries themselves can contribute significantly to the knowledge base of the multinational firm, creating ownership advantages through operations in dynamic host environments. Thus, foreign subsidiaries play a very important role by acquiring and creating valuable knowledge in their host country, and in time, contributing back to the knowledge base of the entire MNEs (Cantwell and Piscitello, 1999; Birkinshaw and Hood, 2001; Almeida and Phene, 2004; Zhao and Luo, 2005) and to the MNE competitive advantages.

Subsidiaries evolve through accumulation of resources and specialized capabilities (Birkinshaw and Hood, 1998). Overall, subsidiary roles evolve as a result of the headquarters' assignment, subsidiary choice and local environment determinism; these three mechanisms interact to determine the subsidiary's role at any given point in time (Birkinshaw and Hood, 1998: 775). Given that market knowledge and commitment increase with the length of operation in the host market, external embeddedness contributes to the ability of the subsidiary to become competence creating (Cantwell and Mudambi, 2005), and in particular its ability to accumulate innovation capabilities (Frost, 2001).

Foreign subsidiaries can source knowledge either internally from the HQ or other units of the multinational network (Forsgren, 2008) or within the host country environment. Externally, there are various channels through which a foreign subsidiary can source knowledge: either through in-house R&D, through foreign linkages to customers or backward linkages to suppliers or business partners (Jindra et al., 2009), through collaboration with business partners or through linkages to universities and public research centers (Santangelo, 2009). If internal knowledge sourcing is strong, this may discourage other means of knowledge sourcing (from Roper et al., 2008).

Developing and conducting innovation activities is not a sufficient means in itself. The underlying assumption is that the company benefits, and in the case of the MNE, not just the subsidiary but the overall multinational network. The ability of the subsidiary to transform knowledge is dependent upon the subsidiary characteristics, its resource-base and capabilities. The first step is how foreign subsidiaries source knowledge both internally within their MNE network and externally within the host economy (Cassiman and Veugelers, 2002; Roper et al., 2008). This allows the subsidiary to develop innovation initiative, transforming this knowledge into new products and processes. In the final step, the firm can exploit such activities through higher performance and, in turn, through contributing to the knowledge base and competitive advantages of the MNE network. Roper et al. (2008) refer to the process as *innovation value chain*. In the next section, a series of hypotheses are built first around the creation of innovation initiatives, and second around the impact of such initiatives within subsidiaries.

10.2.1   Localized Subsidiary Innovation Initiative

Role of local embeddedness

Local embeddedness refers to the extent to which a subsidiary has established relationships with local institutions such as suppliers, customers and research institutions (Mu et al., 2007, p. 82). Through a network of ties as conduits for information flows, subsidiaries are exposed to new developments in the host market. Gaining access to knowledge in diverse environments requires a physical presence because local knowledge is typically *sticky* and tacit (Szulanski, 1996). This is why foreign subsidiaries can become key agents of learning and innovation.

Research suggests that innovation is enhanced when a firm is connected to many others and has diverse contacts (Powell et al., 1996). The combination of weak and strong ties in the environment strengthens exchange of knowledge and promotes trust amongst business partners, leading to a combination of expertise (Anderson et al., 2002; 2005; Yamin and Otto, 2004; Forsgren et al., 2005). The strongly embedded subsidiary is the one that 'maintains frequent and significant interactions with local organizations' (Håkanson and Nobel, 2001, p. 398), which facilitates the development of local competences (Andersson et al., 2001), and in particular of local innovation initiatives. Thus, we posit that:

Hypothesis 1: There is a positive relationship between subsidiaries' local embeddedness (with local business partners and institutions) and subsidiaries' localized innovation initiative.

Role of internal embeddedness

From the evolutionary perspective, productivity of knowledge creation is determined by dynamics between constituents of the system. Technology transfer and acquisition from various sources are constrained or facilitated by competition and coordination within the networked system of knowledge creation (Kogut, 2000, pp. 408–9). MNEs are created from a network of different geographically dispersed organizations which are related to each other through interpersonal ties. The MNE is viewed as a social community with ability to integrate, combine and create knowledge leading to the creation of competitive advantages (Ambos et al., 2006). Knowledge exchanges and intra-unit relationships strengthen the competence advantage of the subsidiary (Kostova, 1999), providing support for the creation of innovation initiatives.

Hypothesis 2: There is a positive relationship between subsidiaries' internal embeddedness and subsidiaries' localized innovation initiative.

10.2.2   Outcomes of Subsidiary Initiative

There are benefits to the action of competence creation within the subsidiary (Cantwell and Mudambi, 2005); such benefits lie in the evolving position of the subsidiary within the overall multinational network (Forsgren et al., 2005). Through enhanced competences and performance, the subsidiary increases its influence over other parts of the MNE. With innovatory capabilities, the subsidiary can transform knowledge into new products and processes, and demonstrate *innovation output*, such as a larger number of patents. The ability to develop new knowledge is also linked to increased performance by the subsidiary itself.

However, the process through which the subsidiary can enhance its position within the network as a result of its newly created competences is not automatic. The subsidiary's participation in localized knowledge flows is not exogenously determined but endogenous to the development of the capabilities, bargaining power and autonomous strategic position of the subsidiary (Mudambi and Navarra 2004). As a result, the subsidiary's increased local embeddedness can also lead to increased tensions with other parts of the firm; in some cases, the subsidiary may experience barriers in planning its portfolio of innovation resources. Subsidiaries' ability to act as a 'technology vehicle' is based on their absorption of knowledge but this can be hindered 'when they behave completely autonomously and strive for their own interests' (Manolopoulos et al., 2005, p.262). Potentially the attempt at devolution from the MNE initiative would be penalized by the restricted access to firm-specific assets within the MNE networks. For instance, it is reported that localized knowledge flows erode the bargaining power and thereby rent appropriability of subsidiaries (Mudambi and Navarra, 2004, p.392).

To overcome such problems, as well as the situation when knowledge exchange within the multinational network is encouraged by the headquarters, the subsidiary will tend to strengthen its relationships with the parent company and other units of the MNE and its position within the network by contributing to the knowledge base of the company. Overall, there are positive impacts of the innovation initiative in the host economy for the subsidiary itself in terms of performance and innovation output, but also for the whole multinational network. Therefore:

Hypothesis 3: Innovation initiative has a positive impact on the subsidiary's ability to generate innovation output, increase its performance and transfer knowledge to the other units of the MNE.

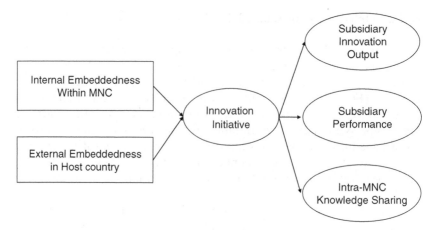

Figure 10.1   Determinants and outcomes of subsidiary initiative

10.2.3   Framework of Analysis

Figure 10.1 presents the model to be tested in this chapter, and covers the *innovation value chain* from the perspective of the foreign subsidiary in a host economy. It shows the drivers to innovation initiatives as well as the impact of the innovation competence for the subsidiary within the host economy and for the entire multinational network.

10.3   METHODOLOGY AND RESULTS

10.3.1   Data

We use the Korean Innovation Survey (KIS) for manufacturing sectors in 2002 and 2005 to test our hypotheses. KIS 2002 reports firms' innovation activities between 1999 and 2001, while KIS 2005 covers the period from 2002 to 2004. This dataset is prepared by the Science and Technology Policy Institute (STEPI) under the Government of the Republic of Korea. It is part of the Community Innovation Survey (CIS) by the OECD and administered under the Law on National Statistics in the Korean context. Participating firms are asked about the importance of knowledge sources, acquisition of technology, technological cooperation, purposes of and barriers to innovation, as well as general information about innovation.

   Although the survey does not allow for the identification of individual responding firms (Veugelers and Cassiman, 2004), it is rich in firm-level information, and provides a large number of responses by MNEs located in South Korea. As such, it is a good source of information on innovation activities conducted by foreign subsidiaries in this country. The dataset contains a total of 423 respondent firms with foreign ownership of 20 per cent or more. However, due to the large number of missing responses, we conducted a careful data screening and decided to only include a total of 113 useable observations with complete answers.

10.3.2 Variables and Measurement

Endogenous and exogenous variables are presented in Table 10.1.

Innovation initiative
Innovation initiative is measured by the extent to which the replacement of existing old-fashioned products with totally new products has been the reason for new technological innovation. For this question, the KIS survey used a five-point Likert scale, from 1 (very low) to 5 (very high). Zero is assigned for 'not applicable'. We consider zero as part of the ordinal scale, assuming that 'not applicable' equals the absence of such an innovation initiative.

External embeddedness
The international business literature has assumed that technological embeddedness is positively related to the increased scope of new product developments (Andersson et al., 2002). The literature on the innovation value chain has suggested that identifying external knowledge resources is the first step of innovation activities (Roper et al., 2008). This chapter therefore specifies innovation initiative as a function of the availability of external knowledge sources. Based on CIS data, we identified four types of external knowledge sources – forward, horizontal, backward, and public knowledge sources (Crespi et al., 2008; Roper et al., 2008).

Internal embeddedness
Foreign subsidiaries also have access to intra-MNE knowledge in addition to local external knowledge. KIS data provides the five-point Likert scale about the importance of knowledge sources, from 1 (very low) to 5 (very high), and zero for 'not applicable', that is, no use of concerned knowledge sources. Using KIS data, we first measure the importance of external technological information by computing the average score of forward information from customers and clients, horizontal information from rival firms in the same market, and backward information from suppliers of intermediate goods and parts. Similarly, the score for public scientific information was computed based on information from universities and

Table 10.1 *Variables, measurements and descriptive statistics*

Short name	Definition	Mean	Standard deviation	Min	Max
Endogenous Variables					
Innovation initiative	Innovation aiming at new product development to replace existing products	3.124	1.753	0	5
Innovation output	Number of patents filed	11.965	32.897	0	205
Intra-MNE knowledge sharing	Importance of intra-MNE knowledge sharing	0.991	1.740	0	5
Sales growth	Sales growth over the past three years	0.347	0.643	−0.774	4.563
Exogenous Variables					
Intra-MNE information	Importance of knowledge from other units of MNE	2.912	1.845	0	5
External technology	Importance of knowledge from public research center	2.582	1.351	0	4.750
External science	Importance of knowledge from public or private institutes and universities	1.422	1.138	0	3.667
Log innovation expenditure	Innovation expenditures	7.247	2.561	1.792	13.816
Log R&D staff	Number of R&D staff	2.955	1.259	0	6.907
Permanent innovation	Presence of permanent R&D department as an indicator of independent knowledge utilization capacity	0.956	0.207	0	1
Appropriability	Concerns about failing to appropriate rents from innovation output	2.708	1.314	1	5
Employment growth	Employment growth over the past three years	0.070	0.245	−0.610	1.133
High-tech industry	Whether or not the industry classification is high-technology by OECD definition	0.434	0.498	0	1

public research centers. The distinction between technological and scientific information was justified based on Manolopoulos et al. (2009).

Previous studies about internal knowledge flows within the MNE structure measured the perceived importance of intra-MNE knowledge flows by asking questions such as: what would the consequence be for other units in the foreign company if they no longer had access to the competencies of a subsidiary? (Foss and Pedersen, 2003). Similarly, to measure the extent to which the subsidiary is embedded in the internal MNE knowledge network, we used firms' responses about the importance of knowledge inflows from affiliated firms within the same MNE group.

Innovation output and exogenous variables

Innovation output can be measured by the number of patents filed by the respondents in the period covered by the survey. We are not oblivious to the drawbacks of patents as the indicator of innovation output. Nevertheless, we justify measuring innovation output by patents because output of innovation activities other than patents is very difficult to observe empirically, and patents are usually filed building on existing knowledge, both visible and invisible (Song and Shin, 2008, p. 296).

Literature has found relationships between innovation output and internal innovation input. Innovation inputs are often specified by *innovation-related expenditures* and the *number of R&D staff* of the firm in Crespi et al. (2008) and Schmiedeberg (2008), among others, which express innovation activities in a form of an innovation production function. KIS provides numeric data for those three variables.

Intra-MNE knowledge sharing and exogenous variables

This chapter measures intra-MNE knowledge sharing by using the responses about the importance of technological cooperation with affiliated firms within the same MNE group. Data is based on the six-point Likert scale where zero indicates the use of intra-MNE knowledge-sharing experiences.

We identified various exogenous variables of external technological cooperation with the help of previous empirical studies. The purpose of exploration of variables is to find a reliable instrument for an endogenous 'intra-MNE knowledge sharing' variable rather than testing each and every factor of external technological cooperation. Therefore, for practicality, we limited our interest to *appropriability* and *absorptive capacity* of the firm, as these are immediately available from KIS data and are considered to be associated with external R&D cooperation in previous studies. The former is measured by the extent to which the possibility of illegal replication of innovation outputs has impeded the firm's innovation process (recorded as a five-point Likert scale, from 1 (very low) to 5 (very high)), while the latter, absorptive capacity, is proxied by the presence of a permanent R&D department and in-house research centers, observed as the binary scale of zero and one.

Subsidiary performance and exogenous variables
Subsidiary performance is measured by sales growth over the surveyed three-year period. The comparison over the three-year period enables changes in performance to be assessed.

The exogenous variables used to explain performance change are the *industry* and *employment growth rate*. To measure the effect of being in the high-tech industry, a dummy variable is created, by assigning 1 for high-tech industry and zero for the others. Industry classification is applied based on 2-digit NACE-Rev. 1 classification of OECD (Schmiedeberg, 2008, p. 1497).

10.3.3   3SLS Model

To test our hypotheses, we used a three-stage least squares (3SLS) model. The model assumes three stages: first, each endogenous variable is instrumented by relevant exogenous variables so as to generate predicted values that will then replace the endogenous variables in the subsequent equation. The second stage is the estimation of a cross-equation covariance matrix of disturbances from the first stage. Finally, the main equation to explain the ultimate dependent variable is estimated based on the covariance matrix and other exogenous variables.

Before running the model, we test how each endogenous variable can be predetermined based on exogenous variables, using determinants identified in previous empirical studies. A test for cross-correlation does not reveal any problems (see Table 10.2).

Dividing firms into high- and low-initiative groups, we found that high-initiative groups tend to use more locally available external technological and scientific knowledge (Figure 10.2). Those firms also reported that they found that intra-MNE knowledge sharing is very important for innovation activities. Consequently, those high-initiative firms filed a smaller number of patents in the survey period but achieved significantly higher performance improvement in the given period of time. Nevertheless, this observation does not represent the *ceteris paribus* effect, that is, the possibility of not accounting for the intervention of other characteristics. The more dynamic relationships among endogenous variables should be further examined with an econometric model.

In the 3SLS model, our main interest is to explain the simultaneous

Table 10.2 Correlation matrix of variables

	1	2	3	4	5	6	7	8	9	10	11	12	13
1. Innovation initiative	1.0000												
2. Intra-MNE information	−0.0269	1.0000											
3. External science	0.1570	−0.1054	1.0000										
4. External technology	0.2755	0.0047	0.4373	1.0000									
5. Innovation output (patents)	0.0061	0.1282	0.2109	0.1042	1.000								
6. Log innovation expenditure	−0.0499	0.2457	0.0465	−0.0679	0.3439	1.0000							
7. Log R&D staff	0.0447	0.1422	0.3334	0.1107	0.4906	0.5178	1.0000						
8. Intra-MNE knowledge sharing	0.1204	0.2307	0.0695	0.1883	−0.0649	0.1218	0.1822	1.0000					
9. Appropriability	0.1476	−0.0329	0.1448	0.0978	0.0016	−0.0483	−0.1221	0.0067	1.0000				
10. Permanent innovation	−0.0833	−0.1510	0.1054	−0.1148	0.0747	0.1716	0.2199	−0.0508	−0.1467	1.0000			
11. Sales growth	0.0443	0.0244	−0.0787	−0.0760	0.1325	0.1903	0.2691	0.2888	−0.1122	0.0635	1.0000		
12. Employment growth	−0.0068	−0.0406	−0.1250	−0.1054	0.0172	0.0639	0.1285	0.1469	0.1215	0.0649	0.4546	1.0000	
13. High-tech industry	−0.0212	0.1200	0.0682	0.0364	−0.0852	−0.0088	−0.0515	0.0354	−0.0231	0.0146	0.0573	−0.1664	1.0000

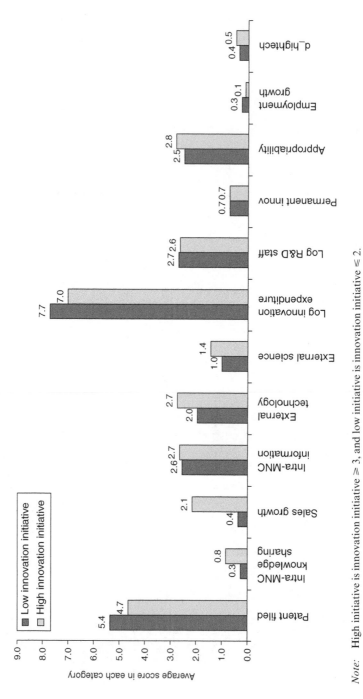

Note: High initiative is innovation initiative ≥ 3, and low initiative is innovation initiative ≤ 2.

Figure 10.2 Comparison of high and low levels of innovation initiative

234

relationships between four endogenous variables, namely, innovation initiative, innovation output, the role of intra-MNE knowledge sharing in respondents' innovation activities and performance change. The iteration command of STATA for 3SLS provided the estimation of Table 10.3. A Hausman test was performed in order to confirm endogeneity of variables so as to argue that 3SLS estimation is more efficient than estimation based on simple OLS. We conducted a Breusch–Pagan test and found heteroscedasticity at the 95 per cent significance level, while heteroscedasticity was not detected when we relaxed the significance level to 90 per cent. The evidence of mild heteroscedasticity means that there may be endogenous variables omitted in this model. For the test of over-identification, we computed the Sargan score and found that this model was not overidentified at the 95 per cent level, that is, the number of endogenous variables used in this model is adequate.

Our dataset is a pooled cross-section data from year 2002 and year 2005, as this method is successful when testing pooled cross-section data (Wooldridge, 2009). To make sure that there are no statistically significant structural breaks between the two years, we perform the Chow test, based on a simple multiple regression.

We start by checking relationships between endogenous variables and related exogenous variables. Model 1 shows the effect of knowledge sources on the innovation initiative of subsidiaries. Coefficients for intra-MNE information and external technology are positive and significant. The effect of external scientific knowledge on innovation initiative is not significant. This empirical result can be compared with Manolopolous et al. (2009)'s finding that firms tend to consider external technological knowledge valuable, even if what actually contributes to performance change is external scientific knowledge from public research centers.

In Model 2, all explanatory variables turned out to be significant except for innovation expenditures. The size of innovation expenditure is positively related to innovation output. As predicted, the number of R&D staff turns out to positively affect innovation output of the subsidiary.

Model 3 shows that high appropriability concerns prevent the subsidiary from sharing knowledge with other units of the MNE, as predicted. The presence of permanent innovation and research departments plays no significant role on intra-MNE knowledge sharing. This could be due to the fact that the number of patents filed absorbs most effects related to a firm's internal innovation capacity.

Finally, Model 4 tests the effects of exogenous and endogenous variables on the performance change of subsidiaries. The two control variables – being in a high-tech industry and employment growth – are both significant and have a positive effect on sales growth (our proxy for performance

Table 10.3   Results of 3SLS model

	No. of observations	R^2	Chi^2	p	
Model 1	113	0.059	10.390	0.016	**
Model 2	113	−0.019	39.380	0.000	***
Model 3	113	−0.475	9.260	0.055	*
Model 4	113	−6.852	143.340	0.000	***

	Coefficient	Std. error	Z	p>|z|	
Model 1					
innovation initiative					
Intra-MNE information	0.098	0.058	1.680	0.093	*
External science	0.078	0.099	0.780	0.433	
External technology	0.249	0.106	2.360	0.019	**
Constant	2.087	0.359	5.810	0.000	
Model 2					
patent filed					
Innovation initiative	9.669	5.597	1.730	0.084	*
Log innovation expenditure	1.798	1.122	1.600	0.109	√
Log R&D staff	10.293	2.411	4.270	0.000	***
Constant	−32.005	14.622	−2.190	0.029	
Model 3					
intra-MNE knowledge sharing					
Innovation initiative	0.731	0.359	2.040	0.041	**
Patent filed	0.015	0.010	1.430	0.152	√
Appropriability	−0.086	0.061	−1.410	0.160	√
Permanent innovation	−0.202	0.341	−0.590	0.554	
Constant	−1.047	1.172	−0.890	0.372	
Model 4					
sales growth					
Innovation initiative	−0.764	0.288	−2.650	0.008	***
Patent filed	−0.002	0.008	−0.270	0.786	
Employment growth	1.115	0.277	4.020	0.000	***
Intra-MNE knowledge sharing	0.778	0.150	5.180	0.000	***
D_high-tech	0.192	0.114	1.690	0.091	*
Constant	1.825	0.895	2.040	0.041	
Hausman test	chi^2(15)=30.05		Prob>chi^2 =0.0117		**
Breusch–Pagan test	chi^2(1)=3.86		Prob > chi^2=0.0495		**
Sargan score	chi^2(3)=6.41		Prob > chi^2=0.92		
Chow test	F(4, 93) =0.98		Prob > F =0.4203		

Note: $* = p < 0.1$; $** = p < 0.05$; $*** = p < 0.01$.

change). Innovation initiative is negatively associated with performance change.

10.4 DISCUSSIONS AND CONCLUSIONS

Our first and second hypotheses consider the factors facilitating innovation initiative at the level of the subsidiary. We find a clear relationship between the level of knowledge received from other units of the multinational network and the innovation initiative of foreign subsidiaries. Results for the external embeddedness, however, point to differences between the external scientific knowledge environment and the external technological knowledge environment. Foreign subsidiaries benefit from public research centers within South Korea. Our third hypothesis analyzes the impact of innovation initiative within the subsidiary.

We find that innovation initiative is positively associated with innovation output (see Figure 10.3). Innovation initiative also raises the profile of intra-MNE knowledge sharing in subsidiaries' innovation activities. Thus, we conclude that innovation initiative is a common cause for innovation output and intra-MNE knowledge sharing.

Our results show that the number of patents filed has no effect on intra-MNE knowledge sharing. This could be because the subsidiary's accumulation of internal knowledge reduces the relative importance of intra-MNE knowledge. Innovation output can operate as a mediator on the indirect relationships between initiative and intra-MNE knowledge sharing.

Our findings are consistent with those of Yamin and Otto (2004) but not with those of Mudambi and Navarra (2004). Whether or not local external and MNE internal knowledge assets are complementary can be interpreted as successful intra-MNE coordination for subsidiaries to carry out dispersed innovation activities, while substitutive relations could indicate either limited mandate of subsidiaries due to the centralized mode of MNE governance or the absence of an intra-MNE coordination mechanism (Grant, 1996). In this case, one can question whether foreign subsidiaries in South Korea are actively involved in coordination with their headquarters or other units of the MNE regarding their innovation initiative.

Performance change measured by sales growth is negatively associated with innovation initiative. Innovation initiative may result in the creation and accumulation of internal knowledge, as supported by the positive relationships between innovation initiative and innovation output. Figure 10.3 shows that innovation output does not mediate the indirect

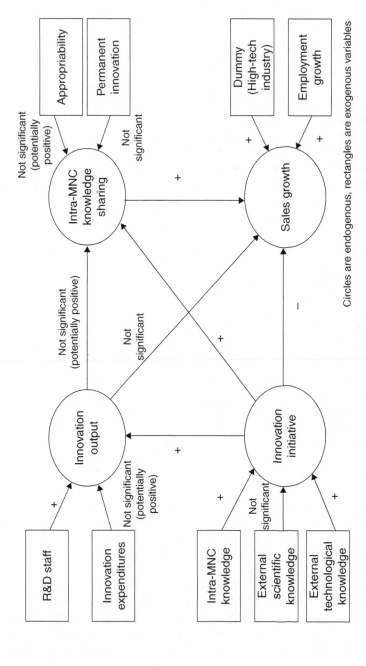

Figure 10.3   Relationships between internal and external sources and intra-MNE knowledge sharing

effect of innovation initiative on performance change. This could be explained by the fact that firms have binary priorities of short-term and long-term goals and the allocation of managerial time on either goal is reflected in the time frame of realized performance change (Liu, 2008).

Innovation initiative and innovation output are related to long-term goals that can differ from sales growth, which tends to be a short-term goal. This can explain why our data fails to observe the link between innovation initiative and performance change. Intra-MNE knowledge does generate a mediating effect in the negative association between innovation initiative and sales growth. This could be because intra-MNE knowledge sharing helps innovative subsidiaries to balance short-term and long-term goals more effectively.

To conclude, this study has provided a useful insight into the innovation initiative of foreign subsidiaries in the South Korean context. Few studies have considered the evolving role of foreign subsidiaries in Korea, their ability to develop innovation initiatives, the drivers behind such initiatives and their potential to contribute knowledge to the multinational network. This is because MNEs have only started investing substantially in South Korea since the late 1990s. By now, however, foreign subsidiaries have developed competences, and have started benefiting from the technological knowledge of their host economy.

The main limitation of the study lies in the use of the Korean Innovation Survey data, as this does restrict the number of variables that can be included in the model. Because there is no access to the name of the firms that take part in the study, it is not possible to add to the existing dataset. Additionally, the large number of missing values lowers the overall number of cases included in the model (although over 423 firms took part in the survey, only 113 cases could be used in the analysis).

REFERENCES

Almeida, P. (1996), 'Knowledge sourcing by foreign multinationals: patent citation analysis in the US semiconductor industry', *Strategic Management Journal*, **17**(special issue), 155–65.

Almeida, P. and A. Phene (2004), 'Subsidiaries and knowledge creation: the influence of the MNC and host country on innovation', *Strategic Management Journal*, **25**(8/9), 847–64.

Ambos, T.C., B. Ambos and B.B. Schlegelmilch (2006), 'Learning from foreign subsidiaries: an empirical investigation of headquarters' benefit from reverse knowledge transfers', *International Business Review*, **15**, 294–312.

Andersson, U., I. Björkman and M. Forsgren (2005), 'Managing subsidiary knowledge creation: the effect of headquarters control mechanisms on subsidiary external network embeddedness', *International Business Review*, **14**, 521–38.

Andersson, U., M. Forsgren and U. Holm (2001), 'Subsidiary embeddedness and competence development in MNCs: a multi-level analysis', *Organization Studies*, **22**(6), 1013–34.

Andersson, U., M. Forsgren and U. Holm (2002), 'The strategic impact of external networks: subsidiary performance and competence development in the multinational corporation', *Strategic Management Journal*, **23**, 979–96.

Birkinshaw, J. and N. Hood (1998), 'Multinational subsidiary development: capability evolution and charter change in foreign-owned subsidiary companies', *Academy of Management Review*, **23**(4), 773–95.

Birkinshaw, Julian and Neil Hood (2001), 'Unleash innovation in foreign subsidiaries', *Harvard Business Review*, **79**(3), 131–7.

Cantwell, John and Ram Mudambi (2005), 'MNE competence-creating subsidiary mandates', *Strategic Management Journal*, **26**(12), 1109–28.

Cantwell, J. and L. Piscitello (1999), 'The emergence of corporate international networks for the accumulation of dispersed technological competence', *Management International Review*, **39**(1), 123–47.

Cassiman, B. and R. Veugelers (2002), 'R&D cooperation and spillovers: some empirical evidence from Belgium', *American Economic Review*, **92**(4), 1169–84.

Cohen, W.M. and D.A. Levinthal (1990), 'Absorptive capacity: a new perspective on learning and innovations', *Administrative Science Quarterly*, **35**(1), 128–52

Crespi, G., C. Criscuolo, J.E. Haskel and M. Slaughter (2008), 'Productivity growth, knowledge flows and spillovers', Centre for Economic Performance, NBER working paper, no. 13959, National Bureau of Economic Research.

Forsgren, M. (2008), *Theories of the Multinational Firm: a Multidimensional Creature in the Global Economy*, Cheltenham, UK and Northampton, MA, USA: Edward Elgar Publishing.

Forsgren, M., U. Holm and J. Johanson (2005), *Managing the Embedded Multinational: A Business Network View*, Cheltenham, UK and Northampton, MA, USA: Edward Elgar Publishing.

Foss, N. and T. Pedersen (2003), 'The MNC as a knowledge structure: the roles of knowledge sources and organizational instruments in MNC knowledge management', DRUID Working Paper, Copenhagen Business School.

Frost, T.S. (2001), 'The geographic sources of foreign subsidiaries' innovations', *Strategic Management Journal*, **22**(2), 101–23.

Ghoshal, S. and C.A. Bartlett (1988), 'Creation, adoption, and diffusion of innovations by subsidiaries', *Journal of International Business Studies*, **19**(3), 365–88.

Grant, R.M. (1996), 'Towards the knowledge-based theory of the firm', *Strategic Management Journal*, **17**, 109–22.

Håkanson, L. and R. Nobel (2001), 'Organizational characteristics and reverse technology transfer', *Management International Review*, **41**(4), 395–420.

Jindra, B., A. Giroud and J. Scott-Kennel (2009), 'Subsidiary roles, vertical linkages and economic development: lessons from transition economies', *Journal of World Business*, **44**(2), 167–79.

Kogut, B. (2000), 'The network as knowledge: generative rules and the emergence of structure', *Strategic Management Journal*, **21**(3), 405–25.

Kostova, T. (1999), 'Transnational transfer of strategic organizational practices: a contextual perspective', *Academy of Management Review*, **24**(2), 306–24.

Liu, Z. (2008), 'Foreign direct investment and technology spillovers: theory and evidence', *Journal of Development Economics*, **85**, 176–93.

Manolopoulos, D., M. Papanastassious and R. Pearce (2005), 'Technology sourcing in multinational enterprises and the roles of subsidiaries: an empirical investigation', *International Business Review*, **14**, 249–67.

Manolopoulos, D., P. Dimitratos, S. Young and S. Lioukas (2009), 'Technology sourcing and performance of foreign subsidiaries in Greece: the impact of MNE and local environmental contexts', *Management International Review*, **49**(1), 43–9.

Mu, S., D.R. Gnyawali and D.E. Hatfield (2007), 'Foreign subsidiaries' learning from local environments: an empirical test', *Management International Review*, **47**(1), 79–102.

Mudambi, R. and P. Navarra (2004), 'Is knowledge power? Knowledge flows, subsidiary power and rent-seeking within MNCs', *Journal of International Business Studies*, **35**, 385–426.

Pearce, R. (1999), 'Decentralized R&D and strategic competitiveness: globalised approaches to generation and use of technology in multinational enterprises', *Research Policy*, **28**(2–3), 157–78.

Powell, W.W., K.W. Koput and L. Smith-Doerr (1996), 'Interorganizational collaboration and the locus of innovation: networks of learning in biotechnology', *Administrative Science Quarterly*, **41**(1), 116–45.

Roper, S., J. Du and J.H. Love (2008), 'Modelling the innovation value chain', *Research Policy*, **37**, 61–77.

Santangelo, G.D. (2009), 'MNCs and linkages creation: evidence from a peripheral area', *Journal of World Business*, **44**(2), 192–205.

Schmiedeberg, C. (2008), 'Complementarities of innovation activities: an empirical analysis of the German manufacturing sector', *Research Policy*, **37**, 1492–503.

Song, J. and J. Shin (2008), 'The paradox of technological capabilities: a study of knowledge sourcing from host countries of overseas R&D operations', *Journal of International Business Studies*, **39**, 291–303.

Szulanski, G. (1996), 'Exploring internal stickiness: impediments to the transfer of best practice within the firm', *Strategic Management Journal*, **17**, 27–44.

UNCTAD (2008), *World Investment Report 2008*, New York and Geneva: UNCTAD.

Veugelers, R. and B. Cassiman (2004), 'Foreign subsidiaries as a channel of international technology diffusion: some direct firm level evidence from Belgium', *European Economic Review*, **48**(2), 455–76.

Wooldridge, J.M. (2009), *Introductory Econometrics*, 4th edn, Mason, OH: South-Western Cengage Learning.

Yamin, M. and J. Otto (2004), 'Patterns of knowledge flows and innovative performance in MNEs', *Journal of International Management*, **10**(2), 239–58.

Zhao, H. and Y. Luo (2005), 'Antecedents of knowledge sharing with peer subsidiaries in other countries: a perspective from subsidiary managers in a foreign emerging market', *Management International Review*, **45**(1), 71–97.

11. Management control in creative firms

Nathalie Beckers, Martine Cools and Alexandra Van den Abbeele

11.1 INTRODUCTION

This chapter investigates the role of management control instruments to stimulate creativity in an organizational context. Creativity and the resulting innovations are of utmost importance for enterprises today (Amabile and Khaire, 2008). Innovation is the process which follows on creativity, and it can thus be seen as the implementation of creative ideas. Creativity is thus a critical step in the innovation process (Shalley, 1991). The results of the creative process can take different forms, ranging from administrative versus technical innovation, product versus process innovation, and radical versus incremental innovation (Damanpour, 1991). Innovating, however, is a risky activity, which needs to be carefully monitored by the management of the organization. This implies that accounting can play an important role to inform internal and external parties about the success of creative activities and the innovative outcomes reached. The earliest studies on the role of accounting for innovation used to focus on firm-wide innovation (West and Farr, 1989) as measured by expenditures on research and development (R&D) activities (Sougiannis, 1994, Lev and Sougiannis, 1996). The financial accounting literature investigates how intangible value drivers and intellectual capital are valued for external reporting reasons (for example Basu and Waymire, 2008; Cañibano et al., 2000; Van der Meer-Kooistra and Zijlstra, 2001). The management accounting and control literature, however, has only recently started to study how innovation and creativity are affected by the design and use of the management control system (MCS) (Davila et al., 2009a). Management control refers to the process of collecting and using information for the coordination of planning and control decisions, in order to make sure that employees act in the interest of the organization as a whole (Horngren et al., 2006). The MCS is therefore the system that includes all the devices managers use to ensure that the behavior of employees is consistent with the organization's objectives and strategies (Merchant and Van der Stede, 2007, p. 5). Management control is one of the tools for implementing strategy, besides human resources management, the organization's structure and culture. It broadly includes strategic planning, budgeting, resource allocation, performance measurement, evaluation and rewarding, responsibility center allocation and transfer pricing (Anthony and Govindarajan, 1995). The management control perspective on innovation and creativity leads to a couple of research questions which have only recently come to the attention of academics: what is the role of management accounting and control in stimulating creativity and innovation? How do firms experience the tension between the need for a MCS to avoid control problems and the fear that such a system hinders entrepreneurial processes?

In the context of this debate, our chapter has two objectives. First, we review the management accounting and control literature to provide an overview of the research findings related to innovation and creativity. We will hereby also consider articles related to the role of management accounting and control in departments for new product development and R&D, as these are the departments in which creativity matters a lot in established organizations. Second, this literature review allows us to identify a number of gaps in the literature and to consequently make some suggestions for future research. We formulate research ideas at four levels of analysis: the individual level, the group level, the firm level and the inter-firm level.

The remainder of this chapter is structured as follows. In the literature review we consecutively consider management accounting and control papers related to innovation, to new product development and R&D, and finally to creativity. In the section that follows, we identify the research gaps and propose how these gaps could be tackled within the management accounting and control discipline. In this section we also report on our exploration with the key informants from the design sector, in order to provide insights in the relevance of our suggestions for practice. The final section provides our overall conclusions.

11.2 REVIEW OF THE MANAGEMENT ACCOUNTING AND CONTROL LITERATURE

In this section, we provide an overview of articles published in the management accounting and control literature related to innovation and creativity. The first subsection focuses on the role of management accounting and control to stimulate innovation. The second subsection presents the management accounting and control articles on new product development and R&D, while the third subsection explains the results in terms of the role of management control for stimulating creativity. We searched the management accounting literature[1] using the keywords 'creativity' and 'innovation' to analyze the articles published until December 2009. We further took into account related articles investigating MCS use in R&D and new product development environments. Overall, the management accounting and control literature tends to support the relevance of control to innovation (Davila et al., 2009b).

11.2.1   Management Accounting and Control Systems and Innovation

In the management accounting and control literature, most studies focus on innovation rather than on creativity. Table 11.1 provides an overview of the innovation-related papers. The MCS papers are presented in terms of their focus on MCS *design* (Panels A and B) versus *use* (Panels C and D). The papers on MCS design either focus on the top level (Panel A) or on the business unit (Bu) level (Panel B). The papers on MCS use discuss either the formal (versus a rather informal) use (Panel C) or a dynamic (versus a rather static) use of cost accounting to innovation (Panel D).

A first category of studies examines the role of management compensation to stimulate innovation (Table 11.1, Panel A). Taking a firm-level perspective, Ittner et al. (1997) examine the factors influencing the relative weights placed on financial and non-financial performance measures in CEO bonus contracts. They find that the use of non-financial measures increases with the extent to which the firm follows an innovation-oriented strategy. A more recent study on management compensation at firm level is undertaken by Xue (2007). Xue (2007) studies a firm's innovation process by examining the relationship between CEO compensation contracts and a firm's choice of obtaining new technology internally ('make') or externally ('buy'). The results show that managers' approach to innovation is largely determined by different types of incentive compensation. Risk-averse and utility-maximizing managers implement the 'buy' strategy if their compensation is heavily weighted on accounting-based performance measures. Managers with more stock-based compensation on the other hand, especially stock options, appear to have a preference for the 'make' strategy. Ghosh et al. (2007) take a different approach: they study the role of management control towards innovation in the tradition of measuring firm-wide innovation in terms of R&D expenditures (Sougiannis, 1994; Lev and Sougiannis, 1996). More specifically, Ghosh et al. (2007) study the relationship between CEO stock ownership and discretionary investments such as R&D and capital expenditures, thereby

Table 11.1   *Management accounting and control systems and innovation*

Paper	Focus/Results	Research set-up
Panel A: MCS design at top level		
Ittner et al. (1997)	Use of non-financial measures linked with innovation-oriented strategy	Use of secondary data (317 firms)
Xue (2007)	Relationship between CEO compensation contracts and a firm's choice of obtaining new technology internally or externally	Use of secondary data (US high-tech industries: 9268 observations)
Ghosh et al. (2007)	Non-linear association between CEO ownership and R&D investments due to a combination of incentive-alignment and entrenchment effects of equity ownership	Use of secondary data (9831 US firm year observations)
Panel B: MCS design at BU level		
Holthausen et al. (1995)	Positive relationship between divisional CEO compensation and future innovation but no relationship with expected innovation opportunities	Use of secondary data (299 US divisions)
Panel C: Formal use of MCS at top management level		
Bisbe and Otley (2004)	Style of use of MCS moderates the impact of innovation on performance: interactive use of MCS favors innovation only in low-innovating firms, not in high-innovating firms	Survey (58 CEOs of medium-sized, mature manufacturing Spanish firms)
Bisbe and Malagueño (2009)	Relationship between interactive use of MACS and a firm's innovation management mode	Survey (57 medium-sized Spanish firms)
Henri (2006)	Interactive use of performance measurement systems fosters organizational capabilities like innovation	Survey (383 listed Canadian manufacturing firms)
Panel D: Dynamic view on MCS use within the organization		
Mouritsen et al. (2009)	Management accounting calculations (and associated management control systems) relate innovation activity to firm-wide concerns	Field study involving 3 small and medium-sized companies
Revellino and Mouritsen (2009)	Examination of how controls change and adapt to the innovation as the innovation unfolds	Single case study

focusing on the over- and under-investment problem. They find a non-linear association between CEO stock ownership and R&D investments. Furthermore, they observe that R&D investments and CEO stock options are positively associated at high levels of option holdings whereas capital expenditures do not vary with CEO ownership. Finally, they conclude that the influence of R&D investments on future firm risk is significantly greater than that of capital expenditures.

In contrast to the firm-level focus in Ittner et al. (1997), Xue (2007) and Ghosh et al. (2007), Holthausen et al. (1995) study whether the structure of executive compensation at the business unit level is related to the expected innovation opportunity set and to subsequent innovative activity (Table 11.1, Panel B). They find no evidence that the proportion of total compensation tied to long-term components has a positive relation with the expected innovation opportunities that divisions are faced with. They do find, however, modest evidence that the proportion of total compensation tied to long-term components has a positive relation with future innovation.

While the previous set of studies focuses on the design of management compensation, a number of more recent studies examine the use of formal MCS at top management level and its impact on innovation (Table 11.1, Panel C). Bisbe and Otley (2004) and Bisbe and Malagueño (2009) build on Simons' (1995, 2000) distinction between three types of control systems: 'belief' and 'boundary' systems frame the strategic domain, while 'feedback and measurement' systems are used to elaborate and implement the strategy. Belief and boundary systems are formal systems that explicitly outline the acceptable domain of activity for organizational participants. Belief systems provide an explicit set of beliefs, by defining basic values, purpose and direction: the way value is created, the level of desired performance and human relationships are taken into account. Boundary systems provide formally stated rules and limits. The proscriptions are tied to defined sanctions and there is a credible threat for punishment (Simons, 1995, 2000). Once these formal sets delineate the activity domain, the feedback and measurement systems help to implement the intended strategy and to adapt to competitive environments. In this context, Simons (1995, 2000) distinguished between the diagnostic versus the interactive use of the MCS. Diagnostic systems aim to follow up to which extent the results fulfill the intended strategy. They focus on deviations and exceptions to monitor and reward achievement of specified goals through the review of key success factors.

In contrast, interactive systems aim to stay tuned to the environment. Such interactive systems focus the attention of top management on constantly changing strategic information. Top managers are strongly involved by paying frequent and regular attention to interactive control systems. In addition, they send messages to the whole organization in order to focus attention on strategic uncertainties. They put pressure on operating managers at all levels of the organization, and in this way guide and provide input to innovation. In terms of MCS use, Simons (1995, 2000) suggests that an interactive MCS contributes to successful innovation.

Bisbe and Otley (2004) refine Simons' claim by studying whether an interactive control system makes companies more innovative, or whether it makes innovative companies more successful in terms of improved performance. Based on a survey involving Spanish CEOs, they come to the conclusion that an interactive use of the MCS only seems to favor innovation in low-innovating firms, but that it seems to discourage innovation in high-innovating firms. While they do not find an indirect effect of an interactive use of the MCS on performance acting through innovation, they do find that the style of use (interactive versus diagnostic) of the MCS moderates the impact of innovation on performance. In a follow-up survey, Bisbe and Malagueño (2009) further investigate the interactive versus diagnostic use of management accounting and control systems to foster innovation. Simons (2000) pointed out that top managers happen to make deliberate and systematic choices as to which individual MCS instruments to use interactively and which diagnostically. Bisbe and Malagueño (2009) find that this choice is associated with a firm's innovation management mode (IMM). IMM refers to commonly occurring configurations of organizational and managerial processes by which innovation arises and is managed (Roussel et al., 1991, Park and Kim, 2005). Three IMMs can be identified, namely intuitive, systematic and strategic IMMs. An intuitive IMM conceives simple and isolated forms of innovation initiatives in a context where a strategic framework for innovation management is lacking. In the systematic IMM, decisions regarding innovation initiatives are mostly taken on a project-by-project basis, while interrelationships among projects and the implications at the firm level are not addressed. In the strategic IMM, firms emphasize the interrelationships among innovation initiatives and seek to create a strategically balanced portfolio of innovation initiatives formulated through the integration of technology and business perspectives. Bisbe and Malagueño (2009) observe that the level of product innovation output is influenced by whether or not the IMM and interactive management accounting and control systems feature similar cognitive models. The sophistication of the information contents provided by the interactive MCS should respond to the priority needs perceived in the IMM. Similarity in patterns between the IMM and management accounting and control systems, on the other hand, does not lead to a beneficial impact on the level of innovation outputs.

Henri (2006) studies the diagnostic and interactive uses of one aspect of the MCS, namely performance measurement systems, in the context of four capabilities leading to strategic choices (market orientation, entrepreneurship, innovativeness, and organizational learning). His results show that an interactive use of performance measurement systems fosters these four capabilities by focusing organizational attention on strategic priorities and stimulating dialogue. He further finds that by creating constraints to ensure compliance with orders, the diagnostic use of performance measurement systems exerts negative pressure on the capabilities. The evidence finally confirms that there is an influence of dynamic tension, resulting from the balanced use of performance measurement systems in a diagnostic and interactive fashion, on capabilities and performance.

Panel D in Table 11.1 refers to two papers by Mouritsen and his colleagues, taking a dynamic view on management accounting and control systems' use in relation to innovation. Mouritsen et al. (2009) show how management accounting calculations, instead of only describing the properties of innovation, add perspective to them by mediating between innovation concerns and firm-wide concerns. The authors interviewed 20 to 25 managers in three small and medium-sized enterprises about their efforts to control and account for innovation. They find that management accounting calculations – sales performance, contribution margin, and ABC margin – relate innovation activity to the firm in two ways. Mouritsen et al. (2009) refer to them as different types of translations. A 'short translation' refers to a single calculation, which helps extend or reduce innovation activities in view of an actual or a possible performance variance. A 'long translation' mobilizes at least two calculations to problematize the role of innovation for corporate purposes differently: these multiple calculations challenge each other and develop organizational struggles concerning the role of innovation, its location in time and space, and this in terms of technological, organizational and environmental issues. In this way, the long translation develops competing contexts for innovation and impacts firms' innovation strategies and sourcing arrangements. When there is extreme pressure for innovation activities to prove their strategic significance, the tensions between calculations are likely to bend innovation activities more to considerations such as growth, productivity, profitability and liquidity. Revellino and Mouritsen (2009) study MCS use in the context of innovation. They undertook a case study focusing on the introduction of the Telepass, which was an important innovation for the Italian 'Autostrade'. They observed that a multiplicity of control instruments, including elements of budgetary planning, strategic vision, user satisfaction, productivity and highly challenging targets, changed and adapted to the innovation as the innovation unfolded. The controls were considered much more as a part of the innovation than as external devices to make it transparent. Revellino and Mouritsen (2009) conclude that innovation and the MCS co-develop, in other words that the MCS should be structured by taking into account the characteristics of the innovation.

11.2.2 Management Accounting and Control Systems in New Product Development Departments

Closely related to the MCS studies on innovation, we group a number of studies on the design and use of the MCS in R&D and new product development departments. Table 11.2 provides an overview of the articles reviewed below.

Abernethy and Brownell (1997) explore MCS design in the shape of accounting versus non-accounting controls in an R&D setting. They find that non-accounting controls, especially personnel forms of control, contribute to organization effectiveness when task uncertainty is high. This is the case when the degree of variety in the tasks encountered (defined as the number of exceptions) is high and the existence of well-established techniques for performing tasks (task analyzability) is low. Furthermore, both accounting and behavior controls appear unsuitable when the number of exceptions is high. As such, they conclude that the number of exceptions has a more significant influence on the suitability of controls compared to task analyzability.

A number of other studies (see Table 11.2, Panel B) focus on the role of the MCS to improve new product development. Davila (2000) examines the relationship between project uncertainty, product strategy and MCS, to explore whether the MCS helps or hinders product development performance. Based on case studies involving R&D managers, marketing managers and business unit managers of new product development teams in both European and US companies, he concludes that project uncertainty and product strategy are relevant to explain the design of the MCS. Better cost and design information appear to have a positive association with performance. Time information, such as information on the time-to-market, on the other hand, hinders performance. Davila et al. (2009a) examine the adoption of MCS in product development in the context of early-stage entrepreneurial companies. Instead of questioning the role of the MCS as a help or impediment towards product development performance (compare Davila, 2000), they start from the acknowledgement that the MCS is important for enhancing innovation (for example Simons, 1995; Cardinal, 2001; Cardinal et al., 2004).

Table 11.2   Management accounting and control systems in R&D firms and new product development

Paper	Results/Focus	Research set-up
Panel A: MCS design in R&D departments		
Abernethy and Brownell (1997)	Higher effects of non-accounting than accounting controls on organizational effectiveness in an R&D setting	Survey (150 senior research officers in the R&D divisions of a large Australian industrial company and a major US scientific organization)
Panel B: MCS design in new product development departments		
Davila (2000)	Exploration of the drivers of MCS design in new product development: better cost and design information has a positive effect on performance, whereas time information hinders performance	Case studies (12 business units in seven companies, both in Europe and the US)
Davila et al. (2009a)	Identification of internal and external reasons for adoption of MCS in product development in early-stage entrepreneurial companies	Survey (69 early-stage entrepreneurial companies)
Drake et al. (1999)	Effectiveness of activity-based costing (ABC) relative to traditional volume-based costing on process innovation is influenced by its interactive effect with incentive compensation	Experiment with 132 MBA students
Hertenstein and Platt (2000)	Investigation of MCS practice and link of MCS to strategy in new product development departments: new product development department reports at a fairly high level in the organization because of the need to integrate new product development and strategy	Empirical study (interviews and survey) involving over 75 industrial design managers

Davila et al. (2009a) gathered field material through a survey and a large number of interviews and identify six different reasons for adoption. These include external factors such as contracting and legitimizing the process with external parties, and internal reasons such as managers' background, learning, the need to focus the company on executing the strategy when it is failing to do so, or reaction to problems. Furthermore, they find an association between different reasons-for-adoption and time-to-adoption. The reason-for-adoption also appears to be associated with the on-time dimension of product development performance.

Another relevant field study is undertaken by Hertenstein and Platt (2000). They investigate MCS practice and the link of control to strategy for new product development. They find that the firms under investigation experienced a need to integrate new product development and strategy. On the one hand, this trend led to higher reporting levels, and to shifts in reporting from engineering to marketing. On the other hand, they observed that the integration between new product development and strategy integration was not well reflected in performance measures. Even though the firms studied used different financial and non-financial performance measures, relatively few firms reported that their performance measures reflected key aspects of their strategies. New product development managers were generally dissatisfied with the performance measurements, and firms were searching for more effective alternatives.

Still in the context of new product development, Drake et al. (1999) undertook an experiment involving MBA students to examine how accounting cost systems and incentive structure choices interact. The authors investigate process innovation in work teams, and classify innovations as either cooperative or individual. Cooperative innovation requires the coordination of at least two team members, while only one person working alone carries out an individual innovation. In terms of the costing systems, they investigate the effect of the traditional volume-based costing system versus the use of activity-based costing (ABC) which focuses attention on activities and resources which are usually under control by multiple people. In terms of the incentive structures, they compare an individual incentive scheme (tournament-based incentives) versus a group incentive scheme (group-based incentives). They assume and find that the number of cooperative innovations, reached when group-based incentives are in place, are higher than when tournament-based incentives are used, and that this result is even stronger when an ABC system is used as compared to a traditional volume-based system. However, while as expected the highest profits appear when ABC is linked with group-based incentives, the lowest levels of profits surprisingly occur when ABC is coupled with tournament-based incentives.

11.2.3 Management Control Systems to Stimulate Creativity

While the accounting literature has focused on the theme of innovation, only a limited number of studies have just recently investigated the

Table 11.3   Management control systems and creativity

Paper	Results/Focus	Research set-up
MCS design at individual level		
Chang and Birkett (2004)	Development of a conceptual framework on the balance between creativity and productivity and exploration of the framework for one professional service firm. The case study shows that after a restructure, competency standards also ensure professional creativity (on top of productivity)	Case study (one large international chartered accounting firm)
Kachelmeier et al. (2008)	Experimental study on the impact of performance-based compensation on worker productivity: participants rewarded for creativity-weighted output simplify their objective by restricting their production to high-creativity ideas, but are unable to translate this focus into a greater number of high-creativity output	Experiment with 78 undergraduate business students
Kachelmeier and Williamson (2010)	Experimental study extending Kachelmeier et al. (2008) by allowing participants to choose between different incentive contracts: participants choosing a creativity-weighted pay scheme are eventually caught up by participants choosing a quantity-only contract, not only in terms of quantity but also in terms of creativity	Experiment with 90 undergraduate business students

preceding creative process (Chang and Birkett, 2004; Kachelmeier et al., 2008; Kachelmeier and Williamson, 2010). Davila et al. (2009b) confirm that the impact of control systems on creativity has been virtually ignored. Table 11.3 refers to the scarce number of papers on the role of MCS to foster creativity at the individual level.

Chang and Birkett (2004) use an in-depth case study approach to explore their conceptual framework integrating and balancing the concepts of creativity and productivity. They hereby build on the literature suggesting that structural capital plays an integral role in knowledge creation and management. The case study consists of an investigation into how a professional service firm configures its structural capital in the form of competency standards: they study the competency standards used by an Australian branch of a large international chartered accounting firm before and after a major firm restructure. Chang and Birkett (2004) find that the competency standards after the restructure have a more balanced set of expectations about creativity and productivity from their professionals, whereas the competency standards before the restructure predominantly ensured professional productivity alone.

In contrast to the previous approach, Kachelmeier et al. (2008) and Kachelmeier and Williamson (2010) provide experimental evidence on the use of MCS instruments to foster creativity. In both articles, the authors investigate the effect of different types of incentive schemes on creativity. At the same time, they acknowledge that worker productivity should be evaluated both in terms of the quantity produced and in terms of the creativity of the outcome, since firms must generate creative innovations while also maintaining high ongoing productivity in order to succeed in a competitive economic environment (Chang and Birkett, 2004). Kachelmeier et al. (2008) are the first researchers to examine how people respond to creativity incentive payments both in the presence and in the absence of quantity incentives.

In this context, they asked the participants in the experiment to design rebus puzzles to find out whether worker productivity differs when compensation is based on quantity, creativity, or the product of both measures. Kachelmeier et al. (2008) in the first place conclude that quantity-based compensation improves quantity and that creativity-based compensation improves average creativity ratings. Combining quantity and creativity measures in a creativity-weighted pay scheme, however, results in creativity-weighted productivity scores that are significantly lower than those generated by participants with quantity incentives alone. Follow-up analysis indicates that participants in all conditions produce a similar number of high-creativity puzzles. However, in addition to these high-creativity efforts, participants with quantity-only incentives in addition produce a significantly larger number of reasonable but more mediocre puzzles. The authors conclude that participants rewarded for creativity-weighted output simplify their objective by restricting their production to high-creativity ideas, but are unable to translate this focus into a greater volume of high-creativity output.

Kachelmeier and Williamson (2010) extend this research stream with an experiment on the implications of contract selection. Again, the participants have the task to design rebus puzzles, but at the same time they are allowed to choose between a contract that rewards creativity-weighted productivity and a contract that only rewards quantity. During a preceding practice period, participants are informed of both potential contracts and then randomly assigned to one of these contracts. In this preceding round, Kachelmeier and Williamson (2010) replicate the result of Kachelmeier et al. (2008) that quantity-only compensation leads to significantly higher creativity-weighted productivity scores than creativity-weighted productivity compensation. In the next round, participants can choose between both contracts. The results reveal that participants who choose the creativity-weighted pay scheme indicate significantly higher self-perceptions of creative ability and generate significantly higher creativity-weighted productivity scores than those who choose a quantity-only contract across the first several units of production. Participants choosing the creativity-weighted pay scheme, however, appear to be unable to sustain their initial advantage, as quantity-only participants eventually produce just as many high-creativity puzzles and significantly more puzzles overall. Kachelmeier and Williamson (2010) conclude that the same advantage can be attained with the quantity-only compensation when participants are allowed to decide upon the compensation contract as when the contracts are randomly assigned.

11.3 RESEARCH GAPS AND SUGGESTIONS FOR FUTURE MANAGEMENT CONTROL RESEARCH ON INNOVATION AND CREATIVITY

Our review of the management accounting and control literature related to innovation and creativity allows us to formulate a number of suggestions for future research. One of the obvious conclusions from our review is that studies on MCS design and use for reaching innovation outnumber the studies focusing on how to foster creativity. It is clear that the MCS literature on the paradoxical balance of creativity and control is still in its infancy. Davila et al. (2009b) confirm that the interaction between organizational forces and creativity – an important field of research in the creativity literature – has yet to be explored. Another observation that we make is that creativity and innovation are typically studied at different levels of analysis: innovation is typically studied at the business unit level or firm level, while creativity has only been studied at the individual level. We identify a need for future research directed at four levels: the individual level, the group level, the firm level and the inter-firm level. In the remainder of this section, we formulate our suggestions for each of these levels.

11.3.1 MCS for Stimulating Creativity at the Individual Level

A first level of analysis that comes into mind when thinking about how to stimulate creativity is the level of the individual. Given that innovative results are the outcome of creative efforts not only by people, but also by the organizational and environmental context, it is not surprising that we did not encounter studies on the innovations reached at the individual level. The few management control papers on stimulating creativity are all situated at the individual level. Experiments like the ones undertaken by Kachelmeier et al. (2008) and Kachelmeier and Williamson (2010) are particularly useful to study how to stimulate individual creativity in an organizational context. It remains puzzling that firms in practice seem to be reluctant to incorporate creativity measures within multidimensional performance measurement systems such as the balanced scorecard (Kaplan and Norton, 1996), notwithstanding published suggestions to do so (Ittner et al., 1997). On the one hand, firms might fear that rewarding employees for creativity might be ineffective, or they might be reluctant because creativity is hard to measure. On the other hand, Kachelmeier et al. (2008) point out the unintended consequences of incorporating creativity measures in multidimensional evaluation and compensation schemes. It could lead employees to suppress less-creative productivity, even if this does not necessarily lead to gains in high-creativity output. A lot also seems to depend on whether output of lesser creativity is valued positively or negatively at the margin. Under the experimental conditions set by Kachelmeier et al. (2008) and Kachelmeier and Williamson (2010), the role of feedback on the participants' progress towards the productivity or creativity goals imposed is ignored, even though feedback is an important aspect of the evaluating and reward system in practice. Kachelmeier et al. (2008) suggest that when given feedback, the participants with the creativity goal might even try harder to be creative, which does not necessarily lead to more creative outcomes (Amabile, 1996, 1998). The sensitivity of incentives to feedback (as suggested by Sprinkle, 2000) is taken into account in an ongoing research project by Beckers et al. (2012) on how to stimulate creativity for groups.

Apart from suggesting that experiments be undertaken to examine various conditions under which individual creativity can be fostered, we call for empirical papers taking into account the complexity of creativity. The MCS literature on creativity considers creativity as a one-dimensional concept. In contrast to the accounting studies discussed (Chang and Birkett, 2004; Kachelmeier et al., 2008; Kachelmeier and Williamson, 2010), various researchers disaggregate this concept by identifying different types of creativity (Sternberg, 1999; Unsworth, 2001; Litchfield, 2008). In addition, innovative results have for a long time been recognized as divergent in nature. Damanpour (1991) classified them as administrative versus technical innovation, product versus process innovation, and radical versus incremental innovation.

Would a different composition of the MCS stimulate different forms of creativity? A study into the use of management control instruments to stimulate various types of creativity is therefore our next suggestion for future research.

11.3.2   MCS for Stimulating Creativity and Innovation at Group Level

In this section we want to highlight the research gap related to the role of management control to foster group creativity, since team-based structures are increasingly used in organizations (Sprinkle, 2003). Very little management control literature examines creativity or innovation at the group level. Drake et al. (1999), focusing on process innovations at the group level, is a notable exception. They stress that past research on innovative behavior has led to conflicting results (Damanpour, 1991) because innovation at individual versus group level received scant attention. A few articles outside the research field of accounting investigate creativity in groups. One example is the study by Leenders et al. (2007), who develop a conceptual model of the effect of design methodology on the creative performance of new product development teams. Although not a management control paper, Leenders et al. (2007) examine the same tension of exerting control versus enhancing creativity, specifically in new product development activities. Their main conclusion is that the creative performance required from new product development teams is driven by the communication structure of the team. A first interesting avenue for future research at the group level is therefore to investigate in the field which types of control systems are appreciated in a teamwork environment. Which management control instruments are used in this environment, and to which degree do team members feel stimulated by them?

A second avenue for future research lies with experimental studies. Drake et al. (1999) provide an accounting experiment and focus on how different types of cost information (especially more rude information under a traditional volume-based costing system versus more detailed and accurate information under an ABC system) stimulate innovation in teams. Studies on the role of management control to foster creativity in a team context, however, are still scarce. Sprinkle (2003) stresses that few studies in managerial accounting have yet examined performance-evaluation and compensation issues in group settings. One exception is a recent working paper by Chen et al. (2012). In their experiment, three-person groups need to come up with a creative destination for a historic building. They manipulate the measurement of creativity (at the individual versus at the group level) as well as the incentive system (as a linear piece rate compensation versus a tournament compensation).[2] They suggest that inter-group tournament pay has the effect that group members feel more like a group, and come up with a more creative group solution. Under individual-based pay, the group members work harder individually, but the outcome is not more creative. Again, this experimental setting leaves room for future management accounting research paying attention to incentive issues in workgroups and teams, especially to stimulate creativity and innovation. One project heading in this direction is a recent study by Beckers et al. (2012). They investigate how small groups working on creative tasks react when feedback is given or not given, and when rewarded with different compensation schemes (for example rewards based on quantity only versus rewards based on both quantity and creativity).

11.3.3 MCS for Stimulating Creativity and Innovation at the Firm Level

As already mentioned, the earliest studies on the role of accounting for innovation used to focus on firm-wide innovation as measured by expenditures on R&D activities. In Table 11.1 we discussed the papers on how to stimulate divisional-level and firm-level innovation from a management accounting and control perspective (Ittner et al., 1997; Xue, 2007; Ghosh et al., 2007). The scarcity of papers leaves ample room for elaborating on this interesting research topic. Also when undertaking a more extensive literature review outside the field of accounting, we could only identify a few papers that explicitly investigate the relationship between incentives and innovation at the firm level. Balkin et al. (2000) report that CEO compensation is related to innovation at the firm level, but only in high-tech firms. And Service and Boockholdt (1998) examine a number of factors such as organizational culture and organizational communications and how these factors encourage successful innovation at the firm level.

Future research can investigate how typical management control aspects influence creativity and innovation at the firm level. This literature has for instance not even answered how budgets – the traditional management control tool – impact creativity (Davila et al., 2009b, p. 296). In Cools and Van den Abbeele (2010) we explore this research question in a number of design firms. We pay attention to the use of formal controls (such as budgeting, formal evaluations of employees' performance) and informal controls (such as trust, organizational culture, attracting the right colleagues) (Dekker, 2004; Merchant and Van der Stede 2007). Another way to expand this research stream is to refine the studies by Bisbe and Otley (2004), Bisbe and Malagueño (2009) and Henri (2006). The focus should hereby not only be on how the design and use of different types of MCS (for example interactive versus diagnostic) impact on divisional and firm-level innovations, but also on how different types of incentive systems (for example firm-level versus individual-based compensation packages) help to foster innovations (for example number of new products introduced, number of patents).

11.3.4 MCS for Stimulating Creativity and Innovation in Inter-firm Cooperation

The management accounting and control literature has recently paid attention to inter-firm cooperation, and to the way in which inter-organizational relationships need to be managed. However, no study so far has investigated how creativity is or can be stimulated in inter-organizational relationships. In other words, what is the influence of the steering by principals on the creativity in the executing design firm? The existing management accounting literature on this topic demonstrates the importance of an effective management control system for collaborative relationships (for example Anderson and Dekker, 2005; Dekker, 2004; Dekker and Van den Abbeele, 2010; Langfield-Smith and Smith, 2003; van der Meer-Kooistra and Vosselman, 2000, van der Meer-Kooistra and Vosselman, 2006). This is especially relevant given the high failure rates for this type of relationship.

One crucial question that has not yet been answered in this literature, is how the creativity of a partner in inter-organizational relationships can be stimulated and controlled at the same time. An important area for future research is therefore to investigate how creativity and innovation within inter-organizational relationships can be managed. In-depth case study research involving both parties in the inter-organizational relationship (that is, the principal as well as the firms working under contract to the principal) would be an interesting avenue to advance this unexplored topic. Another way to advance this topic could consist of an in-depth analysis of contracts between principals and creative firms working for the principal (for example, design firms in creative industries). Recent papers in the management literature have started to code strategic alliance contracts (Argyres et al., 2007; Reuer and Ariño, 2007; Ryall and Sampson, 2009). In the accounting literature, however, inter-firm contracts have not yet been systematically analyzed, especially not in creative and innovative settings. Such detailed contract analyses can provide interesting insights into the formal control mechanisms contracted between principals and the firms working on creative tasks under contract to the principal (for example design firms).

11.3.5   MCS for Stimulating Creativity and Innovation at Top Versus Lower Organizational Levels

Finally, Table 11.1 indicates that management accounting and control studies focus on the link between performance measurement systems and innovation/creativity at one specific level in the organization: the top or the lower – unit or subunit – levels. We wonder whether the MCS of the company can satisfy the needs of both the top level and these lower management levels. While this is quite a general question that remains largely unanswered within the MCS literature, the investigation of the use of the MCS at the top versus the lower levels in the organization related to stimulating innovation and creativity deserves a particular focus. Case studies would provide a suitable way to dig into this underexplored area.

11.4   CONCLUSIONS

In this chapter we review the literature to gain better insights into the contradictory views on management control in a creative environment. On the one hand, MCS seem to be needed in order to create a working environment that allows creative minds to focus on their job. On the other hand, MCS are thought to be hindering creativity, and in that sense seem to be restricted to the minimum. For the literature review we searched the management accounting and control literature related to fostering creativity as well as innovation, since both concepts are highly intertwined. We identified three groups of studies: nine articles deal with the management accounting and control studies on innovation, five papers investigate the use of management accounting and control in R&D settings and new product development departments, and three studies focus on how management control systems can stimulate creativity. In other words, our overviews reveal that MCS studies focusing on how to stimulate innovation outnumber the studies focusing on how to foster creativity. In the second place we identify research gaps related to management control and innovation and creativity meriting future research. We hereby formulate research ideas at four levels of analysis: the individual level, the group level, the firm level and the inter-firm level. Our suggestions include ideas for experiments on stimulating individual and group creativity when feedback and compensation schemes are manipulated. We also suggest paying more attention to the nature of creativity and the resulting different types of innovation, by undertaking field studies on the role of management control towards different types of creativity. The literature would also benefit from studies on how typical management control instruments (especially budgets) influence innovation and creativity at firm level. Do these instruments hinder or foster creativity? We further call for studies paying attention to the different needs for management control instruments between the top and the lower levels in the organization, and to stimulating creativity in inter-organizational relationships. A lot is moving in this interesting field at the moment, but we are still waiting for the answer to our questions.

NOTES

1. We searched the following journals for papers on 'creativity' and 'innovation': *The Accounting Review, Journal of Accounting and Economics, Journal of Accounting Research, Review of Accounting Studies, Accounting, Organizations and Society, Contemporary Accounting Research, Management Accounting Research, European Accounting Review, Journal of Management Accounting Research, Journal of Business, Finance & Accounting, Abacus, Accounting and Business Research, British Accounting Review, Accounting Horizons, Accounting, Auditing and Accountability Journal,* and *Advances in Accounting.* Since our focus is not on management accounting techniques and the diffusion of management accounting innovation, we exclude articles related to these topics.
2. Compensation is based on the outcome of a winner-take-all tournament. In the individual-based (intra-group) tournaments, individuals compete against members of their own group. In the group-based (inter-group) tournaments, groups compete with other groups.

REFERENCES

Abernethy, M.A. and P. Brownell (1997), 'Management control systems in research and development organizations: the role of accounting, behavior and personnel controls', *Accounting, Organizations and Society*, **22**, 233–48.

Amabile, T.M. (1996), *Creativity in Context: Update to the Social Psychology of Creativity*, Boulder, CO: Westview Press.

Amabile, T.M. (1998), 'How to kill creativity', *Harvard Business Review*, **76**(5), 77–87.

Amabile, T.M. and M. Khaire (2008), 'Creativity and the role of the leader', *Hardvard Business Review*, **86**(10), 100–109.

Anderson S.W. and H.C. Dekker (2005), 'Management control for market transactions: the relation between transaction characteristics, incomplete contract design and subsequent performance', *Management Science*, **51**, 1734–52.

Anthony, R.N. and V. Govindarajan (1995), *Management Control Systems*, Chicago, IL: Irwin.

Argyres, N.S., J. Bercovitz and K.J. Mayer (2007), 'Complementarity and evolution of contractual provisions: an empirical study of IT services contracts', *Organization Science*, **18**, 3–19.

Balkin, D.B., G.D. Markman and L.R. Gomez-Mejia (2000), 'Is CEO pay in high-technology firms related to innovation?', *Academy of Management Journal*, **43**(6), 1128–9.

Basu, S. and G. Waymire (2008), 'Has the importance of intangibles really grown? And if so, why?', *Accounting and Business Research*, **38**(3), 171–90.

Beckers, N., M. Cools and A. Van den Abbeele (2010), 'Management control and group creativity', Working Paper, KU Leuven.

Beckers, N., M. Cools and A. Van den Abbeele (2012), 'Creative performance in a group setting: the impact of compensation scheme and relative performance feedback', Working Paper, KU Leuven.

Bisbe, J. and R. Malagueño (2009), 'The choice of interactive control systems under different innovation management modes', *European Accounting Review*, **18**(2), 371–405.

Bisbe, J. and D. Otley (2004), 'The effects of the interactive use of management control systems on product innovation', *Accounting, Organizations and Society*, **29**, 709–37.

Cañibano L., M. Garcia-Ayuso and P. Sánchez (2000), 'Accounting for intangibles: a literature review', *Journal of Accounting Literature*, **19**, 102–30.

Cardinal, L. (2001), 'Technological innovation in the pharmaceutical industry: the use of organizational control in managing research and development', *Organization Science*, **12**(1), 19–36.

Cardinal, L. B., S.B. Sitkin and C.P. Long (2004), 'Balancing and rebalancing in the creation and evolution of organizational control', *Organization Science*, **15**(4), 411–31.

Chang, L. and B. Birkett (2004), 'Managing intellectual capital in a professional service firm: exploring the creativity–productivity paradox', *Management Accounting Research*, **15**, 7–31.

Chen, X., M. Williamson and H. Zhou (2012), 'Reward system design and group creativity: an experimental investigation', *Accounting Review*, **87**, 1885–1911.

Cools, M. and A. Van den Abbeele (2010), 'Management control in creative firms', Working Paper, KU Leuven.

Damanpour, F. (1991), 'Organizational innovation: a meta-analysis of effects of determinants and moderators', *Academy of Management Journal*, **34**, 555–90.

Davila, A. (2000), 'An empirical study on the drivers of management control systems design in new product development', *Accounting, Organizations and Society*, **25**, 383–410.

Davila, A., G. Foster and M. Li. (2009a), 'Reasons for management control systems adoption: insights from product development systems choice by early stage entrepreneurial companies', *Accounting, Organizations and Society*, **34**, 322–47.

Davila, A., G. Foster and D. Oyon (2009b), 'Accounting and control, entrepreneurship and innovation: venturing into new research opportunities', *European Accounting Review*, **18**(2), 281–311.

Dekker, H.C. (2004), 'Control of inter-organizational relationships: evidence of appropriation concerns and coordination requirements', *Accounting, Organizations and Society*, **29**, 27–49.

Dekker, H.C. and A. Van den Abbeele (2010), 'Organizational learning and interfirm control: The effects of partner search and prior exchange experiences', *Organization Science*, forthcoming (available online).

Drake, A.R., S.F. Haka and S.P. Ravenscroft (1999), 'Cost system and incentive structure effects on innovation, efficiency and profitability in teams', *The Accounting Review*, **74**(3), 323–45.

Ghosh, A., D. Moon and K. Tandon (2007), 'CEO Ownership and discretionary investments', *Journal of Business Finance & Accounting*, **34**(5–6), 819–39.

Henri, J.F. (2006), 'Management control systems and strategy: a resource-based perspective', *Accounting, Organizations and Society*, **31**, 529–58.

Hertenstein, J.H. and M.B. Platt (2000), 'Performance measures and management control in new product development', *Accounting Horizons*, **14**(3), 303–23.

Holthausen, R.W., D.F. Larcker and R.G. Sloan (1995), 'Business unit innovation and the structure of executive compensation', *Journal of Accounting and Economics*, **19**(2/3), 279–313.

Horngren, C.T., S. Datar and G. Foster (2006), 'Cost Accounting: a Managerial Emphasis, 12th edn, Upper Saddle River, NJ Prentice Hall.

Ittner, C.D., D.F. Larcker and M.V. Rajan (1997), 'The choice of performance measures in annual bonus contracts', *The Accounting Review*, **72**, 231–550.

Kachelmeier, S.J. and M.G. Williamson (2010), 'Attracting creativity: the initial and aggregate effects of contract selection on creativity-weighted productivity', *The Accounting Review*, forthcoming.

Kachelmeier, S.J., B.E. Reichert and M.G. Williamson (2008), 'Measuring and motivating quantity, creativity or both', *Journal of Accounting Research*, **46**(2), 341–73.

Kaplan, R. and D. Norton (1996), *The Balanced Scorecard: Translating Strategy Into Action*, Boston, MA: Harvard Business School Press.

Langfield-Smith, K. and D. Smith (2003), 'Management control systems and trust in outsourcing relationships', *Management Accounting Research*, **14**, 281–307.

Latané, B., K. Williams and S. Harkins (1979), 'Many hands make light the work: the causes and consequences of social loafing', *Journal of Personality and Social Psychology*, **37**, 822–32.

Lev, B. and T. Sougiannis (1996), 'Penetrating the book-to-market black box: the R&D effect', *Journal of Business Finance & Accounting*, **26**, 419–49.

Leenders, R. Th. A.J., J.M.L Van Engelen and J. Kratzer (2007), 'Systematic design methods and the creative performance of new product teams: do they contradict or complement each other', *Journal of Product Innovation Management*, **24**, 166–79.

Litchfield, R.C. (2008), 'Brainstorming reconsidered: a goal-based view', *Academy of Management Review*, **33**(3), 649–68.

Merchant, K.A. and W.A. Van der Stede (2007), *Management Control Systems. Performance Measurement*, Evaluation and Incentives, 2nd edn, Harlow: Prentice Hall.

Mouritsen, J., A. Hansen and C.O. Hansen (2009), 'Short and long translations: management accounting calculations and innovation management', *Accounting, Organizations and Society*, **4**, 738–54.

Park, Y. and S. Kim (2005), 'Linkage between knowledge management and R&D management', *Journal of Knowledge Management*, **9**(4), 34–44.

Reuer, J.J. and A. Ariño (2007), 'Strategic alliance contracts: dimensions and determinants of contractual complexity', *Strategic Management Journal*, **28**, 313–30.

Revellino, S. and J. Mouritsen (2009), 'The multiplicity of controls and the making of innovation', *European Accounting Review*, **18**(2), 341–70.

Roussel, P.A., K.N. Saad and T.J. Erickson (1991), *Third Generation R&D: Managing the Link to Corporate Strategy*, Boston, MA: Harvard Business School Press.

Ryall, M.D. and R.C. Sampson (2009), 'Formal contracts in the presence of relational enforcement mechanisms: evidence from technology development projects', *Management Science*, **55**(6), 906–25.

Service, R.W. and J.L. Boockholdt (1998), 'Factors leading to innovation: a study of managers' perspectives', *Creativity Research Journal*, **11**, 295–307.

Shalley, C.E. (1991), 'Effects of productivity goals, creativity goals, and personal discretion on individual creativity', *Journal Applied Psychology*, **76**, 179–85.

Simons, R. (1995), *Levers of Control: How Managers Use Innovative Control Systems to Drive Strategic Renewal*, Boston, MA: Harvard Business, School Press.

Simons, R. (2000), *Performance Measurement & Control Systems for Implementing Strategy, Text & Cases*, Upper Saddle River, NJ: Prentice Hall.

Sougiannis, T. (1994), 'The accounting-based valuation of corporate R&D', *The Accounting Review*, **69**, 44–68.

Sprinkle, G.B. (2000), 'The effect of incentive contracts on learning and performance', *The Accounting Review*, **75**, 299–326.

Sprinkle, G.B. (2003), 'Perspectives on experimental research in managerial accounting', *Accounting, Organizations and Society*, **28**, 287–318.

Sternberg, R.J. (1999), 'A propulsion model of types of creative contributions', *Review of General Psychology*, **3**, 83–100.

Unsworth, K. (2001), 'Unpacking creativity', *Academy of Management Review*, **26**(2), 289–97.

Van der Meer-Kooistra, J. and E.G.J. Vosselman (2000), 'Management control of interfirm transactional relationships: the case of industrial renovation and maintenance', *Accounting, Organizations and Society*, **25**, 51–77.

Van der Meer-Kooistra J. and E.G.J. Vosselman (2006), 'Research on management control of interfirm transactional relationships: whence and whither', *Management Accounting Research*, **17**, 227–37.

Van der Meer-Kooistra J. and S.M. Zijlstra (2001), 'Reporting on intellectual capital', *Accounting, Auditing & Accountability Journal*, **14**(4), 456–76.

West, M.A. and J.L. Farr (1989), 'Innovation at work: psychological perspectives, *Social Behavior*, **4**, 15–30.

Xue, Y. (2007), 'Make or buy new technology: the role of CEO compensation contract in a firm's route to innovation', *Review of Accounting Studies*, **12**, 659–90.

12. The TELE case: linking innovation process and culture in a large service company

Jens O. Meissner and Martin Sprenger

12.1 INTRODUCTION

Two trends in innovation management influenced the basic idea for this chapter. First, the increasing number of managerial attempts to design linear innovation management processes that can be derived from literature and practice. Second, the increasing acceptance of an innovation culture dynamics as a key driver for innovations. The two approaches partly contrast each other.

The first approach supposes that innovation processes can be structured in a more or less rigid manner. Exponents of this stream are, for example, Cooper's stage-gate model (Cooper, 1998), the funnel model (for example Terwiesch and Ulrich, 2009) or the open innovation process model (Chesborough, 2003). These concepts are not capable of adequately dealing with innovation dynamics (and sources) that cannot be regulated by a formal structural method, for example a process model. This is usually the case within irregular business circumstances or the exposition to unpredictable societal dynamics. However, in organizational innovation, irregularity is a typical variable.

The second approach is based on culture concepts. Examples of exponents of this stream are Schein's culture model (Schein, 1992), Sackmann's iceberg model (Sackmann, 1991), the cultural core model or Want's corporate culture hierarchy (Want, 2003). These models explain the relevance of implicit, more or less hidden or invisible dynamics of innovation within social structures and organizations. It has been widely confirmed in theory and practice that companies cannot assess the tacit dimension of innovation culture (for example Nonaka and Takeuchi, 1995). However, it can never be systematically assessed and completely explained by management initiatives. Even so, the hidden beliefs and attitudes about innovation and innovativeness massively influence the social processing of innovation projects.

The topic of product development in the sense of innovation management has been picked up by Brown and Eisenhardt (1995). According to
them the empirical literature about product development can be organized into three streams. First is product development as a rational plan.
According to this perspective a product that is well planned, implemented
and appropriately supported will be a success. That is when the product
has advantages in the marketplace, is targeted in an attractive market and
is well executed through excellent internal organization. Selected studies
of this stream are, for example, Cooper and Kleinschmidt (1987) or Zirger
and Maidique (1990). The second stream of research is product development as a communication web. According to this stream, external communication (with suppliers and customers) is critical to successful product
development. Successful product development teams include gatekeepers,
who encourage team communication outside their groups, and powerful
project managers who communicate externally to ensure resources for the
group. Internal communication improves development-team performance. Cross-functional teams that structure their internal communication
around concrete tasks, novel routines and fluent job descriptions have
for example been associated with improved internal communication
and successful products. Selected studies of this stream are, for example,
Anaconda and Caldwell (1990) or Dougherty (1992). The third stream
has been termed the disciplined problem-solving perspective. According
to this stream, successful product development involves relatively autonomous problem solving by cross-functional teams with a high level of communication and with work being organized according to the demands of
the development task. Extensive supplier networks, coupled with overlapping product development phases, communication and cross-functional
groups improve the performance of development teams. This perspective
also highlights the role of project leaders and senior management. There
is an emphasis on both project and senior management, on the one hand,
to provide a vision or discipline to the development efforts, and on the
other hand to provide autonomy to the teams. Examples of studies of this
stream are Womack et al. (1990) or Clark and Fujimoto (1991).

Based on the analysis of literature, Brown and Eisenhardt (1995) developed an integrative model which summarizes the key findings within
the literature (see Figure 12.1). The key to developing such an integrative model was the observation that the streams have complementary
theoretical approaches. The organizing idea behind the model was that
there are multiple players whose actions influence product performance.
Specifically, they argue that the project team, leader, senior management
and suppliers affect process performance (for example speed and productivity of product development); the project leader, customers and senior

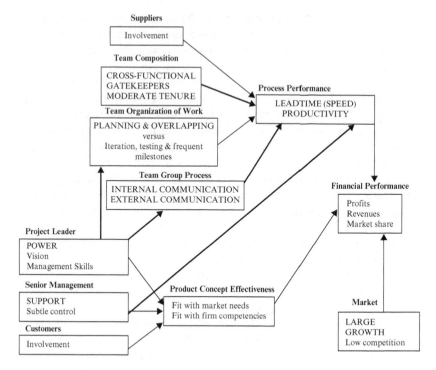

Note: Capital letters and thickened lines indicate robust findings.

Source: Brown and Eisenhardt (1995).

Figure 12.1   Factors affecting the success of product-development projects

management affect product effectiveness (that is, the fit of the product
with firm competencies and market needs); and the combination of an efficient process, effective product and munificent market shapes the financial
success of the product (that is, revenue, profitability, and market share).

A missing issue in this study and in the literature in general is the link
between innovation culture and project management. Classical innovation
management is based on the assumption that ideas can be more or less
easily generated (for example with idea management), or that they can be
handled like a production process (for example stage-gate process). This is
in large part a sterile and dehumanized view of innovation management.
Important questions regarding a company's corporate culture remain
unanswered, for example, how and where did the idea originate, what role
do individuals or groups of people play, and how will the power structure
of the enterprise be decided? This missing link represents the theoretical

field of this chapter. Our research question focuses on how basic assumptions of team members occur in managed organizational innovation activities and how they influence the effectiveness of the innovation process.

In order to answer these questions, a group of researchers analyzed the development process of a new product. More precisely, the innovation process of a telecom enterprise has been studied in the context of a single case study. The goal of the case study was to investigate the specific dynamics of innovation for this company, and to describe their impact on the new product. Of special interest was how innovation behavior and the corporate culture of the firm were interrelated. This case study is part of a research project called Innovation Dynamics in Practice (IDIP). In this project, innovation will be considered from a systemic constructivist perspective (Berger and Luckmann, 1967; Gergen, 1985; Luhmann, 2000; Baecker, 2003; Aderhold and John, 2005), which focuses on the social dynamics in innovation processes, and their impact.

12.2   TELE: AN ENTERPRISE FROM THE SWISS TELECOM INDUSTRY

The case study was completed in conjunction with a major enterprise within the telecom industry in Switzerland. For decades the telecom industry in Switzerland has been a controlled monopoly market. With the revision of the Communications Law in 1998, the market in Switzerland – and in the EU – was liberalized. One of the reasons for this governmental change was the hope that various economic advantages would be realized. The legislator estimated that as a result telecommunication costs would be lowered, and an additional wave of innovation would follow (Abegg, 2005, p. 76). Evidence shows that these goals were not too audacious and have indeed been met. With this liberalization, a number of telecommunication firms have entered the market. Since then, a lot of better-priced, high-quality products and services have become available (Vaterlaus et al., 2004, p. 10).

In general, the telecom market is dynamic, with very fast-paced technological growth. In addition, it is characterized by the convergence of the technologies of: telecommunication, data communication and television. This is because the telecoms of today are offering a new mix of services to their customers, which is in addition to their traditional telecommunications product offerings. Therefore a mixture of technologies are involved, which are tailored to specific customer needs, often in the form of a bundle of services. So it is not surprising that, according to a study carried out by the University of Zurich in 2004, in this mature industry, still a lot of above-average innovation activity prevails (Vaterlaus et al., 2004, p. 10).

The company being investigated, which, for the purpose of anonymity, will subsequently be called 'TELE', is a subsidiary of a large foreign telecom company, but with respect to its daily business decisions, operates more or less autonomously. Especially for innovation projects, TELE has its own allocated budget to develop new products and services. TELE has approximately 1000 employees within Switzerland, who are situated at several locations around the country.

Up until now, TELE has worked more or less only in one business segment. In this segment TELE fulfills the needs of both business and private customers. The share of the company's entire business volume for business customers encompasses a mere 10 per cent. This has a significant impact on the budget allocation within these business units. Therefore, our study focused on the innovation that takes place in a business unit, which receives a significantly smaller portion of the entire corporate budget than the private customer unit.

12.3   METHODOLOGY

We have chosen a qualitative approach focusing on 'building a complex, holistic picture, formed with words, reporting detailed views of informants, and conducted in a natural setting' (Creswell, 1994, p. 2). So qualitative studies focus on meanings as they relate in context. Lincoln and Guba (1985) referred to the qualitative approach as a post-positivist naturalistic method of inquiry.

The present study was applied as a single case study. Yin (2003) maintains that a case study is a research design 'that investigates a contemporary phenomenon within its real-life context, especially when the boundaries between phenomenon and context are not clearly evident' (Yin, 2003, p. 40). Yin also emphasizes the importance of having 'multiple source[s] of evidence' to get a broad comprehension of the observed phenomenon. Thus, in this in-depth case study, the researchers have chosen different methodical approaches for the different phases of the project.

To prepare the project a context analysis was carried out (see Figure 12.2). This was achieved by secondary research such as document and literature studies with a focus on the industrial characteristics. Within the context analysis a detailed analysis of the research partner was also carried out. Therefore we studied annual reports and several internal documents. As a result we obtained a detailed description of the characteristics of the industry as well as a good idea of our partner.

The collection of empirical data happened in two waves. In the first wave, problem-centered interviews were conducted with key persons of the

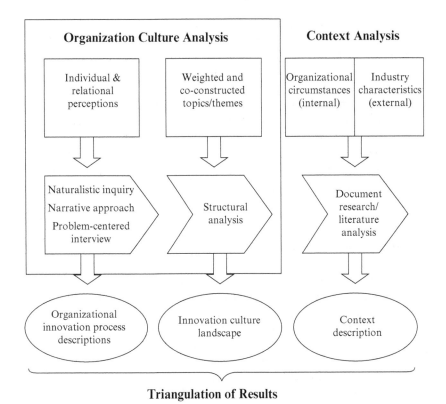

Triangulation of Results

Figure 12.2   Research design of the project

innovation project (for example marketing manager, technical support). The problem-centered interview is characterized by an open structure (Witzel, 1982, 2000) and looks at the individual themes of the interviewed people. For instance, how do they perceive the problem, and what are the consequences? The dialogue is directed to understand the experience and stories of the interviewed people. The researchers always started by asking the interviewees how they personally experienced the project; in other words, they asked them their own personal story. This established a comfortable atmosphere for the interviewees to tell the researchers their side of the story, one without any adverse consequences for them professionally.

In the second phase, a method called 'structuring technique' was applied (Geise, 2006). The structuring technique specifies a means of knowledge acquisition where terms are grouped together according to the relationship of these terms to others already collected (Hackel and Klebl, 2008). With this approach, subjective theories are clarified visually. In this project, the interviewee grouped together 11 terms written down on cards, which had been mentioned previously. The respondents then combined them to form a relationship. With the help of symbols, the relationship was clarified.

For data evaluation the interviews were recorded, and a transcript was drawn up. Later, the content of the obtained data was analyzed. This occurred between August 2008 and April 2009. In a second stage we combined the interviews with the structure analysis technique. This occurred in July 2009 and August 2009. The whole process of data gathering and analysis took over a year. The goal of the analysis was to find out the relevant statements, which could then give advice on the innovation process of TELE.

This was done by a researcher, who then extracted theoretical content in the form of quotations. As a result, a number of statements could be identified, which were later critically appraised with relation to the theme of innovation. Thereafter, in a subsequent meeting, a verbal comparison of the statements was made with the interviewees. Finally, a white paper was drawn up using the respective quotes that the interviewees had given. These quotes focus on the innovation's theoretical aspects and approaches. The process took several weeks to complete. During the whole analysis process, a group of researchers regularly met to discuss and reflect on the results interpreted and crafted-out so far to achieve a maximum degree of interpretative validity (Meissner, 2007).

The examination of the study happened on the basis of the classic quality criteria, which are validity, reliability and objectivity (Petrucci and Wirtz, 2007). Objectivity was ensured by the fact that results were always discussed within the research team. Validity was ensured by the fact that the results were discussed by the test persons and, as mentioned above, during the whole research process by the group of researchers. Finally, the criterion of reliability was maintained by use of the aforementioned structuring technique, which was completed in two stages. In the first stage, the concepts were supplemented by the statements made by the interviewees. Through ordinal classification, the research team could then check whether or not the concepts in themselves were conclusive, based on the network of relationships established in the first phase.

12.4 RESULTS

Based on the collected data, the innovation process could be reconstructed in detail. Typical dynamics could be identified, which are shown in Figure 12.3.

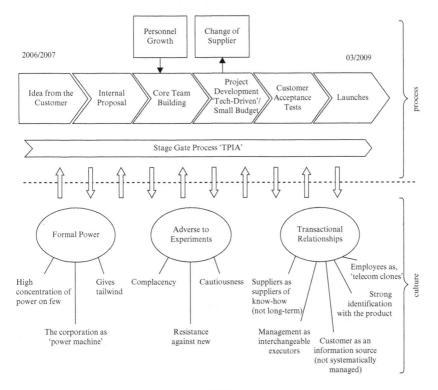

Figure 12.3   *Reconstruction of the TELE innovation process with main cultural themes*

12.4.1 Process Description

The upper half of the diagram shows the different steps of the observed innovation process. The impetus for the development of the new product in this case was not an internal one. The idea for the project arose from a conversation with an important customer. The customer told a segment manager at TELE that he would be interested in a new telecom solution, because the old one was too expensive. Based on the criteria set by the customer, an internal proposal was created.

After they overcame the first stage-gate, a core team was assigned to handle the development of the product. This core team was very heterogeneous and all members were from fairly important departments within the company. From the beginning, the team had members who were qualified and who could contribute something vital to the success of the undertaking. This circumstance is an important prerequisite for innovation.

For an optimal use of know-how, it also seems to be important that people from the different departments are part of the team from the beginning:

> For an optimal [use of know-how], yes, this [is] what I have told you, you should really have one representative of each one [of the] impacted segment[s], [Interviewer: from the beginning?] from the beginning; even from the product conception.

> If you don't have people that understand the business, and know how to use internal knowledge you don't succeed.

In the observed project, this was not done. For example, the marketing communication department should have become involved much earlier in the project than they were. As a result, the influence of this department was minor, and their expertise was not used in an optimal way. The reason for this late involvement lies in the internal process schema. During the whole development process, there were several stage-gates to overcome. In TELE, this process is called the 'TPIA process'. According to this internal procedure, the marketing communication department is not involved from the beginning. Possible influences and improvements from this department's side were therefore not possible. One member of the marketing communication department states:

> To some extent there are certain process cycles and milestones, and the marketing communication department becomes involved at a much later point in time. [Also] we are not involved from the beginning of the project, and therefore, our input is rather limited. [Additionally], the project has been protracted over many years now, and yes, well, the influence that I have had on the project itself, is almost non-existent. This is because this is the way the project was designed from the beginning.

Also noteworthy is the fact that TELE has had several staff changes throughout the whole project process. These changes were made both to the development team, and the management. This lack of staff continuity was assessed by various stakeholders of the project as being problematic:

> Change is another problem if you spend two hours explaining [how things work] to a guy, and then six months later he's gone, and there's a new guy.

In a broader sense, the customers are also a part of the development team. Before the launch of the product, there was a phase of customer acceptance tests. This step can be regarded as a trial run, where the products were tested and improved.

For the development phase, TELE worked together with an external partner, a supplier of technology. In this way, a lot of time and money could be saved, because TELE did not have to build up these skills/competences to bring the product to realization:

> External partners are really important when considering the time-to-market aspect of things, as we don't have to build up all the knowledge and technology, which the partner already has. Instead, we merely have to integrate it, which first of all gives us a major head start on the project. Alongside the time saved, we also receive the external partner's services, which bundled together, result in an interesting package.

The collaboration with an external partner brings not just advantages, but also inherent dangers. This might for example be when the external partner becomes so crucial that they are indispensable in the future. This can become problematic because of technical barriers, or if promises are not kept according to the skill level required (as described in the principal–agent theory), which is precisely what happened to TELE (Jensens and Meckling, 1976). The originally selected partner had to be changed because they did not have the know-how required to finish the job. This change cost TELE a lot of time and money. In the end, however, the new partner was quick and competent.

12.4.2 Culture Description

Based on the data, three prominent and influential cultural factors could be identified: formal power, adversity to experiments, and transactional relationships. These will now be described in detail.

12.4.2.1 Formal power
The analysis of the process has shown that formal power is the most important factor during the whole process. Without the acceptance of the top management, innovations are doomed to fail from the beginning, as it is the board of directors that holds the responsibility for the allocation of resources:

> Without the support of top-management, innovations don't have any chance in our company, which is true, we have, we need to, we have to tell them this is something that we really need, and we have to convince them what is the benefit of this, because when they are not convinced, your project will just be put on the side.

The power in TELE is not shared. Only one authority, organizationally attached to the top management, decides which innovation project will be carried out. Therefore, there is a high concentration of power on a few individuals. This has a decisive circumstance influence on the innovation process in TELE. This also makes the whole process unnecessarily long and more complicated. According to the people involved, the most difficult part was not the product development, but rather assuring the management that this was the right direction for the company to be heading:

> Because the technical part is not the difficult part, it is, I guess the process part which has taken us the longest.

However, if the management is committed to the project, it gives a significant tailwind to the entire success of the project. According to the people interviewed, management support was the most important factor for an innovation project in TELE.

12.4.2.2 Averse to experiments
The innovation project under consideration also comprised the development of a new business segment. This resulted in resistance against the new product. The TELE culture was until then fully aligned to one unique segment. The management board in particular was totally fixed on this. The employees not involved in the project had to, in a first step, understand that a new era was now being ushered in. In TELE, there were two or three staff members who took on this task. They were able to push the development of the product so that it could be finished successfully. According to the people interviewed, this is another prerequisite for the successful completion of innovation projects:

> [. . .] that two flag bearers were needed to bring the project forward.

As previously mentioned, the customer is also a part of the wider development team. However, he is also very helpful in enforcing management support. If there is opposition against the new product idea, the customer, or rather the customer need, is a very strong argument for pushing it through the stage-gates. This strategy is often used by the employees of TELE. One TELE associate states:

> The customer was for me the steamroller/inspiration for me to go ahead in these times. The customer wanted this [product] and was really interested, and wanted to buy thousands of units as soon as the solution became operational. This appeal for the product was immediately internalized and transferred to the marketing segment.

The people in the development circle did not have this resistance against the new product. They were highly motivated to get away from the one, single business segment that the company had been focusing on. The certainty of entering new fields seemed to be a positive thing.

> And the employees, here at TELE are actually really motivated, and also wanted to, so to say, get away from only working in business segment X.

Not only did the management board have this resistance against the new product, but so did the sales department. If the sales team does not understand or know about the new product's features, they will not sell it and will simply resort to selling the proven products that they already know. Regular training sessions to show them the functionality and the advantages of the product are important elements in the whole process:

> We have regular sales training, and we also have an internal sales training department. In conjunction with the marketing manager, the sales training is set up and the sales team is instructed to focus on the benefits and the key factors, so that they are communicated in the best possible way to the customer.

For the salespeople, selling the new product must also be worthwhile in a financial sense. Therefore, giving them the proper incentive to sell the product is also a part of the considerations involved:

> On the one hand, you can have a really great product, but if you don't properly motivate your sales staff by giving them the proper incentives to sell the product, then they simply won't sell it! They will only sell something that will pay off for them. In the implementation phase, these kinds of things are crucial. You have to think these things through beforehand, otherwise they just won't work. If there is some sort of a hindrance then it won't work.

12.4.2.3 Transactional relationships

As mentioned, the idea for the innovation was not an internal one, but rather an idea coming from a customer. During the whole process, the customer had an important role as a supplier of ideas, and as a purveyor of arguments for the implementation of the project:

> I am also even talking to customers, so I am actually also implementing part of the functionality, and then they give me input, and I am also discussing with different vendors to get ideas on innovation.

Even though the customer is an important part, they are not systematically managed. The relationships are more informal, and dealt with by personal contacts among the various salespeople involved.

For the development, TELE worked together with an external partner. The relationship with this partner is not very strong, so there is no interest in building a long-term relationship. The relationship is more results-oriented, in the sense that they are merely a supplier of know-how, which TELE lacked, and which thereby helped them reduce their time-to-market for the product.

> External partners are important. If we don't have the capability to [complete the job] . . . the external partners are important for the technologies we don't [yet] have.
> [Interviewer: OK, is this the only reason?]
> If it was for me, I'm not going to be using an external partner because this is something that you don't control. I am a control freak, I would want to know what happens, and you are always, external partners, unfortunately are there if you don't have the capability to do it, and then but there is also the problem, that depending on the partners, the product might be OK, the product might not be OK.

Within the core team, a very strong identification with the new product took place. According to the people interviewed, this was a significant factor within the project, which allowed the development process to be concluded successfully:

> But then, for us, we are quite happy that we finally have this product, so that we will have something to offer, [that is] new to our clients, we really believe strongly in the product, and we hope that it will fly sooner or later.

12.5   CONCLUSION

In summary, it is striking that a development process in TELE is characterized by skepticism and formal power. Innovative people need not only to have creative abilities, but also a lot of diplomacy and sales skills. In a first step, an innovator has to persuade the management board of his/her idea. This is the most important step in the whole process, because the management board has the authority to approve or deny any undertaking the firm is involved in, and thereby also sets the budget for it. In a second step, after the development, an innovator has to provide the sales team with a thorough understanding of the product's benefits, so that they may in turn sell the product to the customer in the most effective way. While carrying out the project, it is important that the innovator push the development in the right direction. The manager of an innovation project has to be a visionary, a team leader, and a politician, all within the same project.

Compared to the study of Brown and Eisenhardt (1995) presented at the beginning of the chapter, many of their findings could be confirmed. We have found most of the factors of their model in the innovation process in TELE (for example management support or the power of the project leader). One thing that is missing in the model is the factor 'corporate culture'. As we have shown, the 'aversion to experiments' – a cultural issue – had a strong influence on the whole process, which is reflected in the resistance against the new product. But also the 'power culture', which made the whole process unnecessarily prolonged and more complicated, was an important issue as well as the 'transactional relationships'. In the whole process, there was no interest in building a long-term relationship. The culture in TELE is very goal oriented.

To return to our original question, which was: how do basic assumptions of team members in managed organizational innovation activities influence the effectiveness of the innovation process, we can observe the following:

- Management at the beginning was very skeptical as well as the sales department. Of course this has a negative influence on the process, reflected by the long and nerve-racking process.
- The process part is the most difficult stage, rather than the development. Only with a strong belief in the product idea of every team member can this cultural barrier be overcome. This can be seen as a basic assumption for a successful innovation process.
- An innovator needs to know that he/she has to execute different roles, which depends on the different process phases. At the beginning they have to be a politician to gain management support. During the development they have to be a coach and a coordinator. Before the launch they have to be a salesperson.

The results also show the emergence of different meanings, norms and imperatives within the company:

- 'Stage-gate process' as a means and mediator of formal power.
- 'Strategic partnering with the key customer' avoids uncertainty and supports the seriousness of the innovation initiative.
- 'Build a core team and create a shared identity' to counterbalance the top management norm to work on the basis of transactional relationships.

While management theory has started to realize these hybrid requirements of intra-firm innovativeness (for example Almirall and Casadesus-Masanell, 2010), management education seems to be lagging behind. At least, a first yet brief research query concerning the term 'dynamic innovation management role models' (and others similar to this) offered no helpful information for research and practice. This insight can be seen as the main finding of our chapter. Thus, future research should keep an eye on the transformation of this academic knowledge in applied concepts and recommendations for practitioners. Obviously, this is an ambitious aim. But we see no other way to adequately appreciate the innovation management practice we found at TELE – which was an artful and mindful combination of interdisciplinary management skills to bring the innovation to life – against all the powerful internal barriers that the company tried to set up.

REFERENCES

Abegg, C. (2005), 'Liberalisierung von Netzsektoren: auswirkungen auf die unternehmen im Schweizer Alpenraum', IRL-Report 3, Institute für Raum- und Landschaftsentwicklung, Zurich: vdf Hochschulverlag.
Aderhold, J. and R. John (2005), Innovation. *Sozialwissenschaftliche Perspektiven*, Konstanz: UVK.
Almirall, E. and R. Casadesus-Masanell (2010), 'Open vs. closed innovation: a model of discovery and divergence', *Academy of Management Review*, 35, 27–47.
Anaconda, D.G. and D.F. Caldwell (1990), 'Beyond boundary spanning: managing external dependence in product development teams', *Journal of High Technology Management Research*, 1, 119–35.
Baecker, D. (2003), Organisation und Management, Frankfurt am Main: Suhrkamp.
Berger, P.L. and T. Luckmann (1967 [1980]), Die Gesellschaftliche Konstruktion der Wirklichkeit. Eine Theorie der Wissenssoziologie, Frankfurt am Main: Fischer Taschenbuch Verlag, 1st edn (1967): The Social Construction of Reality, New York: Doubleday.
Brown, S. and K. Eisenhardt (1995), 'Product development: past research, present findings, and future directions', *Academy of Management Review*, 20, 343–78.
Chesborough, H.W. (2003), Open Innovation: The New Imperative for Creating and Profiting from Technology, Boston, MA: Harvard Business School Press.
Clark, K.B. and T. Fujimoto (1991), Product Development Performance, Boston, MA: Harvard Business School Press.
Cooper, R.G. (1998), Product Leadership, Reading, MA: Perseus Books.
Cooper, R.G. and E.J. Kleinschmidt (1987), 'New products: what separates winners from losers?', *Journal of Product Innovation Management*, 4, 169–84.
Creswell, J.W. (1994), Research Design: Qualitative & Quantitative Approaches, London: Sage.
Dougherty, D. (1992), 'Interpretive barriers to successful product innovation in large firms', *Organizational Science*, 3, 179–202.
Geise, W. (2006), 'Zur Anwendung der Struktur-Lege-Technik bei der Rekonstruktion subjektiver Impulskauftheorien', in E. Bahrs et al. (eds), Unternehmen im Agrarbereich vor neuen Herausforderungen, Vol. 41,

Münster-Hiltrup: Schriften der Gesellschaft für Wirtschafts- und Sozial-wissenschaften des Landbaues, pp. 121–31.

Gergen, K.J. (1985), 'The social constructionist movement in modern psychology', *American Psychologists*, **40**(3), 266–75.

Hackel, M. and M. Klebl (2008), 'Qualitative Methodentriangulation bei der arbeitswissenschaftlichen Exploration von Tätigkeitssystemen', *Forum: Qualitative Sozialforschung*, **9**(3).

Jensens, M. and W.H. Meckling (1976), 'Theory of the firm: managerial behavior, agency costs and ownership structure', *Journal of Financial Economics*, **3**(4), 305–60.

Lincoln, Y.S. and E.G. Guba (1985), Naturalistic Inquiry, Beverly Hills, CA: Sage.

Luhmann, N. (2000), Organisation und Entscheidung, Opladen: Westdeutscher Verlag.

Meissner, J.O. (2007), 'Multi-stage analysis for knowledge reflection', in A.S. Kazi and P. Wolf (eds), Hands-On Knowledge Co-Creation and Sharing: Practical Methods and Techniques, Knowledge Board.

Nonaka, I. and H. Takeuchi (1995), The Knowledge-Creating Company, New York: Oxford University Press.

Petrucci, M. and M. Wirtz (2007), 'Gütekriterien bei qualitativen Forschungs-methoden', available at: http://www.ph-freiburg.de/projekte/quasus/.

Sackmann, S.A. (1991), 'Uncovering culture in organizations', *Journal of Applied Behavioral Science*, **27**, 295–317.

Schein, E. (1992), Organizational Culture and Leadership, San Francisco, CA: Jossey-Bass

Terwiesch, C. and K.T. Ulrich (2009), Structure: Shaping the Innovation Funnel: Designing Innovation Tournaments that will work for your Business, Boston, MA: Harvard Business Press.

Vaterlaus, S., S. Bühler, H. Telser and P. Zenhäusern (2004), Bedeutung des Telekomsektors für die Schweizer Volkswirtschaft. Internationaler Vergleich – Beitrag zum Wachstum – Rolle der Regulierung, Bern: ICT Switzerland.

Want, J. (2003), 'Corporate culture: illuminating the black hole', *Journal of Business Strategy*, 07-08/2003.

Witzel, A. (1982), Verfahren der Qualitativen Sozialforschung, Frankfurt am Main and New York: Campus Verlag.

Witzel, A. (2000), 'The problem-centered interview', *Forum: Qualitative Sozialforschung*, **1**(1).

Womack, J.P., D.T. Jones and D. Roos (1990), The Machines that Changed the World, New York: HarperCollins.

Yin, K. (2003), Case Study Research: Design and Methods, 3rd edn, Thousand Oaks, CA: Sage.

Zirger, B.J. and M. Maidique (1990), 'A model of new product development: an empirical test', *Management Science*, **36**, 867–83.

Index

dependable variables, count variable
163
dependent variable export performance
satisfaction 144
descriptive statistics 183
design industry 129
development-team performance,
internal communication 265
diagnostic systems 246
diffusion of enhanced intra-MNEs
198
disciplined problem-solving perspective
265
domestic inventions, foreign ownership
31–2
dosage testing 157
drugs discovery 157–8
dummy variables
Anglo-Saxon, Nordic, European
clusters 207–8
'dynamic innovation management role
models' 278

economics of learning 200
economies, newly emergent challenges
China, India 76
education systems 56–7
electrical machinery research 158
electricity network, smart technologies
53
empirical model estimation 181–3
employee training 22
employment as parameter for business
performance 135
employment rate 72
enablers 57
endogeneity 114–16
energy, renewable 53
energy security 78
energy supply 43
engagement hypothesis, imports of
foreign knowledge 104
entrepreneurship 57, 68–70, 75,
248
environmental health 43
environmental issues 78
environmental policy, Belgium 46
estimation issues, Portugal 114–19
estimation strategy 183–5
ethnocentric attitudes 199

EU Industrial R&D Investment
Scoreboard 159
European Innovation Scoreboard 57
European Innovation Scoreboard
(EIS), Belgium's level
venture capital, entrepreneurship
74–5
European Lisbon Strategy 2
European Patent Office (EPO) 27, 160
European Research Area (ERA) 44, 48
European Research and Innovation
Plan 44
European Space Agency (ESA) 48
European Year of Creativity and
Innovation 1
exogenous and endogenous variables
on performance change of
subsidiaries 235
exogenous variables 231, 232
expenses, non-R&D
machinery acquisition, patent
buying 110–11
experimental studies, future research
256
'Expert Group Knowledge for
Growth', EC 2006 5
expertise combination 226
export assistance for SMEs, 132–3
export barriers for SMEs, Flanders 138
exporter orientation 107
Exporters (EXP) Portugal 108–10,
112–14
exporters, importance 103
exporters of technology, main in
Europe
Germany, Sweden, Austria 35–6
export foreign direct investment (FDI)
185, 188
export intensity of an SME, levels
of accidental, exploratory,
experimental, active, dedicated
exports 90, 138
export opportunities 127
export performance and product
sample booths
creative companies 135
export performance, Flanders 137
export performance satisfaction 129,
of SMEs in creative sector 143
reasons for 134

export promotion implements,
Flanders Investment and Trade
(FIT) 143
trade shows, trade missions 132–3
export promotion programs (EPPs),
Flanders 127–9, 138–9, 142
export promotion services in SMEs,
127
exports of high-technology products,
Belgium 72
external embeddedness
forward, horizontal, backward,
public knowledge sources 229
external knowledge sources, four
types
forward, horizontal, backward,
public knowledge sources 229
Extramural R&D Expenses
acquisition of R&D from
institutions 110–11

facilitators 56–7
international linkages 63
FDI *see* Foreign Direct Investment
Federal Cooperation Commission,
Belgium 48
Federal Council for Science Policy,
Belgium 45, 48–9
tax credits for research, 2008
49–50
feedback and measurement systems
246
financial accounting literature 242
financial intermediaries 90
financial success of product
revenue, profitability, market share
266
firms
Belgian groups 94
connections, usefulness of 226
dynamics 68–9
efficiency, increased 22
foreign multinationals in Belgium
94–7
globally engaged, effects 23
heterogeneity 177
resources and export performance,
Flanders 128–9
stand-alone 94
first-mover advantages 9, 155–6

fixed-effect Negative Binomial
regression
basic scientific research 164
FIT *see* Flanders Investment and
Trade
Flanders District of Creativity 133
Flanders, export performance
satisfaction 136–7
Flanders in Action, 'Vlaanderen in
Actie' (ViA)
Green City District 50
Learning Fleming 50
Medical Centre Flanders 50
Open Entrepreneur 50
Powerful Government 50
Smart Logistics Europe 50
Flanders Investment and Trade (FIT)
8, 127–8, 132–3
e-mail addresses of creative SMEs
136–7
Flemish Authority 45
Flemish design sector
export promotion and satisfaction
126
Flemish exports accounts 127
Flemish governmental organization
(FIT)
promotion instruments 133
Flemish Government, STI policies
research and innovation for
Flanders, importance 50
Flemish region economy,
industrialization 77, 87
Flemish research organizations 51
Flemish Science and Innovation Policy
Council
strategic clusters 51
Flemish Universities 51
foreign advanced subsidiaries 212
new technological capabilities
1893–1990 209
Foreign Direct Investment (FDI) 4–5,
19, 105, 173, 188, 198
difference for developed and
developing countries 189
export 180
investment motives 181
inward and outward 76–7
knowledge diffusion literature 183
local 180

product life cycles, shortened 201
product sample booths and export
    performance 142
productivity effects of different FDI
    types 186–90
productivity growth 157
profitability 248
project management, link with
    innovation culture 266
public expenditure on education for
    S&T 58
public expenditure on human resources
    for S&T 58
public research organizations 46
public scientific information
    from universities and research
        centers 229–31
pulp and paper industry 203
Purely Domestic (DOM) Portugal
    108–19

quantity-based pay scheme 253–4

R&D
    capital stock 21–2
    centralization 28
    deficit 4
    expenditure 2, 162–3
        Europe and OECD countries 24–6
        foreign control, 2004 29
        intramural and extramural 68
        in Swedish telecommunications
            industry 203
    expenses, intramural 110–11
    funds from abroad 24
    intensities (R&Ds) 60–61, 99, 175,
        179
        Belgium 59–61
    investments 246
    landscape, Europe less dominance 76
    and open innovation 77
    outsourcing 5
    outsourcing and insourcing, Belgium
        78
    spillovers 20
    staff, number of 231
ratio test log-likelihood 165
rebus puzzles
    on worker productivity evaluation
        253

regional differences in Belgian
    innovation 77–8
regional distribution of R&D
    expenditure
    Nomenclature of Territorial Units
        for Statistics (NUTS) 61
Regional Plan for Innovation, Brussels
    (PRI/GPI), 2006 78
    strategic targets 54
relevance theory 202
Republic of Korea, Government
    228
research
    design 203–9
    and development intensity 90
    findings 163, 166–7
    funding 74
    geographical concentration, Belgium
        61
    ideas, four levels of analysis 243
    innovation in Belgium 85
    joint venture 18
    needs on control and incentive
        mechanisms 214
    productivity 57, 64–5
resource-based model, Flanders 127
resource mobilization 74
reverse diffusion of capabilities
    foreign to headquarters 200
reverse diffusion of knowledge
    greenfield and acquired subsidiaries
        202
reverse diffusion of technological
    capabilities 197, 201–7, 214
reverse diffusion, speed of 210
reverse diffusion within MNEs,
    197
reverse knowledge transfer 202–3
reverse technology diffusion 196
reverse transfer of technology and
    knowledge 197, 200
risk capital provision, Belgium 46

Sackmann's iceberg model, 1991
    264
sale growth in foreign markets 137
sales incentives 275
sales performance 248
sales training for benefits focus 275
Schein's culture model, 1992 264